Playing
Fair

Joy I. Butler, EdD
The University of British Columbia

Human Kinetics

Library of Congress Cataloging-in-Publication Data

Names: Butler, Joy I., 1957- , author.

Title: Playing fair / Joy I. Butler, EdD, University of British Columbia.

Description: Champaign, IL : Human Kinetics, [2016] | Includes bibliographical references.

Identifiers: LCCN 2015049767 | ISBN 9781450435437

Subjects: LCSH: Play--Handbooks, manuals, etc. | Play--Moral and ethical aspects.

Classification: LCC LB1137 .B87 2016 | DDC 372.21--dc23 LC record available at http://lccn.loc.gov/2015049767

ISBN: 978-1-4504-3543-7 (print)

The web addresses cited in this text were current as of March 2016, unless otherwise noted.

Acquisitions Editor: Diana Vincer; **Developmental Editor:** Jacqueline Eaton Blakley; **Senior Managing Editor:** Carly S. O'Connor; **Copyeditor:** Patsy Fortney; **Permissions Manager:** Dalene Reeder; **Senior Graphic Designer:** Angela K. Snyder; **Cover Designer:** Keith Blomberg; **Photograph (cover):** © Human Kinetics; **Senior Art Manager:** Kelly Hendren; **Associate Art Manager:** Alan L. Wilborn; **Illustrations:** © Human Kinetics, unless otherwise noted; **Printer:** Versa Press

Printed in the United States of America

10 9 8 7 6 5 4 3 2 1

The paper in this book is certified under a sustainable forestry program.

Human Kinetics

Website: www.HumanKinetics.com

United States: Human Kinetics
P.O. Box 5076
Champaign, IL 61825-5076
800-747-4457
e-mail: info@hkusa.com

Canada: Human Kinetics
475 Devonshire Road Unit 100
Windsor, ON N8Y 2L5
800-465-7301 (in Canada only)
e-mail: info@hkcanada.com

Europe: Human Kinetics
107 Bradford Road
Stanningley
Leeds LS28 6AT, United Kingdom
+44 (0) 113 255 5665
e-mail: hk@hkeurope.com

Australia: Human Kinetics
57A Price Avenue
Lower Mitcham, South Australia 5062
08 8372 0999
e-mail: info@hkaustralia.com

New Zealand: Human Kinetics
P.O. Box 80
Mitcham Shopping Centre, South Australia 5062
0800 222 062
e-mail: info@hknewzealand.com

E5789

To all teachers who love to watch students learning through play and who are willing to risk new ideas, and to their students, who were born to play well with others.

Contents

CHAPTER **9** **Striking Game: Cricket** **133**
Kevin Sandher

CHAPTER **10** **Inventing Net and Wall Games** **157**
Joy Butler and Tim Hopper

Foreword

This is an important book for several reasons. It written by one of the stalwarts of the TGfU Task Force that became the AIESEP TGfU Special Interest Group. Joy was also the instigator of the International TGfU Conferences that started in 2001; these have all had a powerful impact on the growth of TGfU. In 2016 the 6th International Conference will be held in Cologne; this progress is testament to the growing interest in research on the teaching and coaching of games around the world as well as the need for publications for teachers and coaches.

Joy has been a prolific writer and advocate for TGfU, and *Playing Fair* tackles the idea that young people and players need the opportunity to be fully engaged in their games education. This engagement process is about self-directed learning, player-centered experiences, creating something new and having ownership of the ideas, sharing ideas, constructing something with others, and feeling a sense of personal achievement. It does so in a framework that allows students to learn about democracy in action on the ground as players face decisions that strike to the core of fairness.

These attributes emerged in the 1980s when the Loughborough University–based TGfU team began to promote a different way of thinking about games. As a member of that team, I created projects on what was called games making. In the first instance, it was a tool for assessing players' understanding of games, but it soon became obvious that this approach had much greater potential. The feedback from university students and pupils in schools prompted rethinking and a deliberate focus on the outcomes of young people creating and making up new and original games. Ever since then, the idea of self-directed learning has been a major focus in TGfU.

From experiences of games making and inventing games, young people and players learn far more than a set of techniques and skills to use in a game. They generate personal capital, develop social and cognitive skills and an emotional attachment to playing a game, and recognize that they have inner resources and the need to resolve conduct and moral issues that arise.

I am delighted that Joy has restored the significance of these experiences in *Playing Fair*, provided new insights, and made those insights accessible to a much wider audience. There is much to learn in this approach, and its potential for young people's development should be a central part of their education. Teachers and coaches will gain a great deal from a careful reading of this text because it will awaken the need for giving young people a voice in their own learning and provide rich opportunities for a range of attributes that go beyond motor skills and learning through drills.

Len Almond

Acknowledgments

The ideas in this book are shaped and influenced by caring and thoughtful people who are concerned about the experiences of children in physical education and beyond. My introduction to inventing games was through a workshop given by Terry Williams in 1985 in Kent, UK. My second was the chapter by Len Almond on rethinking games education. Over time I have appreciated the potential of inventing games as a way to teach broader societal issues such as understanding democracy and issues of social justice.

I would like to thank the six teachers I worked with on a project funded by the Social Sciences and Humanities Research Council of Canada. Their discussions, teaching, and feedback on my ideas have helped to refine the inventing games process laid out in this book. The teachers are Anja Berning, Erin McGinley, Kevin Sandher, Sarah Marshall, Scott Samuelson, and Darryl Beck. Sarah Taylor was invaluable as our GRA. Many of them contributed to the book's final chapter.

I would also like to thank the six chapter authors for their involvement and patience: Linda Griffin, James Mandigo, Kevin Sandher, Tim Hopper, Stephen Mitchell, and Bobby Gibson. Thanks to authors who submitted excellent work that could not ultimately be included because of limitations on space. Tim Hopper deserves special thanks for his generosity in setting up an invaluable graphic resource for all the authors to use to illustrate their game setups and for his insights on the SSHRC project.

Special thanks to Becca King and Bette Shippam, who provided constant support and reprimanded chapters with red ink when they would not behave.

I am sincerely grateful for the enthusiasm and dedication of everyone involved at Human Kinetics. They helped make this dream a reality and were unfailingly personable and professional. It always surprises me to see how many people are involved, but I'd like to thank a few in particular: Scott Wikgren (vice president and director) for believing in the project vision some 12 years ago when I proposed it and the diligent editorial team, in particular Diana Vincer (acquisitions editor), Jackie Blakley (developmental editor), and Carly O'Connor (senior managing editor), who have developed and helped shape the book.

Thanks to Bella and Cricket for being patient when long walks should have been in the offing.

Finally, to my partner, Claire. These last four years have been a long haul and there's so much to thank you for: being a smart, insightful first editor; all those discussions over dinner about the book's central points; encouraging me that the book was worth pursuing and that I could do it; and offering hugs when I didn't know I needed them. I would not have finished this without you.

Introduction

This book is predicated on the love of the game. Who has not been caught up in the action as the scores are close and the clock is ticking? Who has not thrilled to the slap of the puck or the sight of the ball slipping by the outstretched hands of the keeper? It is love that wakes us at dawn and sends us stumbling out into the cold. It is passion that fuels hours of practice in search of the perfect moment, the perfect team, and the perfect match, when everything falls into place.

I have loved games since I was a shy 10-year-old girl, and I still love them now that I'm a university professor. I've worked with students in grades 3 through 12 for many years as a practicing teacher and a basketball coach (reaching three school national finals) and, more recently, in research with preservice physical education teachers and teachers in the field. All of these experiences have contributed to my desire to reevaluate and reconsider the purposes of games education and how those purposes can best be achieved.

Most would agree that the inherent qualities of games include play, fun, challenge, teamwork, friendship, and quick thinking. In addition, physical contest has long been regarded by some as an arena for moral and spiritual development. For instance, the ancient Olympic Games were embedded in important religious festivals, and the current Olympic charter refers quite specifically to the ethical and educational dimension of sport as the first fundamental principle of Olympism:

> Olympism is a philosophy of life, exalting and combining in a balanced whole the qualities of body, will and mind. Blending sport with culture and education, Olympism seeks to create a way of life based on the joy of effort, the educational value of good example and respect for universal fundamental ethical principles (International Olympic Committee, Olympic Charter, 2015, p. 13).

Few would argue against the belief that there is a compelling need to address today's problems of antisocial behaviors and bullying in schools. However, these issues are usually addressed after the fact, through antibullying or safe space campaigns. This book offers a way for teachers to address these behaviors by encouraging students to invent their own games. This opportunity helps students to treat each other fairly, consistently, and before the fact of bullying occurs. An inventing games learning context results in a better understanding not only of game structures, game play, and situated skills, but also of self and others, as well as issues of social justice and what makes democracy work (e.g., collaboration, negotiation, inclusiveness, and fairness). The experiences offered in inventing games are nestled in and dispersed throughout the four categories of the Teaching Games for Understanding (TGfU) game classification system (target, striking, net and wall, and invasion games). The teacher's role is to help players to make informed decisions within the context of games and to practice making intentional, reasoned inquiries about game situations, which they can then transfer to other areas of their lives.

Key Concept: Inherent and Intrinsic Value

Inherent value is defined as the objective property of the game itself, something that is part of its essential nature. For example, we might enjoy a particular tennis game because we are playing well or are matched against a close opponent, but we also enjoy tennis because of certain inherent qualities that exist whenever we play, such as being able to strike the ball with varying degrees of force (Butler, 2006b).

Teachers often understand the inherent value of games intuitively and hope that their learners experience these intrinsic values. However, this depends on the experiences presented. If the lesson teaches only techniques (i.e., mastery), the intrinsic experiences that learners enjoy will be limited to an understanding of these technical fundamentals. If the experience is presented in a gamelike situation and provides the qualities of a contest that offers equal opportunity (in the way that a TGfU class can), then students may develop an appreciation for the inherent value of games—the experience of playing for playing's sake.

Teachers and coaches tend to define **intrinsic value** in terms of the properties they have decided will bring about the best quality of experience for their learners. For example, some educators place more value on teaching skill mastery than on decision making in the game context. Others emphasize learner responsiveness to the teacher's or coach's direction rather than developing skills in reading the game and making appropriate game play decisions. Most fall somewhere in the middle, but with preferences that carry through into their teaching and coaching practices. Our desired way of being in the world affects the way we view games and sport.

This book was written to help teachers and coaches teach the principles of game play and those of democracy and citizenship in concrete ways to contribute to systemic change in the school culture. Rather than handing down techniques in isolation, teachers create environments in which students create their own games (within the constraints of the game category) and set up problems and gamelike situations in which students can learn concepts, skills, and strategies in context. Rather than presenting moral content as established dictates or dogmas, the teacher using the inventing games approach involves learners in situations that challenge them to invent their own rules and codes of conduct through a process called democracy in action.

ORGANIZATION

The first five chapters of this book are theoretical and provide the foundation—in other words, the why and the what of implementing inventing games. The next nine chapters provide the practical content— how to implement the ideas presented in the first five chapters. (*Note:* If you use the metric system in your measurements, you can replace the number of yards with meters.) Figure 1 provides a simple graphic overview of the book.

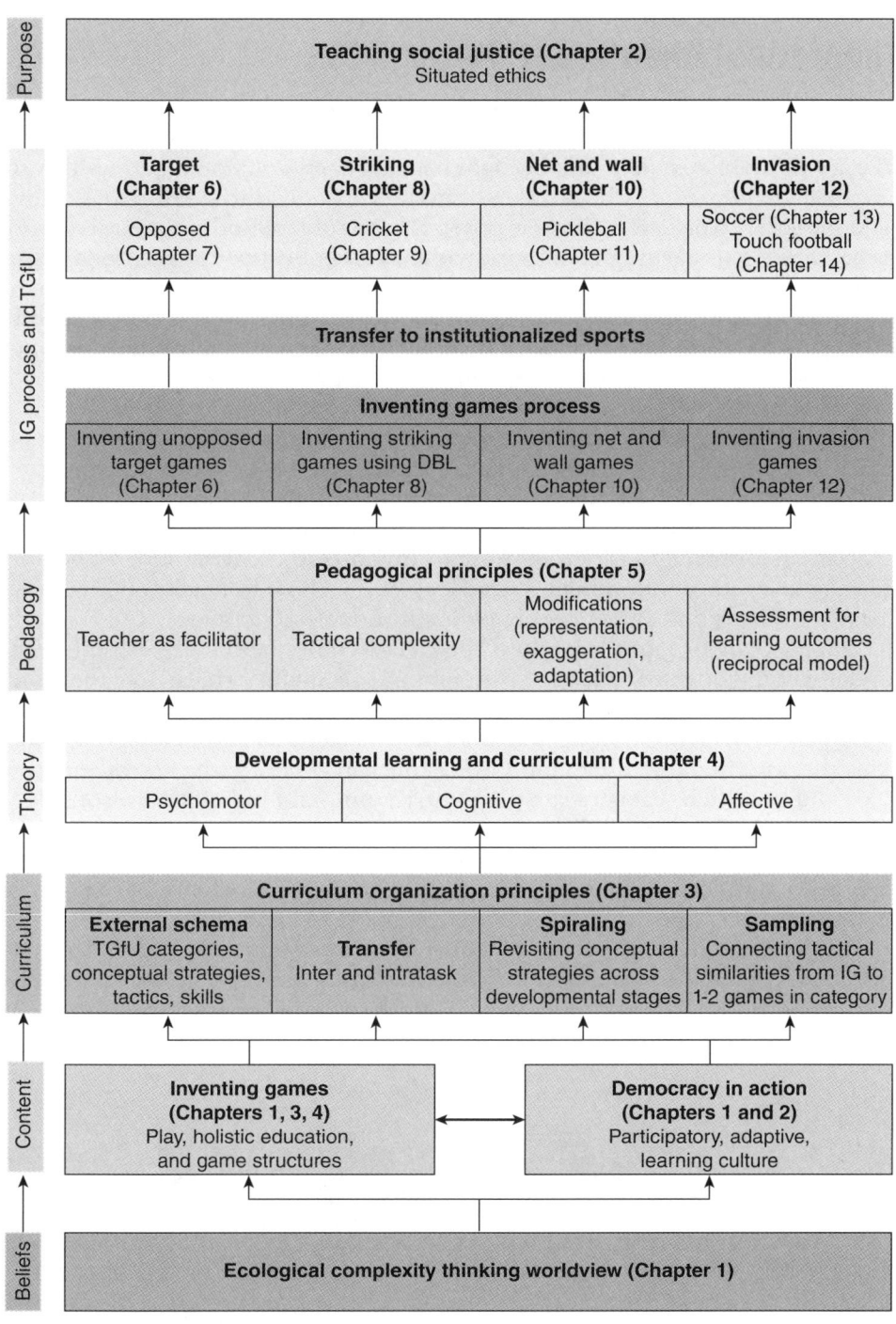

FIGURE 1 Organizational structure of *Playing Fair*.

Theoretical Chapters (1 Through 5)

Notice in the third row from the bottom in figure 1 the two main curricular areas mentioned earlier: inventing games and democracy in action. The two-way arrow indicates their equal weight because they function together in every practical chapter of this book. These curricular areas derive from an ecological complexity worldview (bottom row). Key to understanding this worldview is the belief that learning is both individual and collective (or relational). The inventing games process encourages teachers and learners to focus more on the why than the how, and to think and feel, as well as do. The classroom becomes more participatory and democratic as learners become more autonomous and responsible. The worldview underlying the process of inventing games is described in chapter 1.

Chapter 2 describes how to teach social justice through the practice of democracy in action. It explains how to engage students in the practice of democracy through the invention of games and how to use moments of aporia, or breakdown, as opportunities for learning and gaining new insights.

Chapters 3 through 5 address how to organize the curriculum while considering learners' developmental needs, as well as how to teach the process of inventing games and category-related institutionalized games.

Chapter 3 strips games down to their vital components and examines the fundamental game structures of primary and secondary rules. Together, they create the inherent qualities of the game and provide the means to shape them. These provide the external schema to include conceptual strategies, tactics, and skills that are fundamental to the TGfU game categories, game knowledge, and rules and by which teachers can plan yearly, unit, and individual lessons.

Chapter 4 addresses developmental learning and how the psychomotor, cognitive, and affective domains should work together with curriculum design. The order and flow of the categories presented in this book are based on this rationale.

Chapter 5 examines the four principles that make up the emergent learning focus and pedagogical foundation of the inventing games process: (1) teacher as facilitator; (2) tactical complexity; (3) modification through representation, exaggeration, and adaptation; and (4) assessment for learning.

Key Concept: Institutionalized Sports

Informal games become institutionalized sports when they acquire governing bodies that decide on standardized rules to which all players must adhere. In this sense, particular values and norms become embedded in the organizations.

Practical Chapters (6 Through 14)

The practical chapters are organized according to the TGfU categories: target games, striking games, net and wall games, and invasion games. The order is based on the developmental progressions described in chapter 4. Each game category begins with an inventing games chapter that explains how to teach the primary and secondary rules of the category. Each inventing games chapter is followed by a chapter that describes how to teach an institutionalized games unit so that teachers can link the games knowledge learned in the IG chapters unit to others in the same game category. Teachers can mindfully plan for transfer through both the curriculum and the pedagogical considerations. Because of the limited scope of the book, only one example is given in each category (with the exception of invasion games, for which there are two).

Chapter 6: Inventing Unopposed Target Games

Chapter 7: Innovative Approaches to Opposed Target Games

Chapter 8: Inventing Striking Games: Danish Longball

Chapter 9: Striking Game: Cricket

Chapter 10: Inventing Net and Wall Games

Chapter 11: Net and Wall Games: Pickleball

Chapter 12: Inventing Invasion Games

Chapter 13: Invasion Game: Soccer

Chapter 14: Invasion Game: Touch Football

Key Concepts: Skills and Techniques

A game skill refers to using a technique such as kicking in the context of a gamelike situation. The skill requires the player to interpret the needs of the situation and make the right decision as well as carry out the necessary movements. A technique can be described as part of a skill. Traditionally, game techniques are practiced as isolated actions in closed environments in the hope that they will transfer to the skill in game contexts.

The four inventing games chapters (6, 8, 10, and 12) follow the stages explained in chapter 1. The time spent on each stage will depend on students' game experiences and developmental levels. The practical chapters provide block plans and suggested democracy-in-action topics for a series of lessons for a given grade level. The limitations of the book length do not allow us to provide examples for more than one grade. Each lesson includes an introduction, a development phase, and a culminating activity. The introductory activities usually serve as reviews of previous lessons. They create connections to tactical problems and the development phase and offer activities for warming up the body and the mind. The lesson often begins with a focus game that introduces and emphasizes the concepts and strategies that will be covered in that lesson. The development phase of the lesson includes group work, problem solving, game play, and skill development. Playing the game generates task progressions that help students work on tactical problems and their related skills. These developments are then transferred back into the focus game, as it is played again as part of the culminating activity.

Implementing the principles advocated in this book will lead to the following:

- Learners and teachers who better understand and appreciate the constructs of game play through internal and external schemas (concepts learned emergently through student exploration and those concepts taught or transferred directly by the teacher)
- The transfer of concepts, strategies, tactics, and skills between and among game categories
- Improved performance and engagement among players
- Learners who are more effective and empowered because they understand and value the processes of decision making
- Learners who understand how democracy works from the bottom up
- Learners who begin to understand that democracy is tenuous, that it breaks down in the absence of active social justice, and that we all have a responsibility to construct and reconstruct it, moment by moment

Key Concepts: Strategies and Tactics

In simple terms, *strategy* refers to concepts of the game that are established in advance. These become the big picture ideas, the goals of the plan—the what. Tactics thus become the how of the what. These are the specific decisions made by groups of players or individuals during a game to try to outwit and ultimately beat opponents. Keeping possession (to score) is an invasion game strategy, whereas how players do that represents the tactics (e.g., give and go, fast break, clearing out to create space for a ball handler, screens in basketball).

As a constructivist thinker, I believe that all learning, including learning to play fair, occurs most effectively in playful and meaningful contexts. Throughout this book, I argue that these contexts are provided by engagement in the game. When the game becomes the teacher, opportunities exist for students to explore boundaries, rules, and ethical decisions, both within and beyond game play.

Play, Inventing Games, Democracy in Action, and Worldview

Ms. Craik scans her fourth-grade students, who are playing their invented net games.

A group of shy, uncoordinated girls have made up a game that makes large demands on their balance. A lanky team member spins around three times (with her eyes closed) and calls out the name of one of her opponents on the other side of the net as she releases the ball. Apparently, her challenge is to stay upright and make the pass accurately. Instead, she throws the ball off behind her before staggering dizzily around the court. Although her teammates squeal with laughter, the group is passionately engaged in this odd game of spin and throw.

At the other end of the ability range is a group of boys playing a modified version of Newcomb. They are immersed in a close contest—oblivious to anything else that's going on.

Ms. Craik decides to start with the girls and calls them over for a chat, posing a few questions: How is their game working? Does it involve them all as much as they would like? The girls say there's too much standing about and decide to change the spinning rule a bit to see if the game will flow more easily.

Meanwhile, Ms. Craik has challenged the boys to open up their game. How might they give themselves more time to strategize and structure a more organized offense? After a brief discussion, they decide to introduce a rule that allows two passes before the ball must be sent over the net. As she watches, Ms. Craik prepares questions about how this new rule and constraint on the game opens up the offense for new possibilities.

This vignette provides a quick snapshot of an inventing games lesson focused on net games. We can readily appreciate the diversity of students' skill levels and also how students are the architects of their own games. Through the teacher's skillful questioning, both groups are able to analyze the constraints of their games and change their rules to make them more flowing, challenging, and fun. By working progressively through the constructs of their invented games and the corresponding strategies and tactics, they construct schema from which they can make comparisons to other games they will learn. As they negotiate the construction of their games, they also learn how to work closely with others.

Inventing games and learning about democracy (including social justice issues) might seem an unlikely pairing, because play is often considered frivolous and democratic ideals are often considered the most serious notions children can learn. In this book, we consider how inventing games offers seriously playful opportunities to learn democracy in action, because students learn by doing as they negotiate, debate, overcome conflict, and navigate through a series of problem-solving activities. In the physical environment, emotions are quickly stirred and issues around inclusivity become more visible and more pressing. How better to deal with issues of social justice, such as bullying and accessibility, than in such charged situations? Chapter 2 presents steps teachers can take to become more mindful in dealing with such situations.

Incidents of bullying are very much in the news; the tragic suicides of young people who have been bullied (both face-to-face and online) have shocked the world. As media pundits puzzle to find solutions to the problem of bullying, most educators understand that this is not an easy problem to fix. In a speech reported in *The Vancouver Sun* (June 29, 2013) about violence against women, former U.S. president Jimmy Carter suggested that rather than simply blaming and punishing perpetrators, we should be taking a hard look at overarching attitudes (including religious doctrines) that frame women as inferior. His point was that individual beliefs and actions are nested within, and thus highly influenced by, political, social, and economic structures.

This book does not purport to offer a magic bullet that will eradicate the age-old problem of bullying—for example, by constructing policies to deal with bullies or addressing the topic of bullying discreetly and directly with students. An increasing body of opinion suggests that our current methods (such as punitive zero tolerance, celebrities who speak out against bullying, limiting access to social media sites, or discrete short-term antibullying programs) are not working (Emdin, 2013; Prinstein, 2013). Rather, a comprehensive approach is required across the school curriculum to create sustainable change in the school culture. Physical education is particularly well positioned for such an initiative. Although it has been, ironically, a traditional site of dread for the unpopular and uncoordinated, physical education can offer students opportunities to experiment with, observe, and discuss issues of difference and power. Rather than thinking about these in the abstract, they can experience them firsthand as they practice the democratic principles and skills required to develop an ethic of caring (Gilligan, 1982).

Key Concept: Inventing Games

This book is based on the inventing games (IG) process, a companion to Teaching Games for Understanding (TGfU). The process is explained in the first five chapters as a curriculum model with clearly defined pedagogical principles. Building on the natural instinct of children to play, IG invites them to invent games in the four TGfU game categories. In the process of inventing games and then playing them, children learn about game structures, rules, and the principles of fair play.

This first chapter addresses the reintegration of play into games, the inventing games process, democracy in action, and the worldview teachers require to help their students become game inventors.

REINTEGRATION OF PLAY IN GAMES

Recently, 270 academics, writers, and child development professionals blamed "the marked deterioration in children's mental health" on the lack of unstructured and loosely supervised play (Jacobson, 2008). According to a report produced by Statistics Canada (Ifedi, 2008), the 7.3 million Canadian adults who participated in one or more games ranked "fun, recreation, and relaxation" as the number one reason they played, above the need to stay healthy, meet new friends, hang out with family, or feel a sense of achievement. Yet, sadly, children are turning less and less frequently to games in their free time (Graf et al., 2004). Although organized sport opportunities for 5- to 13-year-olds in North America have doubled in the past 20 years (Hofferth & Sandberg, 2001), teenagers are opting out in large numbers (Ifedi, 2008; Visek et al., 2015). The following list, collected from several reports, summarizes the reasons young people gave for opting out of sports:

- I lost interest.
- I had no fun and it took too much time.
- The coach did not empower players.
- There was too much pressure and worry.
- The coach played favorites.
- The sport was boring.
- There was an overemphasis on winning.
- There was too much sport-specific practice and deliberate practice at a young age.
- The sport programs were badly run.

What better way to recapture and maintain children's interest in and enjoyment of sport than by offering them opportunities to explore and create through play and inventing games? Becoming a good team player takes years of discipline and effort, and becoming a good citizen takes years of civic engagement. The process must be enjoyable to ensure that students stick with it. Without the element of play, activity becomes routine, predictable, and lacking in possibilities. Moreover, democracy depends on human creativity; openness to change, adaptability, and creativity thrive in an atmosphere of freedom and openness, and vice versa. As Shogan (2007) suggested: "If ethics is less about compliance with codes and more about how we explore the ways in which these codes shape our lives, it is possible for people to become more directly involved in understanding and changing their own conduct" (p. 35). In the inventing games process, students are directly involved in constructing the rules that shape the game and their conduct within it. Rather than adopt a zero tolerance approach to bullying, in which bullies are sought out and punished, schools can create curricula that foster respect, fairness, and acceptance.

> ## Key Concept: Sport and Games
>
> The words *sport* and *game* are often used interchangeably. However, although it is true that all sports are games, not all games are sports. Games derive from play and involve competition. Sport games are games of skill that have a large physical component, as opposed to games of chance or board games. Physical educators often refer to games in terms of games education, a subset of the physical education curriculum. The term *sport* is often used in the context of extracurricular activities attached to schools, communities, or private organizations.

Children who are free to play have fun and feel safe. Because they are engaged emotionally, cognitively, and spiritually (as well as physically) in a holistic process, they want to stay in the game. They are more likely to invent variations in game play, alternatives that require quick analyses and creative responses. They are also more likely to experience what Kretchmar (2005) called delight. Moments of delight may happen infrequently in games, but they keep us coming back for more. Learning cannot be compartmentalized into behavioral domains and neatly subdivided into the cognitive, the psychomotor, and the affective, because human systems are nested and interconnected. A student who has just been criticized for poor performance in a skill drill is unlikely to make confident decisions, or decisions that involve risk. Holistic approaches, which take the affective experiences of students into account, are imperative for advancing our understanding of TGfU and learning in general. The next section provides a closer examination of inventing games as a medium for seriously playful learning experiences.

PROCESS OF INVENTING GAMES

Children have always made up their own games during recess and out in their yards or on their streets. The games they invent are usually fun, fair, and inclusive, as players quickly develop and enforce quite sophisticated rules. Inventing games, an offshoot of TGfU, builds on this natural ability while scaffolding tactical principles to help students learn about game structures, rules (Almond, 1983; Castle, 1990; Curtner-Smith, 1996), and the principles of fair play. These principles can be applied not only to game play, but also to their lives as members of democratically organized societies.

Learning Game Structures

Inventing games is not about unstructured play; indeed, the reverse is true. Learners use the process to investigate game structures within the TGfU classification system. Organized by the intent of the game, or the primary rule (see table 1.1), the four categories are target games, striking games, net and wall games, and invasion games.

Key Concept: Teaching Games for Understanding (TGfU)

TGfU was initiated by a small group of educators (Len Almond, David Bunker, and Rod Thorpe) at Loughborough University in the UK in the late 1970s. They had become concerned that the traditional teaching of techniques was failing a large percentage of children who left school without having achieved a great deal of success in games. These educators drew on the child-centered approaches of the 1950s and 1960s, such as movement education, which in turn drew on the ideas of theorists such as Rousseau, Montessori, Dewey, Bruner, and Laban. Building on the work of Margaret Ellis (1983, 1986), Thorpe and Bunker organized games into four categories: target, striking, net and wall, and invasion. They defined each category based on the concepts, strategies, and skills involved, and also on the players' roles. Games could be modified to make them more accessible or more challenging, or to focus on certain concepts, strategies, and skills. The focus of teaching became the game and the player, with an emphasis on player decisions and individual readiness. Teachers became facilitators and designed game contexts and situations to challenge players to improve their performance by developing decision-making skills, skill execution, and tactical awareness.

Table 1.1 TGfU Categories and Primary Rules

TGfU category	Primary rule (intent)
Target games Examples: Archery, bowling, curling, golf, pool	To send an object and make contact with a stationary target in fewer attempts than the opponent makes.
Striking games Examples: Baseball, cricket, Danish longball, rounders, softball	To place the ball away from fielders in order to run the bases and score more runs than the opponents score.
Net and wall games Net examples: Badminton, pickleball, tennis, volleyball Wall examples: Handball, racquetball, squash	To send a ball to an opponent in such a way that the opponent is unable to return it or is forced to make an error. Serving is the only time the object is held.
Invasion games Examples: Basketball, football, hockey, lacrosse, soccer, team handball, water polo, ultimate	To invade the opponents' defending area and shoot or take the object of play into a defined goal area while simultaneously protecting one's own goal.

Layered onto the TGfU classification system is a 10-stage model (see figure 1.1) for the inventing games process. This model was designed to enhance and guide curricular planning; it is not intended to be prescriptive. The application of the stages depends on students' experiences and developmental levels. For this reason, the inventing games chapters (6, 8, 10 and 12) do not follow the stages exactly. It is suggested in chapter 6, for example, that two stages be

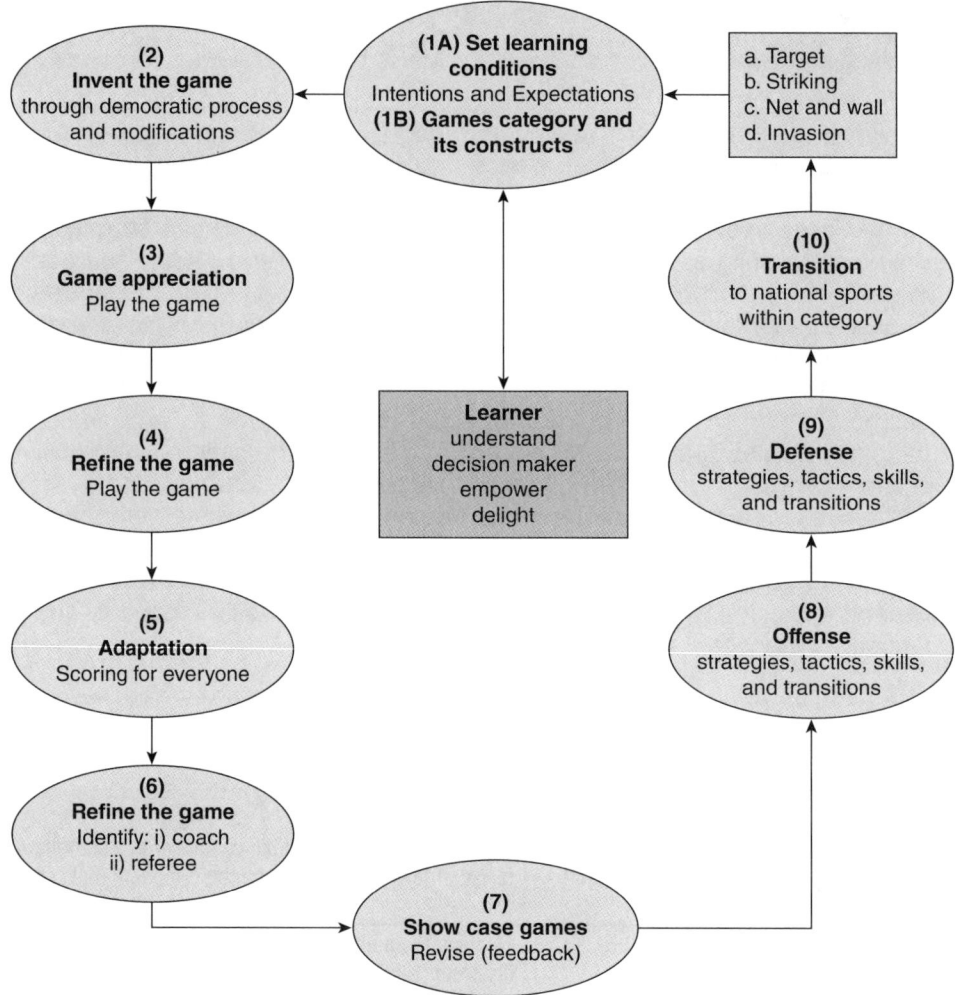

FIGURE 1.1 10-stage model to guide the process of inventing games.
Adapted from D. Bunker and R. Thorpe, 1986, The curriculum model. *In Rethinking games teaching*, edited by R. Thorpe, D. Bunker and L. Almond (United Kingdom: University of Technology Loughborough, England), 7-10.

devoted to refinement, the first in terms of the game and the second in terms of the skills. Although planning is a necessary process, the starting point is not linear or predictable.

The 10 stages of the inventing games process help to break down the intent, or primary rule, of the categories into strategic concepts, tactics and skills, and player roles (see table 3.1 in chapter 3). This reveals commonalities that help teachers transfer learning concepts among and within the categories.

Transfer of Concepts

The transfer of concepts in the inventing games process cannot be left to chance. One serious misapprehension about inventing games is that students will just figure everything out on their own. Teaching for transfer of concepts (related to both game constructs and democracy in action) is a conscious and strategic pedagogical technique. This book addresses this in two ways: by placing inventing games chapters at the beginning of discussions of each game category, and by addressing both external and internal schemas.

Inventing games chapters are placed at the beginning of each of the TGfU game categories so that students can transfer the constructs they learn through their invented games to institutionalized sports within the same category. Teachers use their knowledge of students' invented games to make these connections.

Both internal and external schemas (Schmidt, 1977) have vital roles to play in the transfer of concepts. The TGfU categories (see table 1.1), their essential components (see table 3.1), and the inventing games model (see figure 1.1) serve as external schema that teachers can use to organize and plan student experiences. They also help students create their own internal schemas, based on the cognitive maps they construct from their invented games (this is described in more detail in chapter 3). The two schemas work in tandem.

DEMOCRACY IN ACTION

A historic assumption has been that physical education, and particularly games education, teaches personal and social responsibility. Initially, it was believed (in 19th-century private schools, for instance) that playing games built character, at least in boys (Hellison & Martinek, 2006). Teachers assumed that playing games would teach students how to be good sports in the same way that many teachers today assume that having students work in groups will teach them about effective communication, cooperation, and teamwork. However, as Seefeldt and Ewing (1997) pointed out, "The physical act of performing sport skills will not teach moral action" (p. 7). So the premise of teaching democracy in action is that moral action and democratic citizenship must be a planned and deliberate part of the curriculum.

Inventing games encourages students to understand that with freedom comes a large measure of responsibility. For example, a group of sixth-graders working

Key Concept: Schema Theory

Schema theory was developed by Schmidt (1977). Schemas are generally considered cognitive patterns of domain-specific information that people use as templates to explain, interpret, perceive, encode, and respond to complex tasks and experiences. Schemas also allow people to predict what may occur in future similar situations. People create meaning from situations, data, and events by organizing and determining the patterns in complex sets of information.

through stage 1 of the IG process produced the following list of individual rights for the group (Butler, 2005):

Each member of the group has the right to the following:

- Contribute or decline to contribute to group discussions
- Be heard by others respectfully

The group has a responsibility to the following:

- Include all members in group discussions and decisions and to respect an individual's right not to be involved
- Give decisions due process
- Revisit decisions

Interestingly, this group provides the right to either contribute or decline to contribute, and the insistence on due process and the right to revisit decisions already made reveals a surprising level of maturity for sixth-graders.

The notion of democracy in action counteracts the common assumption that ethics comprises a set of a priori principles. Rather, it suggests that principles, skills, and aptitudes emerge in authentic situations in a participatory, adaptive learning culture. For the purposes of this book, we have limited some of these democratic principles and skills to include the following:

- Group process
- Personal and social responsibility
- Free inquiry
- Decision making
- Social justice

Group Process

From the beginning of the inventing games process, students learn in groups. This requires that they learn how to negotiate, decide on, and adhere to group structures (including methods of reaching consensus), and explore ways of working together and resolving conflicts. Groups usually move through stages, which Tuckman (2001) described as forming, storming, norming, and performing.

- *Forming.* In the forming stage, groups have fresh energy and enthusiasm and focus on orientating themselves to the task. Anything seems possible during this stage, as they read through the inventing games guidelines. Individual group members are also checking out the ways they relate to one another, thoughtfully or not.

- *Storming.* The storming stage can be a time of immense growth as students start to bubble with ideas, perhaps all talking at once. It can also be a time of conflict as they struggle for power. A decision-making policy becomes particularly relevant at this stage.

- *Norming.* Moments of aporia (stuckness, impasse, anger) can render a group unable to proceed in the norming stage. Group policies and rules can help members build trust.

▪ *Performing.* The bonding achieved in the previous stages allows the group to work more closely in the performing stage. Cohesion is witnessed in the showcasing part of the inventing games process. The group is positioned well to refine rules, develop tactics for team play, and, perhaps most important, understand how the democratic process has helped them understand what is fair and equitable.

A team that works through these stages effectively usually moves on to make good and quick decisions on and off the playing field or court.

Personal and Social Responsibility

All games are social, in that they involve relationships with both partners and teams. Learning how to negotiate relationships is a central part of the inventing games process. Learners plunge into collective processes that are no different from real-life situations they face or will face. All collective processes strike a balance between the needs and desires of the individual and the needs and momentum of the group. How much should an individual give up for the good of the majority? How much should the majority take the needs of a minority group into account? Is it OK not to contribute to every decision? What should members do if they totally disagree? How much should members speak, and how much should they listen? How do members of a team support each other? What does it mean to be a good team player?

Free Inquiry

Without free inquiry, there can be no democracy. TGfU teachers believe that knowledge is not fixed and out there, but rather constructed and reconstructed on a daily basis through the debate of ideas (Wallion, 2005). In the traditional classroom, the teacher often decides who should talk and for how long (Butler, 1993). Indeed, lively conversation is often discouraged in physical education; administrators often determine the quality of a lesson based on the amount of silent on-task activity.

In contrast, the inventing games class is a place of lively debate (as well as spirited play) as students articulate and communicate ideas in the expectation that they will be heard and respected. As in real life, communication will fail, tempers will fray, and differences will seem irreconcilable, but inventing games teachers see these moments as opportunities for students to become more articulate, practice active listening, and learn that not all situations can be resolved. Sometimes we have to settle for a compromise, trust others, or delay a final decision until we see how things turn out.

Decision Making

As players ask questions about their actions, such as Should I pass or keep the ball?, they exercise attributes such as social conscience, critical thinking, and commitment (Goodlad, Mantle-Bromley, & Goodlad, 2004). Bunker and Thorpe (1982, 1986b) proposed that all children be involved in decision making through tactical awareness so that they gain understanding and become more engaged.

By making decisions about their invented games, students learn firsthand how games are constructed.

Social Justice

In inventing games, students create ways of being and playing that are inclusive, fair, and attentive to issues of power, privilege, and difference. This is discussed in more detail in chapter 2.

Table 1.2 delineates the IG stages by grade levels and the suggested foci for the democracy-in-action principles.

WORLDVIEW OF AN INVENTING GAMES TEACHER: ECOLOGICAL COMPLEXITY THINKING

At the far end of the gymnasium, the sixth-grade girls confront the boys. "This isn't fair!" Jaclyn yells. "Who put you in charge?"

Josh bounces the ball impatiently. "Let's just get on and play," he says. "We're wasting time!"

As the physical education teacher strides across the gym to address the conflict, she carries not only her whistle, but also her opinion about the purpose of the lesson. This will determine her assessment of the situation: a teacher's nightmare or a teachable moment. She has a number of options. One would be to reprimand her charges and order them back on task. Instead, she asks what's wrong. The outraged girls inform her that the boys have ordered them into defensive roles, keeping the offensive positions for themselves.

What does the teacher do next? This depends on her beliefs about teaching and learning. Those beliefs are situated within, and inseparable from, her worldview, which influences her disposition and teaching style.

The physical education curriculum as a whole has been shaped by a range of worldviews. Health and wellness and outdoor education all draw on a wide spectrum of philosophies and values, from aboriginal ideas about wellness to hard Western science. However, games education continues to dominate the overall physical education curriculum (Lockwood, 2000), and its prevailing value orientation is what Jewett and Ennis (1995) called the disciplinary mastery perspective and what Metzler called the direct instruction model (2005). This perspective comes from a worldview in which truth can be separated from falsehood and knowledge is a body, or corpus, that can be measured, quantified, and transmitted. Because mastery is valued, teachers deliver knowledge, and the disciplinary mastery curriculum emphasizes correct and efficient ways to carry out skills. Ideal learners are compliant, responsive, and able to memorize information—an emphasis on efficiency that can be traced back to the connections between sport and the military. As this worldview translates into practice,

Table 1.2   Inventing Games Stages by Grade Levels and Democracy-in-Action Principles

Inventing games stages			3 and 4	5 and 6	7 and 8	9 and 10	11 and 12	Democracy-in-action principles
1	A	Setting the learning environment; setting conditions for democracy in action	X	X	X	X	X	**Decision making:** Group or partner policy
	B	Defining game category and game constructs	X	X	X	X	X	**Decision making:** Group or partner policy
2		Inventing the game through democratic process and modifications	X	X	X	X	X	**Personal and social responsibility:** Individual responsibilities to the group
3		Game appreciation: Playing the game	X	X	X	X	X	**Personal and social responsibility:** Group responsibilities to the individual
4		Refining the game	X	X	X	X	X	**Social justice:** Inclusion, empathy
5		Adaptation Scoring for everyone		X	X	X	X	**Group process:** Conflict resolution (respect and patience)
6		Refine the game: Identify: i) coach, ii) referee		X	X	X	X	**Group process:** Conflict resolution (respect and patience) **Free inquiry:** Leadership styles
7		Showcasing all the games	X	X	X	X	X	**Free inquiry:** Constructive feedback
8	A	Identifying defensive strategies			X	X	X	**Free inquiry:** Active listening
	B	Refining defensive skills				X	X	**Group process:** Consensus building
	C	Identifying defensive transition strategies (defense to offense)				X	X	**Personal and social responsibility:** Trust
9	A	Identifying defensive strategies			X	X	X	**Free inquiry:** Active listening
	B	Refining defensive skills				X	X	**Group process:** Consensus building
	C	Identifying offensive transition strategies (offense to defense)				X	X	**Personal and social responsibility:** Trust
10		Connecting the invented games unit to institutionalized sports		X	X	X	X	**Social justice:** Modifications and adaptations for equal access

teachers transmit not only techniques, (hoping that these will somehow transfer into game play), but also the knowledge and beliefs that lie unquestioned in their cultural heritage.

In this book, I suggest that inventing games and TGfU are most effectively taught by teachers with a different worldview—that of ecological complexity. Such teachers see good game play as fun, sustainable, and packed with educational potential. They also believe that their actions and decisions can never be entirely separated from those of their learners or from the context within which they occur. They are concerned not only with the short term (the quality of teaching in physical education) but also with the long term (the lifestyles that their teaching may inspire). Such teachers focus on emergent learning as they encourage learners to ask and consider critical questions to construct knowledge and meaning and develop a sense of ownership of their learning. Rather than fixing errors, teachers who have an ecological complexity worldview work to make sense of their learners' interpretations and perceptions, and they offer them opportunities to practice the critical analyses, interpretations, dispositions, and attributes that they will need to be engaged global citizens.

We can surmise that if the teacher in the preceding scenario has a disciplinary mastery perspective, she will implement a quick remedy to move the moment of aporia, or stuckness, along—perhaps by assigning offensive and defensive roles equally to girls and boys. However, if she is interested in sustainable and emergent learning, her actions might look very different. Seizing the opportunity to offer another layer of learning, she would invite them to engage in a critical dialogue and seek ways to reframe and resolve the situation. This scenario is further explored in chapter 2, where steps are suggested for addressing such situations. As noted earlier, ethical situations are much more difficult to circumvent or ignore in a physical learning environment than they are, say, in a civics class. Students who pay lip service to social justice in their written or oral communications may be the very ones who refuse to pass the ball to girls, or to less popular students, or who privilege the large and the strong in other ways.

Inventing games is not just a fun experiment. Rather, it is part of an integrated, considered physical education curriculum based on the following considerations within an ecological complexity worldview.

- *Learning is an active process.* Learners bring information from their earlier experiences and engage with others to coconstruct a game and arrive at new understandings.

- *Knowledge and empathy are developed as students try out various roles such as player, referee, coach, scorekeeper, and manager* (see the practical chapters 6 through 14).

- *Learning is best when it is deadly serious and very playful at the same time* (Sara Lightfoot cited in De Castell and Jenson, 2003). Democratic citizenry depends on human creativity, and conversely, creativity thrives in an atmosphere of freedom, play, and openness.

- *Students learn how to learn.* As students construct meaning from their shared invented games, they also construct structures of meaning that shape their future learning. Children learn through their interactions with others. As they internalize the knowledge and skills through these interactions they can eventually use this to guide and direct their own behavior and actions (Vygotsky, 1981).

■ Self-organization of groups: Students self-organize to co-create prescriptive and proscriptive rules and regulations and to create and play games (chapter 3).

■ Internal schemas (chapter 3) document learning of individual and group understanding of game concepts through mind-mapping and debating ideas.

■ *Learning is a social activity*. Effective communities of practice emerge as teachers purposefully plan students' experiences and interactions.

■ *Coemergence of learning*. Learning emerges as individuals relate in community, causing new patterns and structures to emerge.

■ *Learning takes time*. By teaching to increase learners' capacity for understanding rather than only their retention of content, and understanding that this understanding is transferable, teachers don't feel pressured to cover every activity in the curriculum.

■ *Linear and nonlinear planning*. Teachers still plan, but they see planning as a starting point to an unpredictable, nonlinear journey.

■ *Learning requires good scaffolding*. External schemas, combined with developmental awareness, provide this scaffolding.

■ *Student ability is determined by curriculum design* (Butler, 2006a). Good players draw on a range of skills (not just specific techniques). These include decision making during game play, teamwork, and positioning off the ball. The skills of negotiation, decision making, and invention are of equal value in this process.

■ *A participatory democratic classroom lies on the edge of chaos and order (disequilibrium), a dynamic that promotes growth and evolution*. Teachers must be willing to experience discomfort and avoid the temptation to fix problems immediately.

■ *Democratic citizenry requires ethics of responsibility and care*. Teachers must pay attention to their cultural frames and blind spots, and look for ways to address the social and ecological implications of learning (Davis, Sumara, & Luce-Kapler, 2008).

SUMMARY

Physical education can play a vital role in the 21st century. At a time when personal interactions are increasingly conducted through social media and smart phones, physical education offers the opportunity to navigate challenging tasks through face-to-face negotiation and discussion and in a context where it becomes difficult to smooth over or ignore such problems as unfairness and injustice. When students work together to invent their own games, they learn ways to cooperate in order to resolve conflict, make good decisions, and develop group processes that are fair and effective. They learn to adapt creatively to changing situations in order to stretch their understanding and ability. This inventing games curriculum is underpinned by TGfU game structures or schemas, which provide a framework that helps learners make sense of their experiences and allows for progression and transfer, through which students construct their own internal schemas. As with any worthwhile learning, students may encounter moments of challenge, aporia, and frustration, but more typically, game play is flowing and fun as it catches players up in the moment. Instead of directing and disciplining students so that they can replicate the "correct" way to do things, the successful inventing games teacher engages students, drawing their attention to the possibility of game evolution, productive discussion of issues of fairness and justice, and skill development. This requires close attention to learning possibilities as they appear on the fly and to the broader goals of the physical education curriculum so that students might develop into engaged citizens and active learners who take responsibility for their actions and development. The teacher who manages this kind of attentiveness can be said to embrace an ecological complexity worldview.

Teaching and Learning Social Justice Through Inventing Games

The sixth-grade class is inventing games, within the category of invasion games. The students have discussed and decided on the basic structures of their game (boundaries, goals, ball) and agreed on five rules. Now it is time to try it out. They race off to set up their equipment, and as Mr. Uppal scans them quickly, he notices that one group is already playing. He moves toward them to praise their initiative, but is confused when he sees that they are throwing the ball at each other. His heart sinks. His first instinct is to put a stop to this game; dodgeball is not allowed in many North American schools for good reasons. Instead, he bites his tongue and pulls the group together.

Mr. Uppal: Hey! Well done! You are the first group to get playing! Can someone explain the game?

Sophie, the biggest girl in the group, shoots up her hand.

Sophie: Well. It's based on dodgeball, but we changed it up, 'cause in real dodgeball you can get hurt. We're using these soft, squishy balls, and the rule is that you have to aim below the waist and we have a rescuer that brings people back to life.

She smiles happily at her teacher.

Mr. Uppal: You explained that very concisely, *and* I understood it!

Sophie and the group laugh.

Mr. Uppal: So where did the ideas come from?

Sophie glances at the other kids in the group.

Sophie: I remembered it from summer camp.

Mr. Uppal: The whole thing?

Sophie nods. She knows she's on shaky ground here. Mr. Uppal looks around the group.

Mr. Uppal: So did you all agree on this?

One of the boys speaks up—a little too quickly and loudly.

John: Yeah. We all really, really like dodgeball, but we know you don't, so we made it really safe and everything.

Mr. Uppal watches the others carefully.

Mr. Uppal: How about the rest of you?

A couple of the students keep their faces expressionless. They don't nod, but they don't disagree either. Mr. Uppal knows better than to put them on the spot.

The charter of the International Olympic Committee (IOC) articulates a high regard for human rights (Seaman, 2009), including the right to practice sport. The Olympic spirit depends on fair play and mutual understandings that preclude discrimination of any kind. This notion that all people have equal power—to live freely, to vote, and to speak—is central to democracy. Without social justice, there can be no equality. Yet rights imply civic responsibilities in that they must be actively taken up through involvement in the community, and teachers can help students buy in to such engagement.

The inventing games process offers teachers an opportunity to teach consciously to promote ethical awareness and active, engaged citizenship, which Freire (1989) called dialogic education. Varela (1999) stated that ethical awareness is developed through actions carried out in context; a helpful term for this is *democracy in action* (see chapter 1 for more details). As students negotiate, debate, overcome conflict, and navigate through problems together while inventing games, they enter a microcosm of community life, encountering the challenges and joys of civic responsibility.

The inventing games process helps teachers do the following:

- Promote democratic and emancipatory processes in teaching and learning.
- Equip students for democratic collective learning by helping them discuss and actively listen to new ideas, perspectives, and experiences.
- Provide students with opportunities to make decisions that are fair, equitable, and sound, while helping them develop the aptitudes they need to do so.
- Plan for student learning about social issues by having students work authentically and equitably while inventing games.
- Address moments of aporia (i.e., stuck places) by considering democracy in action.

The vignette at the beginning of this chapter illustrates these premises. The teacher, Mr. Uppal, resists his urge to resolve the situation, and instead opts to engage the students in discussion. Following is a continuation of his dialogue with the students:

Mr. Uppal: Can anyone remind us what this unit is called?

Sophie: Inventing games.

Mr. Uppal: Yes, OK, but in which category of games?

Sophie: Invasion games.

Mr. Uppal: Yes, good. So remind me what some of the characteristics are for invasion games.

Tamson: There is a goal at each end.

Mr. Uppal: Yes, good. And what's the purpose of the goals?

Tamson: To send the ball into the goals to score and beat the other team.

Mr. Uppal: Right! So where are the goals in this game?

Sophie: Mmm, we don't have any.

Mr. Uppal: Well you kind of do . . . .

There is a little pause.

Sophie: Oh right. We use each other as the goals!

Mr. Uppal chooses not to address this, but notes it for later discussion.

Mr. Uppal: OK. So can you quickly regroup and redesign your game to include goals—one at each end?

About 15 minutes later, the group is fully engaged in the newly adapted game complete with two goals (mini soccer nets). Throwing at human targets is still part of the game, and most of the students are flushed and beaming with joy.

Mr. Uppal: I see you've included the goals at each end. So how have you included these in your game?

Sophie: We used—

Mr. Uppal: Thanks, Sophie, but let's have someone else explain this time.

Tamson: I can explain! If we manage to get the ball past all the opponents and it lands in the goal, we score 5 points. If we hit one of the opponents, we get 1 point. They still have to sit down and they can still be rescued.

Mr. Uppal: That sounds pretty good! Thank you, Tamson. The next step now is for you all to ask yourselves six questions. These are all listed in your games sheet. I'm going to invite the whole class to do the same task.

What Mr. Uppal does first is draw the students' focus to their own game constructs. They are able to see that their original dodgeball game simply does not meet the constraints of the invasion game, and they are willing and able to adapt it to fit these constraints. However, the issue of human targets has still not been addressed. Rather than tackling this head on, Mr. Uppal poses six questions to help all the students in his class (not just the most vocal) engage in dialogue about the educational value of the games they have designed.

Mr. Uppal (addressing the whole class and passing around a handout that he now reads): Here are your six questions:

- Is this game fair?
- Is it safe?
- Is everyone involved?
- Is it challenging?
- Does it flow?
- Is it fun?

He keeps a sharp eye on Sophie, who seems reluctant to spend time on this task.

Sophie: Yes to all of them! Let's get on with the game!

Mr. Uppal: Perhaps that's true for you at the moment, Sophie, but I want each group to discuss this point by point. Remind me, now—how did your group make decisions?

Sophie: We agreed that after a discussion we would vote.

Mr. Uppal: Well great! So let's have the recorder write down the number of votes for each of the questions on the sheet. That'll help you keep track. You have three minutes to finish this.

When the class reassembles, Mr. Uppal asks if the answers were unanimous, and most students nod. Mr. Uppal turns to the dodgeball group.

Mr. Uppal: How about you, group 1? Who was the recorder?

John: We had 6s on most questions, but we had only a 3 on if it was safe and only a 4 if it flowed.

Mr. Uppal (turning to the rest of the class): What do you think this group needs to do now to get their scores up to 6?

Several students (raising their hands): They should change their rules!

Mr. Uppal: I agree. Not everyone's happy with the way things are working, group 1. See if you can fix it. I'll be over in a few minutes to help. The rest of you can get back to your games and consider tweaking them to make them even better!

We can see how the inventing games structure reinforces the democratic process by flushing out the views and opinions of all members of the group. Rather than making this process personal by isolating and emphasizing individual opinions and objections, Mr. Uppal keeps it objective by pointing out that consensus has not been achieved. Students can see that the game does not follow the guidelines and is thus an anomaly in the class. By supporting those in the minority, Mr. Uppal makes it easier for students to disagree with the way things are.

When Mr. Uppal returns to group 1, a discussion about human targets is in full swing:

John: I think Mr. Uppal wants us to take out the human targets rule.

Sophie: But that would change the whole game!

Tamson: Yeah! I like it!

Amy: I don't. I always get hit.

There is a brief silence.

Sophie: Well, move out of the way!

Amy: You think I don't try? You think I'm useless!

Mr. Uppal: What have you decided—any rule changes?

Sophie: We can't agree.

Mr. Uppal: Who can summarize the discussion so far?

Sophie: Well, some of us still want to keep the human target rule in, and some want it out. They say you don't like it.

Mr. Uppal: Well, it's true. I don't. But if all six of you decide to keep it, then that's your decision. No one forced you to play this.

Tamson: Why don't you like it?

Mr. Uppal: Well, it's complicated, but there's no game I know of where players deliberately aim to hit a player. I think the reason for that is that it encourages people to throw balls at someone else, and it can hurt them, not necessarily physically either. I've seen kids use this game as an excuse to bully others. And that's pretty unpleasant.

Mr. Uppal quietly leaves as the students continue the discussion.

Tamson: What about if we tagged someone with the ball instead, rather than throwing it at someone?

John: The loose balls take up a lot of time to collect, and that's why we lose the flow of the game.

Sophie: OK. Let's try that!

Mr. Uppal deliberately refrains from telling his students what is right early in the process, preferring that they figure it out for themselves and take ownership of their decisions. First, he engages the students in a little deconstruction of the games construct; then he reinforces the democratic decision-making process they have agreed to follow. This allows dissenting opinions to be heard and respected. In turn, students can think more broadly about the social issues involved. Only at this point does Mr. Uppal offer his own ideas and experience, which the students are more ready to hear and understand.

This example provides a good illustration of democracy in action. Nieto (2000) and Freire (1989) pointed out that reflection is not the result of intellectual effort alone. It occurs through praxis, or the union of action and reflection on the world in order to transform it (Freire, 1989, p. 51). Bringing these insights into the educational realm, we can offer students opportunities to examine, discuss, and reflect on content; grapple with ethical responsibility; analyze critically; and enact the democratic ideals of equality, freedom, and justice. The learning process must not be just practical (e.g., how to vote and offer opinions), but also, as Mathews (1996) suggested, cognitive and affective (e.g., how to keep an open mind, stand in another's shoes, and make decisions with others).

REVISITING THE TRUE MEANING OF COMPETITION

Without competition, there is no game. However, the various interpretations of the word *competition* have led to some confusion. Critics of new approaches to sport education often fear that innovators are against any form of competition. However, it is truer to say that most are reacting to a narrow interpretation of the term. Adages such as "Winning isn't the best thing—it's the only thing" and "Win at all cost" reveal a zero-sum view of competition (i.e., whatever is won by one opponent is directly lost by the other). However, other interpretations exist, and as Stoll and Beller (2000) suggested, it is in the interests of our students that we explore them. Nastasi (1992) and Siedentop, Hastie, and van der Mars (2011) offered alternative and more expansive definitions of competition.

Key Concept: Cooperation

For a team to compete (i.e., meet, come together, or strive against others to attain a goal), they must work together. In inventing games, the decisions learners make in groups off the court or field when creating games can readily transfer to the game itself.

The words *compete* and *competence* derive from the Latin word *competere*. Etymologically speaking, *to compete* means "to strive to achieve a goal." Competition provides a space where people strive to become competent (the best they can be), and opponents are a necessary part of this process. If this is understood, competitors can appreciate their opponents and thank them for their help at the end of the game. When it is not understood, the opponent is reduced to anonymity, and respect, fairness, equality, and honor are traded in for a victory. This leads to unfair practices such as stacking teams and cheating.

A second meaning of *competition* is "to come together." In competition, people come together to showcase their talents, meet like-minded people, and celebrate a shared culture.

TEACHING SOCIAL JUSTICE AND DEMOCRACY IN ACTION

To embrace human rights is to become aware that without social justice there can be no fairness or equality; consequently, democratic processes cannot function. Essential to the definition of democracy is the notion that all people have equal power to live freely, to vote, and to speak. With these rights comes the civic responsibility to exercise these rights through active interest and involvement in the community. Teachers play a crucial role in preparing students to do this.

There are two key aspects of teaching for social justice through the practice of democracy in action. The first is addressing societal inequities through antioppression education. The second is using some of the pedagogical tools to teach social justice—in this case, democracy in action, situated ethics, and inventing games.

Understanding Societal Inequities

As Young pointed out (1990), the democratic process breaks down when unfairness and an imbalance of power occur. Let's consider the nature of power in relation to the games curriculum.

■ *Power over, or coercive power.* This is the power structure in hierarchies. The school administration, which controls the curriculum, is supported by the school board, local government, and the law. Sometimes the culture of the school reinforces practices that seem to go without saying. These might include the disciplinary mastery approach to teaching sport, or inequitable practices such as dodgeball.

- *Power from within, or empowerment*. As educators, we seek to empower our students through active creative experiences such as singing, writing, solving problems, making art, and dancing. Through inventing games, we offer active creative experiences in the ethical domain, as we encourage students to speak up, listen, negotiate, and make decisions that will enhance the effectiveness of the group.

- *Collective power*. Collective power is the power people gain when they act in concert. In the inventing games process, students begin to understand that they are part of a community they can trust. They come to accept that they sometimes need to set aside their own interests in favor of common goals. They learn when to take care of themselves and when to take care of others.

- *Power with, or social power* (influence, rank, status, or authority). Social power determines how much weight an individual opinion carries, how much members are listened to in a group, and how much they are respected. As young people struggle to reach the expectations of adulthood, they rely heavily on their peers to establish self-esteem. Young people who see themselves as outsiders and not accepted by their peers are more likely to withdraw, become depressed, and become targets for bullying (Boyce, King, & Roche, 2008).

- *Earned and unearned social power*. Unearned power is privilege, the power you get not from anything you are have done or created, but from who you happen to be—your gender, your race, your social class, the wealth you've inherited, the opportunities handed to you. With privilege often comes entitlement, a feature of hierarchy (Starhawk, 2011, p. 45). This often plays out along the lines of gender and race in physical education classes.

Teaching for Social Justice

Left unaided in group decision-making processes, students fall back on informal or culturally determined systems of interaction, ranging from the much-loved football huddle to a reliance on acknowledged leaders. These systems are products of cultural, generational, and gender norms. Although there is much to celebrate in all social institutions (church, family, state, school), the active and engaged citizen must always examine them for bias. The challenge for the teacher is to find ways to limit privilege while helping students find positive ways to be rewarded for their efforts.

Very often, we learn about what we believe when we confront real-life situations. In inventing games, these situations arise frequently and naturally as students encounter moments of aporia (rupture or stuckness). When we are faced with situations that challenge what we know, we struggle to make new sense of the universe and push beyond our current moral constructs. Varela (1999), who called this new, more conscious, sense of what is right ethical know-how, believes that it evolves over time through small decisions and actions, rather than being handed down as a set of a priori principles. As students invent and negotiate to create their games, they develop their capacity for personal and social responsibility, free inquiry, decision making, social justice, cooperation, and competition (see chapter 1).

Key Concept: Aporia

Aporia is a term that describes the moment of disruption caused by disagreement, or a place of stuckness caused by not knowing what to do next. This experience contributes to a greater understanding of how democracy works and how the absence of social justice may cause it not to work. Moments of aporia are signposts that indicate the opportunity to make connections between game structures and democratic principles.

Skills for Democracy in Action

Just as in Teaching Games for Understanding (TGfU), ethical understanding, tactics, skills, and effective game play develop through well-designed gamelike activities and structured group processes.

Students take responsibility by doing the following:

- Taking on roles such as recorder, equipment manager, and coach
- Paying attention to social relations
- Helping to resolve conflict

They learn good judgment by doing the following:

- Realizing that sometimes they must put the good of the group before their personal benefit
- Contributing ideas and actions for the greater good of the group

They become models and teachers for others by doing the following:

- Making mistakes and acknowledging them so that their realizations become part of the group's learning
- Modeling behaviors such as listening, respecting, understanding, and forgiving
- Demonstrating integrity
- Developing, discussing, and refining values
- Bringing practical experience, skills, and training to game play
- Bringing special talents and passing on newly developed skills
- Mentoring and accepting mentorship
- Making thanks and appreciation part of the experience of healthy competition

They learn that conflict can provide opportunities for learning by doing the following:

- Learning to trust each other and the group process
- Addressing conflict honestly, respectfully, and directly
- Resolving difficulties and moving on

Key Concept: Situated Ethics

The notion of situated ethics counteracts the common assumption that ethical behavior occurs when we apply a set of a priori principles, such as the Ten Commandments, to a given situation. Rather, it suggests that such principles emerge over time and in context. Some (although by no means all) ethical principles form the basis of democratic culture, along with certain skills and attributes that make democracy work.

Skills for Group Process

As they work together to invent their games, students also construct group structures that represent and serve the needs of all members. The teacher's role includes drawing attention to successes and challenges, and supporting students as they develop fair and effective ways of working, such as the following:

- Agreed-upon structures and processes for making decisions
- Clear and transparent agreements about how people gain decision-making power
- Clear ways for people to take on tasks and responsibilities
- Clear agreements about the scope of each member's authority
- Clear structures of accountability: Who do people report to? How, when, and in what form is an accounting given?
- A group culture of appreciation and thanks to those who make contributions and take on tasks
- A culture of tending to and mutually caring for those holding responsibility
- A fair and transparent systems of rewards
- Training and mentoring to help people take on new responsibilities

The teacher must also be vigilant in rewarding and encouraging the development of skills and strategies that support the process of the group, including the following:

- Doing what they say they'll do quickly and effectively
- Asking for help and guidance when needed
- Passing on tasks they cannot do
- Making sure others complete tasks
- Handling crises calmly when they arise
- Planning, strategizing, and looking ahead

Pedagogical Steps in the Inventing Games Process

There are often clear signals that the game has stopped being fair or that learners are stuck: the game falters, voices are raised, or someone has walked off with the ball. Rather than seeing these moments of aporia as an educational failure, teachers who are focused on emergent learning see them as opportunities for learning.

Teaching democracy in action makes many more demands on the teacher than running drills, refereeing dodgeball, or coaching. However, teachers can take certain steps when a group encounters a moment of aporia or difficulty, such as the encounter described in chapter 1 in which sixth-grade girls confronted the boys in their group who had grabbed all the offensive positions and relegated the girls to defense. Following is an outline of the steps a teacher might take in this situation:

1. Assess the emotional state of the group. Are members able to debrief and negotiate in their heightened state? Might a cooling-off period be necessary?

2. Ask pertinent questions. Following are some examples:
   - How were the decisions made about who played?
   - Who took the most power in making these decisions?
   - Who benefited? Who did not?
   - What other ways of determining players' positions might be considered?
   - Why is it important to include everyone in decision making and take some time to hear all views? What other situations mirror this one?

3. Define the moment of breakdown in communication. In this instance, it might be when the boys imposed a ruling that did not involve the girls in a fair process or when the group decided that offense was more desirable than defense.

4. Identify the democratic principle that was violated, and remind the students that they had agreed to adhere to that principle. Why was it set aside? In this instance, the group had settled on a democratic decision-making process. The reasons the boys ignored it are complex; they reflect the socialization and enculturation of both boys and girls.

5. Identify a democratic attribute or value that might make the inventing games process work more smoothly. In this instance, possible responses are respect, empowerment, and fairness. Democracy does not work when power inequities exist among voters.

6. Consider how the situation might be resolved. Possible solutions are reestablishing and reinforcing the negotiated group decision-making process and applying it to decisions about player roles.

7. Consider policies or practices that might help prevent this situation from recurring. How might the group become of aware of players' grievances, and how might they be addressed?

8. Have students write about the experience to clarify what they learned and, in particular, to identify the principles, concepts, and structures they encountered. In this way, students can develop their own schemas of ethical situations and principles of democracy in action to guide their thinking and reactions. Individual writing can help less vocal students identify their thoughts and feelings, which may help them be more articulate and confident in future discussions.

9. Resolve to learn. Hopefully, the teacher will resolve to better educate the class about offensive and defensive roles. This is a good opportunity to discuss mutually supportive teamwork.

Figure 2.1 illustrates the rationale behind the preceding steps. The horizontal line provides the learning situation through the inventing games and democratic processes. The vertical line indicates issues regarding social justice and situated ethics. In the scenario of the indignant girls, the

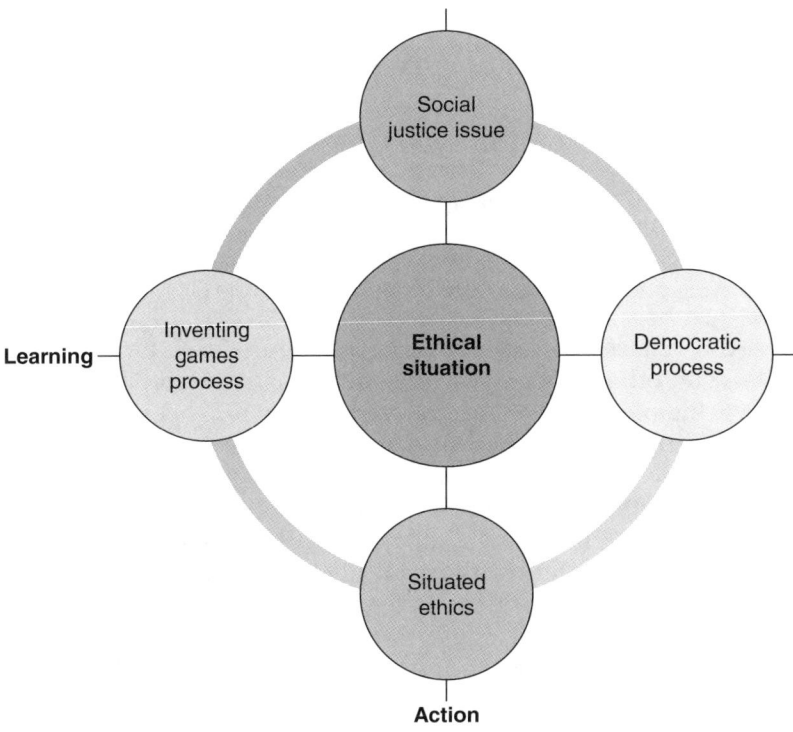

FIGURE 2.1 Components of ethical situations.

following concepts might emerge from a dialogue resulting from skillful teacher questioning:

- *Social justice issues:* Social power, fairness, gender inequity
- *Democratic principles:* Group process, decision making
- *Game constructs:* The assumption that offense positions are more important and more desirable than defense positions

Other Topics for the Democracy-in-Action Classroom

Many of the topics teachers are exploring with students in our current research program focus on forms of power. These have included the following:

- Why do students stack teams to annihilate their opposition?
- What happens when students use each other as human targets—for example, in dodgeball?
- What happens when smaller students, students from minorities, or less skilled players are not selected for teams, or not equally included in game play?
- What happens when someone doesn't participate in decisions and then complains about them?
- What is cheating, exactly? Is it ever OK to keep quiet about an action that is unfair?
- Why do we need referees? How should they be treated?
- How can a group make fair decisions?
- Does everyone have the same rights, including the right to be heard?

Teacher-researchers found the worksheet in figure 2.2 to be useful for understanding how an ethical situation, the social justice issue it raises, and the democratic principles involved are related. This worksheet uses the example of students stacking teams (when students are left to choose their own teams) and offers possible responses and solutions.

Applying this kind of critical analysis to moments of aporia requires attentiveness and mental agility, but this should not discourage teachers from initiating these discussions. Although we may not always know the answers going in, this is perhaps the point. As with most learning, meaning is constructed in the process and through authentic engagement. I am continually surprised by the innate sense of fairness of most young learners, as well as by their aptitude for quite sophisticated ethical dialogue.

Name: _____ Grade: _____

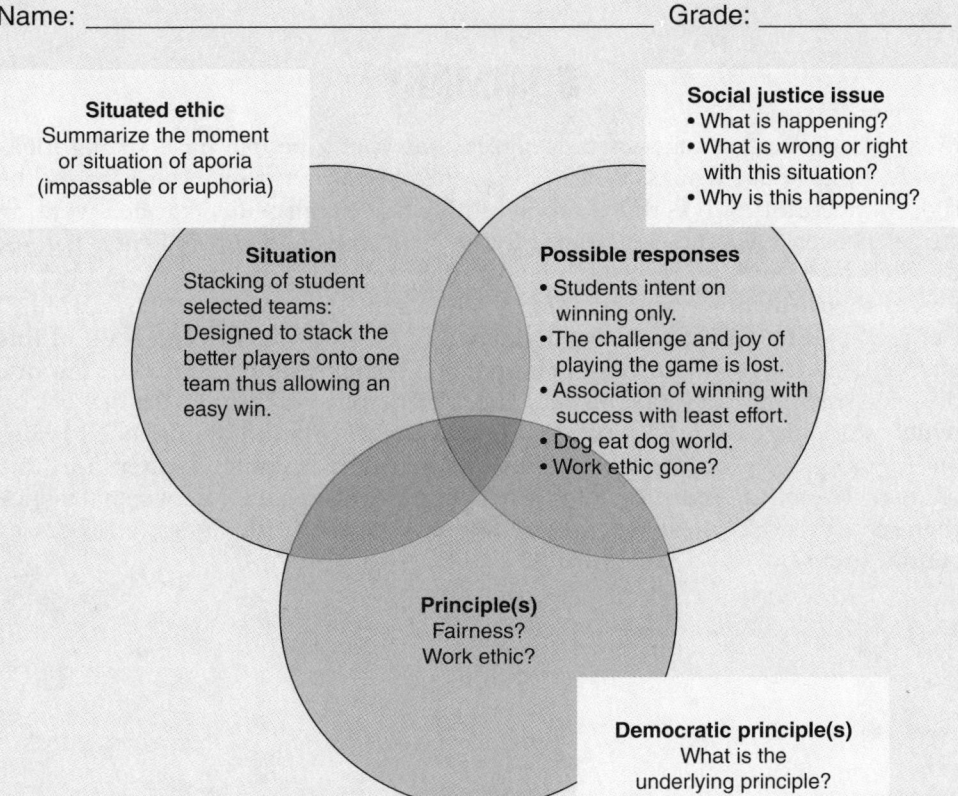

Situated ethic
Summarize the moment
or situation of aporia
(impassable or euphoria)

Social justice issue
• What is happening?
• What is wrong or right
  with this situation?
• Why is this happening?

Situation
Stacking of student
selected teams:
Designed to stack the
better players onto one
team thus allowing an
easy win.

Possible responses
• Students intent on
  winning only.
• The challenge and joy of
  playing the game is lost.
• Association of winning with
  success with least effort.
• Dog eat dog world.
• Work ethic gone?

Principle(s)
Fairness?
Work ethic?

Democratic principle(s)
What is the
underlying principle?

How can this situation be sustained or resolved?

Teacher-centered process	Student-centered process

FIGURE 2.2 Worksheet for understanding the relationship between social justice issues and democratic principles in an ethical situation.

SUMMARY

Most parents and teachers would agree that young people have strong ideas and feelings about what is fair and that they are able to voice these, given the right opportunities. It is these opportunities that are provided by the inventing games process. As students negotiate the structures and rules of their games, they learn to think more broadly about their own responsibilities and behaviors as their learning transfers into the situations they encounter in "real life." Democracy-in-action principles described in chapter 1 and referenced in this chapter include group process, personal and social responsibility, free inquiry, decision making, and social justice. These principles represent a framework on which students can build ideas and organize information about social issues and democratic process. A key point underlies the arguments offered in this chapter: To embrace human rights is to become aware that without social justice there can be no fairness or equality and consequently, democratic processes cannot function.

Scaffolds for Learning: Schema, Transfer, Classifications, and Rules

"Yes. I've heard of the TGfU approach to teaching games," said Jenny. "It's OK in theory. In fact, I'm all for problem solving—I use it all the time. But students need to have the basics in place first, especially the younger ones. This exercise really helps them with their fundamentals."

Jenny was teaching tennis to sixth-graders and had the class in two groups lined up at the back of either court. The first player in line hit the ball over the net, and the first player in the line on the other side tried to hit it back. Players who were successful got to take another turn and keep going until they missed. Those who missed, even on the first try, had to run to the back of the line and wait to take another turn.

I was video recording this lesson, and here are some of the things the camera caught: girls who chatted animatedly when they were in line but stepped up sullenly for their turns and took halfhearted swings that rarely connected; a short uncoordinated kid who tried and tried, but never once connected with the ball; a boy who missed the ball consistently all through the class, but took his racket after everything was over and banged three balls off into the nearby woods.

As I watched the recording, I wondered what the students had learned—that the best get better and the worst don't deserve a second chance? That tennis is a dreary game? That tennis is not a game, but a chance to hit the ball back to an opponent rather than to score points? That physical education is an opportunity to catch up on gossip? That hitting the ball can be fun, but only if the teacher doesn't see you?

Before moving to the curricular implications of the inventing games experience, it is important to remind ourselves that any games education program, including this one, is only part of a well-balanced physical education curriculum. Any credible physical education program offers a rounded experience that encourages learning and participation in lifelong activities and healthy lifestyles. Yet in many schools, traditional games still dominate the curriculum.

Although the focus of this book is games education, it is not intended to endorse an imbalanced curriculum or to minimize the learning that occurs in other areas of the physical education curriculum, such as outdoor learning, outdoor environmental education, educational gymnastics and dance, health-related fitness, and swimming.

This chapter describes how a games education curriculum incorporating inventing games can be organized within both a Teaching Games for Understanding (TGfU) classification system of games and a TGfU pedagogical approach. The external schema of the TGfU conceptual framework is explained through primary (main intent) and secondary rules. Also discussed is the transfer of learning through a spiral curriculum and sampling.

TGFU CLASSIFICATION AND INVENTING GAMES

TGfU is one way to classify games. Other systems include the game category system (Nichols, 1994), core content (Allison & Barrett, 2000), developmental games (Donnelly, Mueller, & Gallahue, 2016), and one based on Suits' essentialist theory of games (Vossen, 2004). I use the TGfU classification to organize content because they make the most sense to me in terms of intent. The TGfU categories (target, striking, net and wall, and invasion) offer a comprehensive and logical structure to organize the games curriculum, unlike the traditional organization around the seasonal cycle of professional sports. Although teachers and students alike have become used to playing certain sports at certain times of the year, this reinforces hegemonic gender and geographic stereotypes, while serving no clear educational purpose. If other games are offered to provide a fair range of activities, the curriculum becomes overcrowded and uncongenial to innovation.

Inventing games units work best when they are nested within comprehensive and balanced experiences offered in the TGfU categories. As students learn to create and develop the constructs of their own games within the constraints of TGfU categories, they form solid ideas about their own games and others within the category. The teacher plans the curriculum to teach for transfer so that students forge strong connections between their own invented game constructs and the constructs of other games within the category. In effect, they

Key Concepts: Rules and Regulations

Whereas rules outline the intent of games, regulations may be put in place to prevent the exploitation of loopholes found in the rules (Shogan 2007, p. 26).

- *Descriptive rules* help officials and organizers identify and standardize such things as the length of warm-up time permitted before matches, the size of teams, the acceptable placement of numbers on playing shirts, substitution protocols, equipment dimensions, playing area dimensions, and the color of match balls.
- *Prescriptive rules* prescribe actions that players may perform when engaged in a particular game. Prescriptive rules describe what an action is—what must be done.
- *Proscriptive rules* proscribe actions that a player must not perform during a particular game.

create schemas of constructs and concepts (such as strategies, tactics, skills, and techniques) for each of the four game categories.

Primary Rules

Determining what unifies the games in each category (their intent) gets to the heart of how games are constructed. The unifying ideas for each category are known as the primary rules. My conversations with teachers and preservice teachers not familiar with TGfU in determining the primary rules often go like this:

Q: What do you notice about the categories? What are the unique criteria for including games in each category?

A: All the games in the striking category require the ball to be hit with an implement.

Q: Yes, that does seem to be true. Is that criterion unique to that category, though? Take a look at all the other categories. Are there games in other categories that require a ball or object to be hit with an implement?

A: You hit a ball with a mallet in croquet (target), a stick in hockey (invasion), and a racket in tennis (net). So they all meet the criterion of hitting with an implement.

Q: OK, so maybe that criterion is not unique to the striking category or sufficient to explain its intent. However, before we dismiss this idea completely, can you think about who has control of the implement in these games?

A: It's only the batting team that has the striking implements. The fielding team doesn't. They have gloves—well, except in cricket. But I guess the wicketkeeper has big gloves.

A: And in the examples of hockey, tennis, and croquet, all players have implements.

Q: This idea (that only offense players use implements) seems to be unique to the striking category, but it's not a big enough idea to explain the games' intent. Let's put this aside as a secondary rule.

A: Maybe it's the playing area that defines the category. In the invasion category, all the games are played on rectangular fields . . . oh, but that wouldn't include team handball and water polo!

A: Maybe it's the number of players. The net and wall games are organized by the number of players on a team. They are played either as individuals or as dual teams.

A: But that wouldn't include volleyball.

Once the more tangible ideas of skills, implements, player numbers (team vs. individual), and location are worked through and given a secondary rule status, the task of identifying the primary rule is then tackled. The conversation usually shifts to a more abstract arena, particularly after the word *intent* is used for guiding the focus of the discussion. Examining the intent of the games in each category then generates definitions.

Secondary Rules

The heart of a game is defined by its primary rule (intent). For example, in all invasion games, the intent is for players to score more goals than their opponents by invading their opponents' defending area in order to score a goal while simultaneously protecting their own goal. Players strive to meet this rule more often, more quickly, and more accurately than their opponents by setting goals linked to the secondary rules. This will become more apparent as we examine the three different type of secondary rules.

For simplicity, we can organize the secondary rules into three categories: descriptive, prescriptive, and proscriptive.

Descriptive Rules

In the process of inventing a game, students have a lot of fun deciding on the secondary rules. These are often descriptive, and we often see them in rules and regulations handbooks for institutionalized sports; they spell out the dimensions of the playing area; the number of players; and the size, weight, and height of the equipment. They set the conditions and contexts for the primary rules or intentions of games, conditions that we manipulate when we try to make the game more or less challenging and accessible for students. For instance, when striking at a ball proves too challenging for participants, we might modify the secondary, or descriptive, pitching rule from hitting a thrown ball to hitting a stationary ball from a tee or kicking at a large rolled ball. This enables participants to pursue the same intent and make the same kinds of decisions, but at an easier level. Softball and baseball have institutionalized modifications of the same game intent by using different-sized balls, fields, and pitches.

Descriptive rules also define the space in which the game is played. Whether the playing area in invasion games is water (water polo), ice (hockey), grass (field hockey, soccer, and lacrosse), or a wooden floor (basketball), play is confined to the area between the goals (and in some cases, such as ice hockey and lacrosse, behind and around the goals). This generates interactions between the opposing teams that are not seen in other games (except inadvertently in striking games). In net games, the net separates opposing teams, removing one aspect of game play—the possibility of opposing players impeding each other directly as in invasion games. Descriptive rules (or regulations) can also speak to the intent of the game. A goal at each end requires teams to both defend their own goal and attack their opponents' using the space in between to maneuver the object to shoot or regain possession. Once the descriptive rules of the game are established, we can also organize the secondary rules into prescriptive and proscriptive rules. A balance between them creates game flow and harmony.

Prescriptive Rules

The actions and experiences enjoyed in games are set by prescriptive rules. These are the rules that state what players must do. For example, in field hockey, international hockey federation rule 9.2 states that "players on the field must hold their sticks and not use them in a dangerous way." Rules 9.3 through 9.18 all start with the statement *players must not*. These "must not do" statements (i.e., proscriptive rules) set boundaries for what players *can* do in rule 9.2 (prescriptive rule).

Consider another example from the game of basketball. In the United States, NBA rule 4, titled "Definitions," defines the actions of basketball. For example, section III addresses dribbling and includes this definition: "A dribble is movement of the ball, caused by a player in control, who throws or taps the ball into the air or to the floor." Because this describes what the player can do, it is a prescriptive rule. The NBA definition goes on to say that the dribble ends when the dribbler does any of the following:

- Touches the ball simultaneously with both hands
- Permits the ball to come to rest while he is in control of it
- Tries for a field goal
- Throws a pass
- Touches the ball more than once while dribbling, before it touches the floor
- Loses control
- Allows the ball to become dead

These seven actions define what players may not do and still be considered as dribbling the ball; hence, they are proscriptive rules.

Prescriptive rules shape the actions of the game. The actions of serve, volley, drop, forehand, backhand, and smash are common and unique to the net game category. Passing, receiving, dribbling, and shooting are common and unique to the invasion category.

Proscriptive Rules

As described in the preceding discussion of dribbling, the rules that place a limitation on actions are proscriptive rules. We will come across this term again when we examine the kinds of constraints we can construct to enable students to learn efficiently and effectively. As we have noted, proscriptive rules define what players *cannot* do, and they link to the primary rules of games. They open up possibilities for what they *can* do (once they know what they cannot do). These constraints enable specific types of games to be played. For instance, the constraint of the net enables players to work closely together on one side of the net without any chance of physical contact with the opposition (except perhaps inadvertently when blocking at the net). The constraint in striking games of one team sending up one batter at a time and the other team fielding all players limits team interaction and focuses attention on the batter, who initiates play. Golfers cannot throw the ball into the hole in golf. Players cannot touch the net on a serve in all net games. Field hockey players cannot use the rounded side of the stick in field hockey, nor can they score a goal from outside the semicircle.

The logic behind proscriptive rules usually draws from principles of fairness, equity, challenge, and precision. Proscriptive rules result from a collective agreement to pursue the game with some limitations. The most efficient way to play golf (get the ball into 18 different holes using fewer strokes than one's opponent) would be to throw the ball from the tee to the hole. The enjoyment, of course, comes with the challenge of selecting the right club for the distance and executing the perfect swing.

UNDERSTANDING GAME CONSTRUCTS THROUGH INVENTING RULES

In inventing games, students take ownership of rules, understanding that they are somewhat arbitrary, yet they create competitions that are challenging, fair, and enjoyable. Students participate in games by agreeing on the essential intent of the game. When they invent their own games, they learn how to construct both primary and secondary rules. For example, as they come to appreciate the primary rule of defending their own goal and attacking the opponents' goal, they make the inference that there must be a goal at opposing sides of a playing area, which is different from the setups of games in other categories. In this way, inventing games helps students understand the structure of the game categories from the inside out, rather than experiencing them as something given. They come to understand the interconnections of descriptive rules, prescriptive rules, proscriptive rules, and the essential intent of the game. Also, they create situations that often prove highly suited to their developmental readiness.

Later (in this chapter and in chapter 4), we examine in more detail how the curriculum might be put together using inventing games. For now, it is important to know that the inventing games units are best placed at the beginning or near the beginning of teaching units in each of the categories. The reason is that, once the primary rule is established, it is easier to understand the category based on common concepts, strategies and skills, and player roles (see table 3.1). These commonalties illuminate relationships between the game categories, and the notion of transfer becomes part of the teacher's plan for learning. Table 3.1 also summarizes the essential constructs of the game categories. These constructs create an external schema that can form the basis for curriculum development for grades 3 through 12.

STRUCTURING THE INVENTING GAMES CURRICULUM

How now should we approach organizing the curriculum? The following questions provide a start for educators:

- Which category should be taught first?
- Should all categories be taught concurrently to give students experience in each?
- What sequence helps learners understand the relationships of concepts, skills, and strategies?
- What is reasonable to expect from students in terms of problem solving?

Table 3.1 Essential Components of Games Education

	Target	Striking	Net and wall	Invasion
Examples of games	Archery, billiards, bowls, bowling, croquet, curling, golf, pool	Baseball, cricket, Danish longball, kickball, rounders, softball	Net: Badminton, pickleball, tennis, table tennis, volleyball Wall: Handball, racquetball, squash	Basketball, field and ice hockey, football, lacrosse, soccer, team handball, water polo, ultimate
Primary rule	To send away an object and make contact with a specific, stationary target in fewer attempts than opponent.	To place the ball away from fielders in order to run the bases and score more runs than the opponents.	To send the object back to opponents so that they are unable to return it or are forced to make an error. Serving is the only time the object is held.	To invade the opponents' defending area to score a goal while simultaneously protecting own goal.
Concepts and skills	• Sending away skills: Drive, release, deliver • Accuracy • Direction and distance	• Placement of the ball in field skills: Striking, body positioning, hand positions on the bat • Decision-making skills: Observation, listening, receiving and throwing • Covering bases skills: Sprinting, ready position, moving sideways • Base-running skills: Sliding, sprinting	• Spatial awareness skills: Throwing, catching on bounce and volley, serving and receiving serve • Positioning on court • skills: Running, stopping, changing directions • Position of body skills: Balance, footwork, hitting the ball in relation to the body • Trajectory skills: Throwing and catching • Depth skills: Hitting with specific force, lob shot, drop shot, spin shot, volley, drive, dig • Angle skills: Control of racquet, angle of racquet, volley, forehand and backhand	Offensive concepts • Keeping possession skills: Sending, receiving, traveling • Penetration or invasion skills: Accurate passing and receiving, dodging, changing of speeds Defensive concepts • Zoning, defending players in area skills: Shuffle, change of speed, running in different directions • Defending a specific player skills: Footwork • Transition concepts skills: Peripheral vision, footwork, running, quick change of direction
Players' roles	• Same skill required for all players • No interaction	Variation in roles for defensive team (e.g. pitcher, catcher)	All players require same skills as they rotate positions. (e.g., all serve and receive)	• Designated goalkeeper • Defensive and offensive role or player • Midcourt (both roles)

(continued)

Table 3.1 *(continued)*

	Target	Striking	Net and wall	Invasion
Playing area	• Playing area is shared • Players take turns • Variations from golf courses to ice sheets	• Playing area is shared • Offensive team has designated track to run • Running track varies	• Area is divided by a net • Opposing players are separated	• Area shared by all players • Rectangular • Often outdoors
Offensive strategies	Hitting a target • Archery Gold • Bowling Jack • Curling Button • Golf Hole • Pool Pockets • Skittles Pins	• Fielding positions • Forcing play • Holding runner from stealing • Staying on offense turn for as long as possible	• Placing ball farthest away from player(s) • Placing ball close to boundary lines • Moving to volley position at net • Intercepting • Anticipating • Employing spikers	• Keeping possession • Moving ball or puck to specified area • Rapidly changing from offensive to defensive • Transition • Organization of players moving from offense to defense and vice versa
Defensive strategies	• No defensive strategies in individual games • Team games, obstacles put up to prevent own target from being hit	• Stealing • Leading • Tagging up • Quick and accurate receiving and sending skills	• Returning object and keeping it in bounds • Anticipating where opponents will return object	• Intercepting ball or puck before it goes over the line or into the goal • Pressuring opponents into making mistakes • Closing down distribution options

"Stages for children inventing games," J. Butler, *Journal of Physical Education, Recreation and Dance*, 84(4): 48-53, 2013, Taylor and Francis, adapted by permission of Taylor and Francis (Taylor & Francis Ltd, http://www.tandfonline.com).

While teachers provide an external schema by laying out the common layers of games, it is important to note that students will be creating their own internal schema based on the cognitive maps they construct as they invent their own games. Figure 3.1 shows some of the questions teachers might ask students as they enter the invasion games unit.

Throughout inventing games units, students are encouraged to explain their ideas and offer examples of overarching principles. For examples, students may explain why goals in invasion games are at opposite ends, or the fact that offense requires keeping possession of the ball while trying to score goals. This is explored further in the practical chapters (6 through 14).

TEACHING FOR TRANSFER

One serious misapprehension about inventing games is that students will just figure everything out on their own. Transfer cannot be left to chance, and both

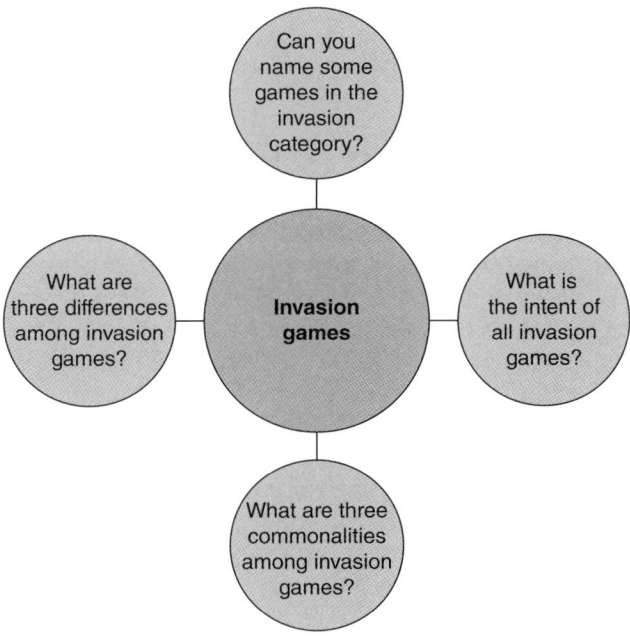

FIGURE 3.1 Mind map for the characteristics of invasion games.

internal and external schemas have a vital role to play. The TGfU classifications and the conceptual framework serve as external schemas that teachers use to organize and plan learning experiences.

As students match their internal schemas with the external schemas in place, and teachers group games in developmentally appropriate orders (see chapter 4), teaching for transfer becomes possible. According to Schunk (1996), positive transfer is more likely to occur when learners recognize common features

Key Concept: Transfer

The notion of the transfer of ideas, practice, or training has to do with the way a learned response in one situation influences a response in another situation (García López & Jordan, 2009). In bilateral transfer, what players learn with the hand (basketball) can be transferred to the non-dominant hand or feet (soccer). Grouping soccer and basketball offers this kind of learning. Intertask transfer of skills and concepts means that the solid foundation of learning one skill or concept will transfer to another, decreasing the time needed to learn in a new context. For instance, the volleyball spike and the tennis serve are very similar. The give and go in soccer is similar to the give and go in basketball. Intratask transfer is often considered as progressions move from simple to more complex.

among concepts, principles, and skills; consciously link the information in their minds; and see the value of using what was learned in one situation in another situation. Transfer can be either intertask or intratask depending on the focus.

Intertask Transfer and Tactical Complexity

Intertask transfer occurs when the learning or performance (or both) of one skill, concept, strategy, or tactic influences the learning or performance (or both) of the same skill, concept, strategy, or tactic in another set of conditions—or the learning of a different skill or concept. For example, a give-and-go tactic in basketball using the hands to make passes can transfer to the same conditions in soccer using the feet to make passes. Tactical complexity describes the combination of tactical concepts (scoring and preventing scoring), movement concepts (body, space, effort, and relationship), and ability and skills (i.e., psychomotor, cognitive, and affective) in a game (Howarth, Fisette, Sweeney, & Griffin, 2010).

Encouraging students to reflect on their games' rules can help them recognize that their creations are based on game concepts. Through careful questioning, the teacher can help them develop mind maps so that they can transfer these concepts to other games.

Table 3.2 provides examples of transfers in concepts, strategies, tactics, and skills. The last row in table 3.2 indicates occasions in which a negative transfer may occur. For example, it is probably not a good idea to follow a badminton activity with squash or tennis. In badminton, the player needs to be able to flick the wrist, whereas this action is not helpful in squash or tennis and could in fact cause injury.

Intratask Transfer

Intratask transfer is transfer within the same task, often between levels of difficulty. It occurs when the relationship between two types of practice is considered. See table 3.3 for further examples. A movement education approach is helpful with young children in practicing and exploring objects while keeping the element of tossing and catching the same. For example, children can toss and catch a beach ball, gatorball, or Wiffle ball while figuring out the differences between them. In bowling, changing the size of the ball, the size of the pins, the distance between the bowler and the pins, and the use of walls may help children build extensive schemas for understanding the properties of bowling, through concepts such as reading trajectory, temporal awareness, and anticipation.

Figure 3.2 provides a mind map that will help learners reflect upon a particular skill—in this example, catching. Hopper's (2003) 4Rs are used to generate questions that students can ask themselves about each stage of executing the skill. This focuses students' reflections on the effective sequencing of catching. Each part of this sequence is accompanied by possible teacher questions that may help learners respond or elaborate upon their initial responses. Once these questions have been developed, learners are invited to summarize their understanding in context of their performance and progress. The sequence can be applied to other skills, though space precludes the inclusion of other examples.

Table 3.2   Intertask Transfer and Nontransfer Examples

	Target	Striking	Net and wall	Invasion
Intertask transfer: Strategic concepts	Accuracy, distance, direction, force, opposed and unopposed game strategies	Batter's placement of the ball away from fielders Base running Covering bases	Spatial awareness using depth (front or back of court) or width (side to side) concepts Covering space	Keeping possession Penetrating defense to score Obtaining possession Preventing scoring
Intertask transfer: Tactics	In opposed games, covering target (curling and croquet)	Closing fielders into the batter to force the batter to hit hard Stealing bases	Playing at the net	Short passing Give and go Double-teaming Overload zone in goal with defense
Intertask transfer: Skills	Sending skills Golf putt and croquet swing Curling and bowling swing	Hook in cricket and baseball swing Throwing skills in all striking games	Volleyball spike and tennis serve	Water polo and handball throwing Lacrosse and hockey manipulation of sticks
Nontransfer examples		Batter drops the bat in baseball and Danish longball but carries the bat in cricket and rounders	Badminton and squash or tennis racket use	Netball and basketball rules of on-ball space Field hockey and ice hockey manipulation of sticks

Table 3.3   Intratask Development of Skills

	Target	Striking	Net and wall	Invasion
Intratask transfer: Strategies	Force: Windup Distance: Reading direction	Reading, placement, anticipation, reacting, trajectory, and temporal awareness	Reading, placement, anticipation, reacting, trajectory, cover, and temporal awareness	Add off-ball strategies to strategies for other categories
Intratask transfer: Progressions within skills	Change size of ball, size of pins, distance, and use of walls	Catching: Progressions through changing ball size and distances to targets Batting: Progressions made from batting from tees to batting pitched balls	Use larger balls for throwing and catching game, change height of net, change from short paddles to rackets, change ball density and size	In addition to changes in equipment, change number of players and rules to simplify or challenge players

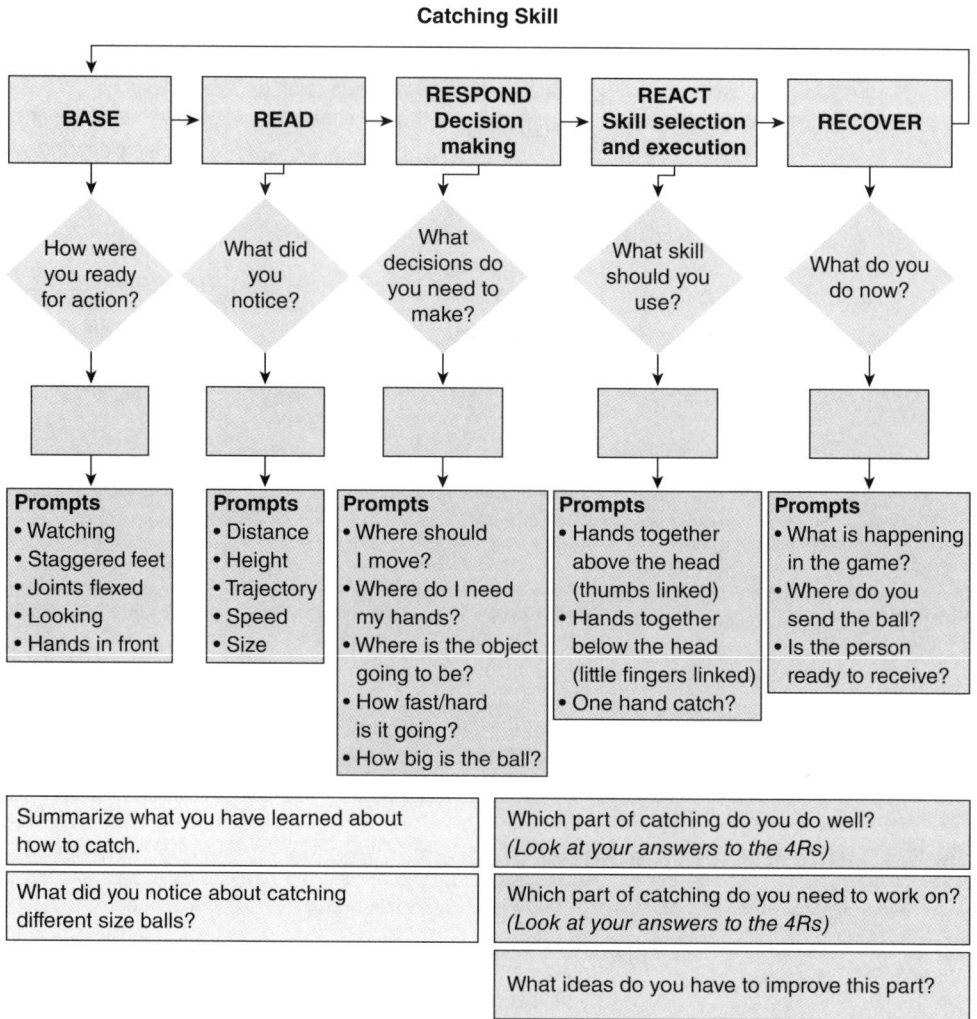

FIGURE 3.2 Mind map for a catching skill.

Most physical educators are familiar with the notion of simple to complex. Rink (2014) described the following four stages of game skill development:

1. Manipulating skills
2. Combining skills
3. Simple strategies in small-sided games
4. Full games

Following is an example of an intratask development of the skill of passing in invasion games:

Stage 1

a. Stationary players pass in pairs while increasing the distance.

b. One player moves to receive the ball in either direction.

    c. Both players move as they pass and receive the ball.

    d. Players pass and cut for the return pass toward the goal.

Stage 2

    a. Players dribble and then pass to stationary players.

    b. Players pass to moving players.

    c. Players receive, dribble, and pass.

Stage 3

    a. Players play 2v1 using all conditions in stages 1 and 2 with a passive, then warm, then active defender.

    b. Players play 2v2.

    c. Players play 3v2 with an emphasis on off-ball movement.

    d. Players play 3v3.

Stage 4

Players play small-sided games (5v5) with an emphasis on the give and go.

In net games, for example, the concept of spatial awareness might be taught as follows:

1. Have students play a 1v1 game using modified conditions (e.g., high net, large ball, enabling rules) to explore space for winning points. They should practice looking for space away from the opponent to send the ball while simultaneously covering (defending) their own court area to allow easier access to the opponent's ball placement.

2. Exaggerate the court space to illustrate the depth concept or width concept, and explain the concept of space either in front of or in back of the court, or laterally (i.e., the width of the court). This is discussed in more detail in chapters 10 and 11.

In the same category of net games, we can see how skills can be developed alongside concepts. For instance, when narrow court space is exaggerated to develop the concept of depth, the skills of performing lob and drop shots can emerge quite naturally. Students see the relevance of the concept and then the skills they need to perform well in the game. The progression of skills can go from simple to complex and from slow to gamelike pace.

CURRICULUM ORGANIZATION

Chapters 6 through 14 provide practical examples of how TGfU can be translated into concrete activities within each game category. When it comes to overall planning, however, two key principles must be considered: spiraling and sampling.

The spiral curriculum allows for revisiting the development of ideas and concepts. Such repetition facilitates learning across developmental stages (Bruner, 1977). This does not mean simply repeating curricular units or modules. When teachers pay attention to the scope and sequencing of concepts and skills, it becomes possible to organize the curriculum accordingly.

The notion of sampling is taken from Thorpe, Bunker, and Almond's *Rethinking Games Teaching* (1986b), which Almond stated was inspired by "Bruner's spiral curriculum and theory of instruction (motivation, representation, structure, and sequence)" (Almond, 2010, p. viii). Using the game classification system, teachers can select a few games with tactical similarities. For example, following an invented invasion games unit, a teacher might want the students to bring their newly developed skill of maintaining offensive control of the ball to other games in the invasion category. The teacher could create lessons on passing and receiving, moving in space (i.e., where the body moves), relationships (i.e., whom one passes to or receives from), and ball control across one, two, or three other games. The curriculum schedule could be organized so that students could transfer the tactical and movement concepts learned in their invented games to other games.

The sixth-grade yearly plan shown in table 3.4 (based on Bruner's work) uses sampling to develop concepts and skills. For example, following an inventing games unit in invasion games, students might sample soccer and field hockey either in the same unit or as two games packaged together to draw out the intertask transfer of game constructs, strategies, tactics, and skills.

The sixth-grade physical education program shown in table 3.5 offers students three sessions of 50 minutes per week and would meet the minimum requirement of 150 minutes recommended in Canada (PHE Canada). It is based on distributed practice theory; activities are offered once a week for six to eight weeks.

Inevitably, curriculum decisions are affected by school structures and settings—for instance, whether practice is distributed (classes are spread out at intervals, such as weekly) or blocked (the unit might use physical education classes until the total number of lessons available is spent). As a general rule, activities with a more psychomotor focus (learning technique such as dance steps) rather than a cognitive focus (learning game strategies) are better learned in massed practice blocks. In the case of a TGfU approach to learning games (in which students are learning skills in gamelike situations and processing game problems), the answer lies somewhere in the middle. Much depends on the facilities available in the school and when they can be used, the weather, the number of staff members available, their experience, and their views about learning. That said, one of the benefits of the inventing games approach is its flexibility and versatility. Given a modicum of equipment (or even no equipment)

Table 3.4   Sixth-Grade Yearly Plan for Inventing Games Using a Sampling Technique

Inventing game (IG) category	Sample game 1	Sample game 2
Target	Bowling (unopposed)	Curling (opposed)
Striking	Danish longball	Cricket
Net and wall	Net games intro	Pickleball
Invasion	Soccer	Field hockey

Table 3.5 Sixth-Grade Yearly Plan for Physical Education

	Fall (Sept-Oct)	Fall (Oct-Dec)	Winter (Jan-Feb)	Spring (Feb-April)	Early summer (April-June)
Target	Inventing games: Unopposed			Opposed games	
Striking			Inventing games: Danish longball		Cricket
Net and wall		Inventing games: Net games intro	Pickleball		Volleyball
Invasion	Inventing games	Floor hockey		Soccer	
Outdoor education and swimming	Outdoor education				Swimming
Educational gymnastics		Educational gymnastics (weight transference)			
Dance			Dance (creative)		
Health-related fitness (HRF)				HRF	

and even a small space, learners invent games that are fun and educational. After all, they've been doing so for centuries in even the most difficult and cramped situations—in school yards, industrial wastelands, and refugee camps.

SUMMARY

In this chapter, we have seen the ways in which the schema and classifications offered by TGfU provide a scaffold for learning that promotes the effective transfer of concepts and skills. Game classifications are organized by the intentions of the games, which generate the primary and secondary rules that define them. In order to invent their own games, students design and revise their own rules as they strive to get closer to their own hopes and intentions to make their games fun, fair, and flowing. Paying close attention to these rules and seeing how their revisions and adjustments impact their game helps them to understand the game categories from inside out. As teachers design the curriculum, they can sequence from simple to complex the introduction of games categories to maximize student understanding and the transfer of key concepts. Skills are developed alongside concepts as they are needed in the games and as they become developmentally appropriate. In the inventing games curriculum, as in the TGfU curriculum, key concepts and skills are revisited through the spiral curriculum and through the introduction of sampling of related institutionalized sports.

Developmental Learning and Curriculum Design

It's a sunny Saturday morning, and the kids are playing soccer in a recreational league. As usual, a group of parents have turned out to help out as referees and coaches. Ricky intercepts the ball and heads off toward the goal. His mom, Judith, is thrilled. "Go Ricky! Go!"

Dave, Ricky's coach, hops up and down enthusiastically. "Nice move, Ricky. Now keep your head up and look for a pass!" Ricky and his teammates thunder down the pitch toward the goal, and the defenders swarm out to meet them. "Spread out!" yells Dave. "Move away from the ball! Use the width!" But as if the ball is a magnet and they are iron filings, every single player except the goalies descends on the ball, which is soon hidden behind a blur of skinny kicking legs. There is much shoving, until the ref finally ends the melee and awards a free kick.

Dave is in despair. "I don't get it!" he says to Judith. "I tell them every practice and every game to spread out and pass the ball. How hard can it be? It's like they become deaf when they get possession!" Judith laughs. "They see themselves scoring a goal," she says. "And what counts more than that when you're seven years old?"

This chapter continues the discussion of curriculum design for inventing games in concert with the ecological complexity teaching perspective described in chapter 1. Briefly put, ecological complexity frames human beings as complex systems developing within other complex systems, such as the environment, social classes, geographic locations, nutrition status, gender and social norms, and parental values. TGfU educators, therefore, consider the varying needs of students as they develop across all three behavioral domains: psychomotor, cognitive, and affective. As TGfU teachers consider the totality and complexity of learners' experiences, they sequence game categories from simple to complex, as shown in figure 4.1, and build a curriculum with these considerations and this order in mind.

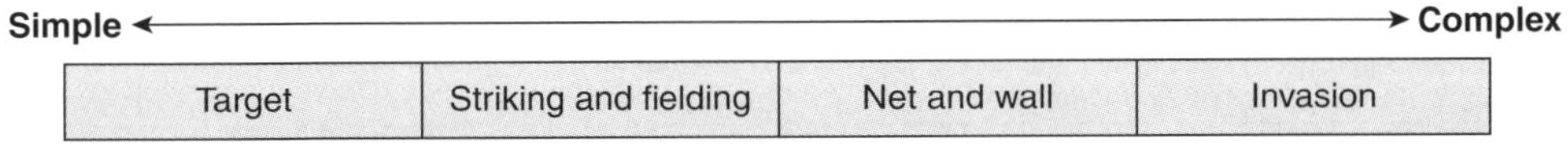

Simple ←——————————————————————————————→ Complex

Target	Striking and fielding	Net and wall	Invasion

FIGURE 4.1 Game categories in developmental order.

Individual experiences in the three domains cannot be separated from each other, because they are inextricably woven together. In the preceding vignette, the young players' lust for goals and their difficulty in grasping and executing team tactics contributes to their tendency to play "magnet soccer." Nonetheless, I have chosen to consider each domain individually to illustrate the complexities of their relationships (see figure 4.2). Taken in combination, the three domains and the TGfU categories create a two-dimensional curriculum model that is useful and descriptive, but recognizes the complexity of human movement and experience in games. Movement occurs along a continuum from simple to complex, and from general to specific, within each domain. A third dimension regarding ability or experience can then be added. This chapter defines each domain and discusses its implications for learners and the curriculum planning process. The later practical chapters build on this introduction to illustrate how teaching is informed by our understanding of the domains.

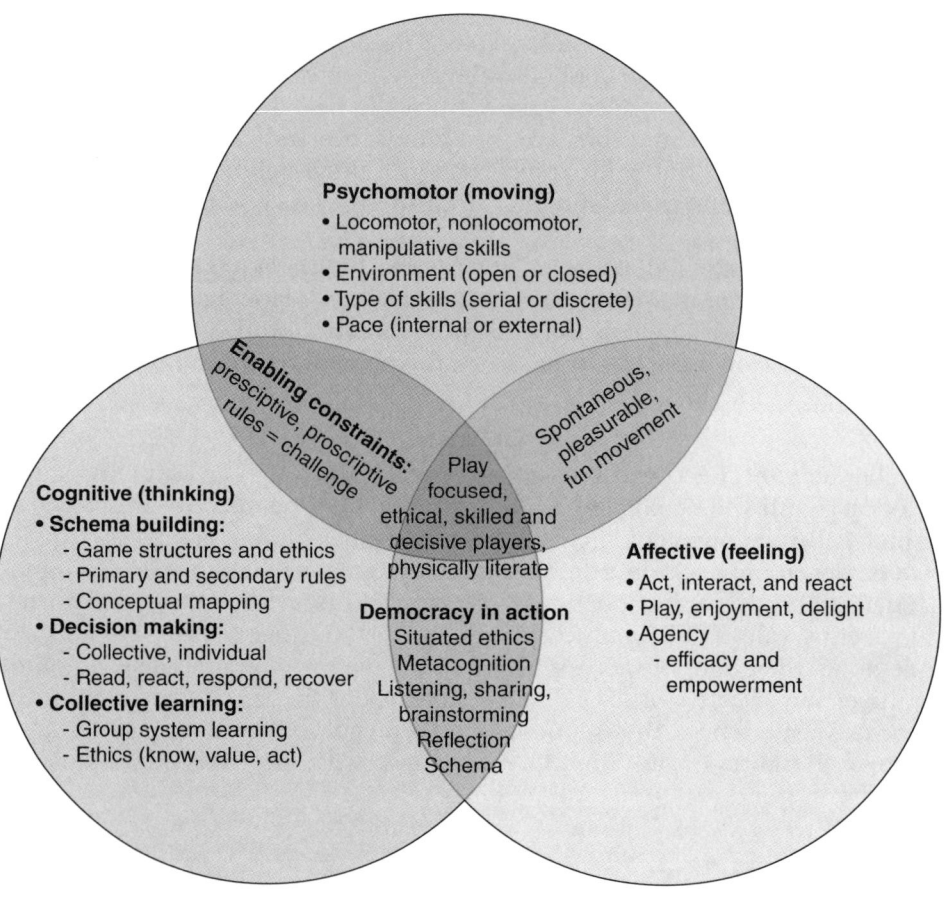

FIGURE 4.2 Venn diagram showing the behavioral domains.

Key Concept: Developmental Learning

There is a growing consensus that human development, rather than being a process of genetic unfolding, is a complex, multicausal process (Davis, Sumara, & Luce-Kapler, 2008; Horowitz, 2000). As noted earlier, the rationale for curriculum sequencing is rooted in the understanding of human beings as complex systems living and learning within other complex systems. One such system is the organic developing human body, which includes the equally organic and developing human brain. There is considerable variation in development influenced by a number of the factors mentioned earlier.

PSYCHOMOTOR DOMAIN (MOVING)

The word *psychomotor* reflects the interaction between the mind (*psycho*) and human movement (*motor*) (Payne & Isaacs, 2005, p. 29); in other words, the cognitive and physical domains.

In the context of games education, experiences and functions of movement include manipulative and locomotor and nonlocomotor skills, which, combined, are known as *motor competency* (Mandigo, Francis, & Lodewyk, 2009). Although children mature, grow, and learn at different rates, motor development theorists suggest that most learn fundamental skills (locomotor and manipulative skills) in the same sequence and the same phases (see Centres, Canadian Sport for Life's Long-Term Athlete Development plan; LTAD, 2005, Balyi et al, 2013).

The Teaching Games for Understanding (TGfU) classification system allows us to classify games according to their intentions, or primary rules, rather than teach them separately and in isolation (see chapter 3). This opens up pedagogical considerations such as the complexity of the psychomotor skills required in each of the four categories and ways that these might be organized to elicit transfer of their learning. Table 4.1 offers three variables to consider: (1) whether skills are locomotor, nonlocomotor, or manipulative skills; (2) whether they are internally or externally paced; and (3) whether the environment in which they are performed is open or closed.

Locomotor, Nonlocomotor, and Manipulative Skills

Target games usually include more sedentary locomotor skills or fundamental movement patterns such as walking. Running for any length of time is rare in target games, and the only manipulative skill involved is sending. Nonlocomotor activities include twisting, pulling, bending, holding, releasing, and swinging, which contribute most to the execution and understanding of the target games concepts of direction, force, and distance. A good example is archery, which begins with the sideways stance to the target, entailing an upper-body twist, a pulling action as the bow is drawn, a holding action as the bow is anchored, and then a releasing action that sends the arrow to the target. Players learn accuracy and precision by performing nonlocomotor skills.

Table 4.1 Psychomotor Variables for Each TGfU Game Category

	Target	Striking	Net and wall	Invasion
Locomotor skills	Step, walk	Run, step, jump, change direction	Run, jump, sidestep, shuffle	Run, jump, sidestep, shuffle
Nonlocomotor skills	Twist, pull, bend, stretch, hold, release, swing	Twist, pull, bend, stretch, hold, release, swing	Twist, pull, bend, stretch, hold, release, swing	Twist, pull, bend, stretch, hold, release, swing
Manipulative skills	Send, bowl, toss	Send (bat, throw), receive (catch)	Send (volley, bump, dig, lob, drop, spike or smash, clear, drive, serve), receive (as for send)	Send (kick, throw, hit, pass, head), receive (trap, catch), travel (dribble, cradle, carry)
Internal or external pace	Internal: Players control the pace at which skills are executed. No time restrictions, except as culturally defined (e.g., time on tee or putting green).	Internal and external: Both batters and pitchers try to control the pace of skill execution. Fielding is externally controlled.	External: The environment (which includes opponents) controls skill performance. Players must pay attention to external events to control their rate of movement.	External: The environment (which includes opponents) controls skill performance. Unlike net and wall games, in which an opportunity to reset occurs after each point, invasion games continue until the ball is knocked out of bounds, an infraction occurs, there is a time-out, or the period ends.
Environment	Closed: Stable and predictable.	Closed or open: Opening up a stable environment to make it less predictable (e.g., changing batting placement, introducing base stealing).	Open: The environment is constantly changing, so movements must be continually adapted. Skills are predominantly perceptual and externally paced.	Open: The environment is constantly changing, so movements must be continually adapted.

Striking games fit neatly into the next level in the psychomotor domain. They include sending with a bat or hand but also receiving (i.e., catching with or without a glove). Locomotor activities are combined with manipulative skills in complex situations. The batter might combine a striking action with a sprint to first base; the fielder, a run with a catch and throw to a base. Players' success in striking games depends on their ability to construct a sequence of locomotor and manipulative skills quickly and effectively. The inherent nature of striking games allows players to reset or regroup after each play, whether on offense or defense, thus giving them the opportunity to reflect on their actions.

Net and wall games are yet more challenging than the previous two categories in terms of the locomotor and manipulative skills required, because there is no time for long deliberations. Players are in constant motion in more confined spaces, which requires more agile movement, precision, and accuracy in the timing of movement to the ball and away from it, as well as the need to read ball trajectories and ball speed more quickly. The addition of the net introduces more aerial movements and more combinations of locomotor and manipulative skills.

Invasion games sit at the most challenging end of this developmental continuum. Because playing areas are large, players must sustain locomotor activity, send accurately, travel, and receive for undetermined amounts of time. Even though players handle the ball on average only 4 percent of the time, they are continually engaged in locomotor activity.

Internal or External Pace

Internally paced skills are controlled by performers, who start the action at their own pace. For example, archers generally decide when to release the arrow. Externally paced skills are controlled by the environment, which includes other team members, opponents, and coaches.

Closed or Open Environment

The game environment includes the following:

- Concrete elements such as these:
  - Playing area (size, shape, and texture)
  - Line markings (color, width, depth)
  - Structures (goals, targets, pitching mounds, bases, stands, nets)
  - Equipment for maneuvering the object (bows, tennis rackets, lacrosse sticks)
  - Uniforms or player attire (raising questions of class, race, and gender)
- Weather, both indoors and outdoors (the effects of light, noise, wind, temperature, moisture)
- Space elements (shared, divided, or parallel)
- Spectator elements (motivation)
- Positive elements (support, guidance, efficacy, agency, empowerment provided by teachers, coaches, and parents)
- Occasion elements (importance given to players, coaches, teachers, parents, school, community)

Based on the preceding elements, the playing environment can be described as stable (closed) or unpredictable (open). Target games such as golf and bowling consist of closed skills and emphasize nonlocomotor skills. Games with fewer variables are naturally easier to negotiate than those that have many. The skills involved in an unpredictable environment are generally described as open (Morris, 2002). Invasion games have the most unpredictable environments because all players occupy the same large spaces. Net games, on the other hand, reduce unpredictability by keeping the players on either side of the net.

Like net games, striking games keep the players in defined areas, although the opposing team players can be in the same space between the bases. Players in open environments are required to adapt their movements moment by moment to situations that change both spatially and temporally. TGfU advocates believe that students learn best when performing closed skills in open environments based on their experiences and abilities.

COGNITIVE DOMAIN (THINKING)

Piaget (1952) suggested that we make sense of our world by synthesizing new experiences with our current understandings (a process he called adaptation). We either fit new ideas into our present set of rules (or schemas), or we create a new set of rules that better account for what we perceive. Piaget referred to these latter processes as assimilation and accommodation.

Consider, for example, a young girl whose only experiences with sand have been in a sandpit playing with her toys. Her experience of the sand is that it is stationary, coarse, and dry (since it is always covered at night). When this child is taken to the beach, she finds that the sand has no wooden confines. She sees other children making sandcastles or digging channels to direct the seawater. When she makes a sandcastle, she finds that the sand behaves differently from her previous experiences; it is wet in some places and dry in others. Faced with many layers of learning possibilities, she must either construct a new understanding of sand, one that accommodates her new experiences, or ignore them to retain her original understanding.

Rather than taking students through a series of steps, TGfU teachers increase the constraints of their students' sandpits to help them adapt and expand their current constructions of knowledge. This is not an easy task for several reasons. In physical education, children can often understand something without being physically able to do it; yet, as physical educators, we often rely on our observations of children's actions to know whether learning has taken place. Piaget (1952) argued that understanding occurs when students decode, conceptualize, and apply content and then reflect on it. Albert Einstein may have captured it best when he said, "Most teachers waste their time by asking questions that are intended to discover what a pupil does not know, whereas the true art of questioning is to discover what the pupil does know or is capable of knowing" (Calaprice, 2011, p. 99).

Scaffolding is a process by which teachers can help students through the stages of learning by offering them activities that allow them to build meaning as they transition through early childhood, middle childhood, and adolescence. Like other social constructivists, TGfU teachers pay attention to their students' developmental stages and create appropriate challenges. These challenges are structured according to game classifications, their primary and secondary rules (see table 4.2), and students' cognitive and motor learning development, as well as their levels of sophistication in democratic and social processes. Table 4.2 shows how cognitive demands made on students move from simple (in target games) to more complex (in striking and net and wall games), and culminate in the most demanding game category, that of invasion games.

Table 4.2 Cognitive Demands for Each TGfU Game Category

			Target	Striking	Net and wall	Invasion
1	Primary rule: Score more points than opponent(s) by . . .		. . . sending the object closer to the target than opponent(s) or in fewer strokes (immediate and obvious).	. . . placing the ball in the field of play to gain time to run bases.	. . . sending the object back to the opposite side so that opponent(s) is/are unable to return it or is/are forced to make an error.	. . . maintaining possession long enough to score in the opponents' goal while defending own goal.
2	Secondary rules		Simple	Complex	Simple	Complex
3	Cognitive development stage for entry		Preoperational	Preoperational	Preoperational	Concrete operational
4	Motor learning stages	Cognitive	Sequence parts of the skill and introduce the primary rule.	Modify equipment and rules to allow the batter time to think about where to place the ball. Practice throws.	Use modifications to slow game conditions.	Use modifications to slow game conditions (increase players' thinking time for off-ball or on-ball movements, play 1v1 or 2v1).
		Associative	Refinements: Timing and coordination of nonlocomotor skill.	Combination skills: Hit and run, run and throw to target, throw to target and run.	Combination skills: Sequence of read (opponent's action) and move, hit and move to base, base and read become more fluid.	Combination skills: Carry and pass, carry and shoot, play 2v1 or 2v3.
		Automatic	Further refinements to aid the precision of closed-skill performance (habitual).	Smoother transitions between receive and throw and hit and run.	Transitions between actions (read, move, send, base) become faster.	Automatic selection of skills for efficient and effective movement; more time for thinking ahead tactically.
5	Thinking time for decision making (procedural skills, how to)		Time to think about skill selection. Focus is largely procedural in this category.	Quick decision making required.	Quick decision making required; selection of skill appropriate to the situation.	Quick decision making required in four phases of play: Offense, defense, transition from offense to defense, and transition from defense to offense.
6	Thinking time for decision making (declarative skills, what to do)		Pauses between opponents' actions. Time to think about action, strategy, and opponent at all points of the game.	Play stops between pitches, so time is available to reorganize fielders based on knowledge of the batter.	Play continues until a point is won. Decisions are based on anticipation and reading opponents' actions.	Play continues until an infraction or goal occurs, so the time to process is limited, the pace is fast, and transitions are continuous.

(continued)

51

Table 4.2 *(continued)*

		Target	Striking	Net and wall	Invasion
7	Reading the game	Read: Assess the distance and direction to the target. Respond: Apply appropriate force and direction when sending the object. Reflect: Receive feedback from the accuracy of the throw to target.	Fielder (example): Read: Assess the trajectory of the ball and decide whether to catch or cover. Respond: Move to the ball to square up for a catch. React: Make minor adjustments to the ball. Read the movement of the batters to decide where to throw. Recover and reflect: Move back into the field for the next batter.	Pickleball (example): Read: Anticipate where the ball is going to land and move to it. Respond with the selected skill (e.g., forehand). React: As the ball enters the player's area, the player reacts to the force and direction of the ball, adjusting to execute the appropriate skill. Recover: Move to the base position to receive the next shot and start the read phase once again.	Off-ball offensive player (example): Read: Be near the ball handler to offer passing support. Respond: Determine the space to cut into and signal physically and verbally. React: Sprint into the space looking to receive the pass; receive the pass. Recover: Dribble the ball while moving in to the read phase. Review and reflect: Actions and decisions at end of game.
8	Collective learning (democracy in action)	Exhibiting fairness in turn taking and sharing space and equipment. Waiting for partners to finish their turns before collecting objects. Etiquette: Thanking the opponent for playing.	Building on turn taking in batting order. Cooperation and communication for fielders: Covering space and each other. Complying with batting out rules (e.g. cricket players acknowledge outs before umpires).	Doubles and team players negotiate space and tactics.	Responding to and accommodating teammates' needs (e.g., throwing catchable passes) while being aware of opponents' play. Negotiating tactics with teammates.

Schemas provide frameworks for thinking about new knowledge (see chapter 3). In TGfU, the external schema is made up of the TGfU game classification, its four categories, and their primary and secondary rules (see table 3.1 in chapter 3). Learners build internal schemas of understanding based on these external schemas.

Primary and Secondary Rules

The primary rule defines and unifies the intent of all the games in a category. These become more complex along the continuum. Secondary rules provide constraints to enhance fair play. Some rules are easier than others for students to understand. Those of target games are simplest, and those of invasion games are more complex. Even so, our physical education and recreation programs are filled with invasion games, even though they are the most cognitively challenging.

Cognitive Development Stage

As the opening vignette demonstrates, third-graders see their role in soccer as quite simple: kick the ball into the net. Other concepts such as spatial awareness, team play, and defensive strategies are too much for them to consider while playing. Because of their simplicity in terms of rules and intentions, target games and net games are easiest for students to grasp.

The terms of preoperational (ages 2-7) and concrete operational (ages 7-11) are used here to define the levels of cognition needed for access to the category. In his description of the characteristics of the preoperational stage, Piaget often emphasized limitations, as he discussed what children cannot do in the preoperational stage but can do in the concrete operational stage. For example, he explained that children cannot "decenter" their attention from one aspect of a problem to another in the preoperational stage. As described in the vignette, children's attention is so focused on scoring at this stage that they are unaware that better possibilities (such as passing) might exist to ultimately improve the team's chances of scoring. In the concrete operational stage, on the other hand, children become more able to mentally modify, organize, or even reverse their thought processes. Children in this stage can anticipate probable events and think at least two steps ahead to make a pass if the situation calls for it, rather than haphazardly kicking the ball at the goal. Games in the first three categories can be accessed in the preoperational stage since the strategies are less complex than in invasion games.

Individual Motor Learning Stage

Traditional games teachers tend to believe that children must be proficient in skills before they can grasp more conceptual learning (about tactics and strategies). This is supported by Fitts and Posner's (1967) work on the three stages of motor learning: cognitive, associative, and automatic. Unfortunately, an overly simple application of this model has led to the teaching of skills unconnected to game play.

In TGfU, the equipment and the number of players are modified to match students' skill levels. This simplifies the cognitive stage of motor learning, so that learners can be introduced to the game situation sooner. In other words, when teachers offer game and gamelike experiences, players can attend more closely to game play. In net games, this might be achieved by providing modifications such as throwing and catching a playground ball for third-graders or using a pickleball bat for fifth-graders. First the game is made accessible; then skill sets and challenges (e.g., throwing and catching, hitting the ball with a flat hand) are introduced.

Learning skills in the context of the game makes more sense to students; they see connections more clearly and are thus more motivated. Even better, they understand the necessity of skills practice. When the focus is first on game play, students think about emergent possibilities. When the focus is on getting the skills right, they are forced into closed mind-set thinking. Even when they get it right, they don't know what to do with it.

Thinking Time for Decision Making

Both procedural knowledge (how) and declarative knowledge (who, what, where, when) systems need to be practiced simultaneously in the learning situation. TGfU advocates believe that it is neither effective nor motivational to insist that students learn skills (procedural knowledge) before they learn strategies (declarative knowledge). Rather, they teach through modified game situations to enable students to make better game play decisions, improve their skills, and find fun and enjoyment in actual game play. Target games require more procedural knowledge, whereas games at the other end of the continuum require declarative knowledge. Both target and striking games involve discrete skills that can be practiced even in gamelike situations.

In inventing games, students can transfer their understanding of game structure from their invented games to institutionalized sports, because they form declarative inference rules that can be converted into procedures. For example, using a give and go is effective for losing a defender in a 2v1 setup. This can be transferred to similar situations that require different skills (e.g., kicking rather throwing or using a stick). How to implement the strategy while making quick passes and running then needs to be worked out (procedural).

Reading the Game

Hopper's (2003) four Rs (read, respond, react, and recover) provide another way to build schemas for understanding game play. To add an assessment component, I have added two Rs.

- Players *read* the game play and decide what to do based on cues in the game situation.

- Players *respond* with their decision on the appropriate movement or skill.

- Players *react* to the dynamics of the ball (or object) by adjusting their execution of the movement or skill.

- After execution, the players *recover* with the appropriate movement or skill to set up for the *read* phase once again.

- Players can *reflect* on and *review* their decisions and actions either during game play (depending on the category) or at the end of the game through conversations, self-reflections, and observations by peers, teachers, coaches, or digital recordings. These additional Rs can usefully connect to formative assessment.

Collective Learning: Democracy in Action

Although target games are often highly individual, they still require taking turns, working side by side, and watching and learning from competitors. Most striking games demand high degrees of reliance and communication with other team members, and most net games, even singles, require close observations of competitors, as well as the ability to read and predict their tactics and strategies. In invasion games, of course, collaboration and team play are crucial.

AFFECTIVE DOMAIN (FEELING)

The affective domain involves the development of motivation, self-esteem, self-confidence, beliefs, and attitudes and is associated with personal identity development or socialization. As students play games, their physical performance and cognitive understanding are intimately connected with their social development and emotional states.

Although most physical educators acknowledge the importance of building confidence, motivation, and self-esteem, planning for affective learning is oddly absent in traditional physical education curricula. These items sometimes show up as lesson objectives, but I have noticed that few preservice teachers have plans to teach for their achievement. Although team play and cooperation are clearly vital to successful game play, they have been insufficiently explored or theorized. For this reason, teachers need to consider what it means to learn with others, and why it is so important.

The importance of imitation and rehearsal in learning in the physical domain is quite obvious when we consider the intricacies of synchronized movement such as paired diving, swimming, boxing, and figure skating. It is also extremely important in game play, in which players must read the intentions of other players. However, there is a broader moral, social, and ethical dimension to collective engagements, which might be summarized by the word *empathy*. The desire to fit in and the need to identify with a social group are so strong that the "major influence on the development of one's 'personal preferences' on music, recreational activities, ideology, world view and so on is neither genetics nor parents but peer group" (Davis, Sumara, & Luce-Kapler, 2008, p. 70). Moreover, our 21st-century global culture is extremely diverse in terms of the backgrounds and cultures that influence our students. Variations in degrees of physical ability, gender, race, and class exist in all learning situations, and the physical education curriculum needs to be flexible and expansive enough to respond. These variations cannot be effectively addressed by a neoliberal tip of the hat to multiculturalism (such as units on folk dancing, or games from other countries).

Identity formation is the fundamental development focus of the affective domain during the adolescent years. Students initiate identity work as they think about their competencies and attributes, set short- and long-term goals, and evaluate their personal beliefs. Physical education has a vital role to play in helping students with this important work. The TGfU curriculum values the ability to work cooperatively and make smart, democratic decisions as much as it does the performance of physical skills. In doing so, it reaches and teaches a broader range of learners than do traditional approaches, which tend to appeal to talented athletes.

The affective domain and developmental considerations can be taken into account when planning curricula. Criteria to consider (see table 4.3) include the number of players; social interactions; space; enjoyment and delight; and agency, efficacy, and empowerment.

Number of Players

As noted, younger students cope less effectively with multiple interactions than older students do. For this reason, we develop physical education lessons with individual activities for those in the younger grades, building into pairs and small groups as they mature socially. We reduce the number of players in invasion and striking games to offer maximal participation and time on task. Target games, once again, are more suitable for younger students, because they are played largely in parallel, side by side or one at a time, which gives them more time to think and observe. This process can be exaggerated by asking students to explain their thinking and observe their partners' actions and decisions. Net

Table 4.3 Affective and Developmental Considerations for Each TGfU Game Category

	Target	Striking	Net and wall	Invasion
Number of players	Individual and small groups	Teams (3 to 11 per side)	Singles Pairs Teams (volleyball)	Teams in full games (5 to 15 per side)
Social Interactions	Turn taking at target	Teams alternate offense until a side is out; some contact between teams.	Constant motion until a point is won. No contact between opponents. A net divides teams or opponents.	Constant motion until a goal is scored in the opponents' goal. Constant interactions.
Space (share, negotiate)	Side by side	Defense team is in the field; 1 to 4 batters either up to bat or on base, all others are waiting to bat.	Divided by a net. No physical interaction.	All players are in most of the defined space.
Enjoyment, delight, play, and fractal time	Accuracy, social interactions between shots	Strike of ball, placement of ball into field, organization and synchronicity of ball and players in fielding.	Shot selection at a given moment, anticipation, parry and counter, challenge of space.	Challenge, evenly matched, flow, spontaneity, well-rehearsed game play, creative play.
Agency, efficacy, and empowerment	Recognition of one's own place and that of the other player(s)	Cover for others in the field, bringing runners home, scoring for the team.	Team play, cover space, anticipation.	Assisted play, scoring, goal prevention, initiative, flair.

games could be sequenced second in the affective domain (rather than third, as they were in the other two domains). This is because they allow a natural development into pairs and, later, small groups (e.g., volleyball). Striking games and invasion games include larger number of players, although teachers can manipulate these to balance the flow of the game with maximal engagement.

Social Interactions and Space

Because the rules of target games invite players to take turns, players develop a sense of fairness in terms of how much time each person is allowed. Striking games generally involve more players, but have a clear sense of order because the members of the fielding team wait their turns at bat and come into contact with their opponents only incidentally. Turns at bat are also systematized with a batting order. Net games involve very little contact with opponents. However, every player on the team must be involved for the game to work.

Invasion games rely more on spontaneous movement and interaction than other games do. Although the rules enforce specific areas of play for different players, restrictions about their involvement are few. There is no equitable turn taking, and the playing areas are not so clearly divided. The number of possible interactions is infinite, and the willingness of each player to engage in creative play becomes imperative. Unfortunately, what has tended to happen in teaching invasion games is that teachers and students focus only on what happens when a player has the ball or object. As we know, during 96 percent of the game, players are off the ball in situations that require as much, if not more, thought and strategy.

Enjoyment, Delight, Play, Fractal Time

The energy, focus, and effort in a game waxes and wanes both individually and systemically. In inventing games lessons, students are constantly challenged to create games that flow. Through their interventions, teachers have students revisit the rules of their games to make them more enjoyable and engaging. In this way, they exploit the potential of fully embodied learning and explore its subtleties. Students inventing and playing their invented games lose track of time, as time becomes fractal and one moment breaks open into another (i.e., one moment exists within the other; Luce-Kapler, Sumara, & Davis, 2002, pp. 360-361). When students ask, "Is it time to go in already?!" teachers know that they have achieved flow. Indeed, as affect theorists (Gregg & Seigworth, 2010) have suggested, the experience of being awash with intense emotions, such as happiness, can radically affect our experience of time. It is this kind of play and this kind of game—enthralling and seamless—that begins to define what we mean by the word "flow."

Agency, Efficacy, and Empowerment

Having personal agency means that we can exercise freedom, control, self-influence, intentionality, forethought, self-reactiveness, and self-reflectiveness. It also includes the ability to use information and resources wisely; to self-regulate;

to act on beliefs, goals, expectations, values, and expectations; to explore and influence environments; and to set personal standards for behavior. As Bandura (1986) noted, people try harder when they believe they have a chance of success. In TGfU, modifications to rules and equipment create a can-do environment in which learners believe that they can achieve their desired outcomes. Self-efficacious students such as these recover quickly from setbacks; they are also more motivated and more likely to challenge themselves. As they work with and observe others, they develop tolerance for difference, sensitivity, and empathy.

When they invent games, students take ownership and become self-regulating as they make up and test their own rules and evaluate their effectiveness. They make choices and discover how they work out. They can achieve success at all developmental stages, and as they try out various roles (e.g., coach, leader, referee, equipment manager, player), they try on a range of possible selves. In this way, they develop new attributes that can be useful in other contexts.

Inventing games units creates classroom conditions that nurture self-determination by allowing students to make choices, demonstrate competency in a range of roles, and participate in supportive peer relationships. As students learn through fluid, dynamic game play, they become engaged and activated by its intrinsic delights. Such things as effort, improvement, and mastery are natural outcomes of creative play, rather than chores to be dutifully accomplished.

CONCLUSIONS

One of the most striking discoveries I have made in my research is that students usually know what is good for them. In the TGfU learning environment, they often select helpful tactics and strategies, make good decisions, reflect wisely on them, and know when they need to work on particular skills. In inventing games, they unfailingly select games that best suit their developmental levels. I often marvel at how students modify the constraints available to them to produce games that perfectly suit their own stage of readiness. That said, the teacher still has a vital role to play in the context of transfer and development. Although learners may make some connections between learning in one game or situation and learning in others, the teacher can draw their attention to many more. Stepping back into the role of observer and commentator, teachers can draw on their deep knowledge of strategies, skills, and game constructs to help their students construct schemas of games structures and knowledge, perhaps by pointing out parallels and contrasts between invented games and institutionalized ones in that category, or across categories, or by suggesting relevant strategies, modifications, or skills that might lead to more successful play.

Table 4.4 presents developmental considerations for curricular design in a quick reference. The table topics are expanded on in each of the subsequent practical chapters.

Table 4.4 Developmental Considerations for Curricular Design

	Modifications (simplifying)	Modifications (challenging)	Adaptations (creating an even playing field so that students of various abilities can play together)
Rules	Proscriptive rules (what not to do—enabling constraints). Example: Defenders cannot tackle the person with the ball.	Prescriptive rules (what to do—enhancing constraints). Example: Use only the left hand to shoot.	Apply different rules for each set of opponents. Example: Only team A can tackle defenders; team B can only intercept.
Players	Decrease numbers to allow greater participation and more time on the ball.	Increase numbers to increase the complexity of plays.	Play 2v1 to emphasize offense or defense in team games, or 2v1 in tennis for easier coverage and to challenge a single player.
Playing area	Decrease the size or length of playing area or the relationship to the target for simple running and passing games.	Increase the size of the area and distances between bases, goals, and net game courts to increase the challenge for runners.	Combine the two modifications for playing area to allow expert player A to play regular player B (e.g., in tennis, player A has a smaller court area than player B in which to play the ball).
Equipment	Use larger equipment surface areas to increase success (larger balls, bats, rackets), higher nets for net games to increase time for decision making, and lower and larger targets.	Use smaller equipment (balls, smaller-surface-area rackets and bats, lower nets, smaller targets) to increase difficulty.	Vary the size of sending equipment to increase or decrease the challenge (e.g., one team has larger rackets, or one team has larger-faced sticks).
Scoring or modifying goal	Use scoring systems that allow multiple chances to score and provide added incentives (e.g., closer to target).	Use narrow areas, smaller targets, etc.	Require one team to score more points than the other to win a set.

SUMMARY

Although it is almost a truism to say that human beings are complex, this has often been overlooked as far as curriculum design in physical education is concerned. In many physical education classes, the physical readiness of students to perform is still privileged over their cognitive, emotional, and social readiness. Yet in all of these areas, development is much more than a simple unfolding of a genetically determined map. Rather, it is a multicaused interplay of genetics and environment, body and brain, and individual and community. The emergent learning-focused teacher allows for variation in development across all of the domains discussed in this chapter, which also offers some advice as to how the IG curriculum might best be structured given these considerations. Specifically, it considers the physical, cognitive, and emotional demands each games category makes on students. I also suggest that our profession might usefully pay more attention to the social readiness of our students, in terms of the development of such qualities as empathy, confidence, motivation, and self-esteem. Though these have been discussed in the literature, insufficient attention has been given to the conscious planning of their introduction and inclusion in the physical education curriculum.

Pedagogical Principles

Linda L. Griffin and Joy Butler

Janice and Mohinder are not having a great game of tennis.

Mohinder: We keep hitting the net, Ms. Marshall. And when we manage to get the ball over, we're so surprised that we miss it. Tennis is *hard!*

Ms. Marshall offers a higher net, padder bats, and a foam ball with a bit of bounce. When she returns, they have played some pretty spirited rallies and seem happier. Mohinder, being taller, won most of these by running up to the net and smashing the ball. Ms. Marshall waits until it happens again and stops the game.

Ms. Marshall: So Janice, how did Mohinder win that point?

Janice (giggling): She runs up and whacks it! It's because she's so tall!

Ms. Marshall: OK. I'm setting up a problem for you two to solve. (She moves the tapes to make the court just a little longer and skinnier.) I want you to try and figure out what you can do when a player comes up to the net like that. Where's the space for you to win a point?

Ten minutes later, Janice and Mohinder have it all figured out.

Mohinder: One way is to send the ball off to the side. We tried that first, but it's hard when the court is thinner.

Janice: The other way is to put it way up high over the other person's head. I like watching Mohinder having to gallop back to get it. It's time for payback!

Ms. Marshall: How did you have to hit the ball to make that shot?

Mohinder (scooping with her padder bat): Kind of underneath and upward.

Ms. Marshall: Which method did you prefer?

The girls look at each other thoughtfully.

Janice: It depends.

Mohinder (nodding): If the person stands kind of a little bit to one side, you can sometimes sneak the ball past them quite easily.

Ms. Marshall: And how did you say you hit the ball for that shot?

Janice (swinging her bat): Sort of hard and quick.

Ms. Marshall: Good. You two just figured out how to make what's called a passing shot. The one that goes over someone's head is called a lob. When do you think that is most useful?

Janice: If the person is right bang at the net. It's not quite as easy to do as that other one—the passing shot—'cause it's hard to get it exactly right. It's like when we did target games last year and we had to send the arrows up really high when you moved the target way, way back, and it was really hard to hit it.

Mohinder (chiming in): And even if you do get the lob to land in court and at the back, someone who's short and quick like Janice can maybe still run back and get it.

Ms. Marshall (nodding): Good work, you two. So now let's move the court back to where it was. You might want to hang on to the foam balls for a while or try the Wiffle balls. You've really come along. Well done!

As suggested in the previous chapters, sport-related games offer a medium for understanding and experiencing the democratic process, self-regulating learning, and developing problem-solving skills. This chapter presents four pedagogical principles to help teachers plan and design games lessons that help students become more reflective and self-directed. Pedagogical principles guide the practice of teaching. They help teachers develop pedagogical strategies such as considering the actual learning environment and the nature of students' experiences of, engagement with, and responses to the lesson. The principles outlined in this chapter have been adapted from Thorpe, Bunker, and Almond's work (1986) and are based on a belief system about games teaching and learning that was discussed in chapter 1—ecological complexity thinking.

TEACHING AS FACILITATING

Active learning is the signature pedagogy of Teaching Games for Understanding (TGfU) as the teacher adopts the role of facilitator. A game-centered approach shifts the pedagogy from teacher centered to student centered by placing responsibility on students. The teacher facilitates the process by setting problems, goals, and boundaries that guide the tasks; students grapple with these tasks as they seek solutions. To be good game players, students need to be good problem solvers. The teacher acts as a connector and integrator by encouraging students to share their perspectives and experiences, stimulating their thinking, encouraging explorations, and making associations. The following suggestions further outline the role of the teacher in games education:

■ Teach students their roles and responsibilities in an active learning lesson. Decide what rules, routines, and expectations you need to put in place so that students feel safe and are willing to engage. Students also need time to adjust to their new roles. Be patient with them and yourself.

■ Think through the organization of space, students (individuals, pairs, or small groups), and equipment. Planning helps you to stay in the role of facilitator, and as we all know, teachers always need to be nimble.

■ Select a task or problem for the students to perform or solve. Consider how much you actually want to say about the task because you want students to grapple with it. As a facilitator, you can ask questions that will help students explore possible solutions. You can also facilitate practice by shaping the games (i.e., simplifying or challenging game conditions) to meet students' developmental needs. Students need to be able to define the problem, gather information about the problem, identify the options, make decisions, and put their decisions into action.

Questions are an excellent way to engage students and as facilitators, teachers need to know when to ask questions and when to provide answers. The literature on game-centered approaches has consistently emphasized the importance of high-quality questions (Den Duyn, 1997; Bunker & Thorpe, 1982; Mitchell, Oslin, & Griffin, 2013). The number and types of questions are a central element of the planning process. Following are six types of question stems and the possible game aspects they can cover:

■ Tactical awareness: What do you . . .?

■ Skill and movement execution: How do you . . .?

■ Time: When is the best time to . . .?

■ Space: Where is/can . . .?

■ Risk: Which choice . . . ?

■ Rationale: Why are you . . .?

To develop the role of facilitator, teachers need to reflect on their teaching and consider a shift to the pedagogy of engagement (Almond, 2010). Pedagogical engagement is a teaching method that focuses on teacher–student interactions, cooperation and collaboration among students, and the active engagement of students in the learning process. Following are suggestions for engaging students (Almond, 2010):

■ Reach out and connect with all students.

■ Engage students constructively.

■ Draw out students to increase their confidence and potential.

■ Extend students' capabilities.

TACTICAL COMPLEXITY

Tactical complexity involves the tactical concepts (i.e., scoring and preventing scoring) and movement concepts (body, space, effort, and relationship) of games combined with learners' abilities and skills (i.e., psychomotor, cognitive, and affective) to implement the concepts (Howarth, Fisette, Sweeney, & Griffin, 2010). At the heart of tactical complexity is the game classification system

(Bunker & Thorpe, 1982; Mitchell Oslin, & Griffin, 2013). The classification system provides an organizing structure for a game-centered approach to teaching and learning. The hope is that students make connections that lead to the transfer of concepts, strategic principles, and tactics within each classification. Transfer is discussed in chapter 3.

As discussed in chapter 4, games can be viewed along a continuum of tactical complexity. The word *tactical* refers to the planning and maneuvering (i.e., actions, conditions, goals) needed to accomplish the game's intent; the word *complexity* refers to the number of interrelated game variables. Games with fewer variables are easier to adapt (i.e., shape) for learners.

It can be a challenge for teachers to understand students' developmental needs where tactical complexity is concerned. Not much has been written on this topic, and strategies and tactics are not only complicated and subtle, but need to change moment by moment as the game evolves and possession changes quickly between teams. The value of having students invent games is that they begin to wrestle with these principles themselves and prove more adept than teachers might think at analyzing game play.

MODIFICATIONS THROUGH REPRESENTATION, EXAGGERATION, AND ADAPTATION

Proponents of the game-centered approach argue that all students can play a game that is modified to facilitate meaningful play. They also believe that learning occurs in context (Ellis, 1986; Thorpe, 2001). To achieve the right context, TGfU teachers embrace the pedagogical principle of modification through representation, exaggeration, and adaptation.

- *Representation:* Maintaining some contextual aspect of the game but slowing play down. Simply put, teachers do less to get more play for their students.

- *Exaggeration*: Overemphasizing some aspect of play to encourage a particular tactical or movement experience.

- *Adaptation:* Increasing the challenge once a student has achieved success. Changes are made in relation to game constraints (e.g., space, score, rules, number of players) to ensure that the game remains competitive (Hopper, 2011).

These concepts help teachers navigate the complexities and social dimensions of games education. The modification principle also keeps students engaged by building on their game competence. Modifications may be made to a simple game, one tactic or movement concept, or a game situation. Modification may mean beginning with few skills, few rules, and few players, thus slowing down the pace and tempo of the game. Modified games or game forms should be representative of the advanced form (i.e., the regulation game) and contain the same tactical structures, but be played with adjustments to meet students' developmental needs (e.g., size, age, ability).

In the inventing games process, modification allows teachers and students to change secondary rules to help players solve tactical problems more efficiently and effectively (Thorpe & Bunker, 1989). These are discussed in chapters 3 and 4 in more depth. Following are six aspects of the game or game form that can be exaggerated to draw attention to particular tactical problems:

■ *Rules*. Rules can be changed to emphasize certain game aspects.

■ *Number of players*. Small-sided games or game forms (3v3 or 2v1) slow down the tempo and flow of a game, thus limiting the tactical complexity, which, in turn, simplifies the decision-making process.

■ *Playing area*. Altering the size of the playing area or changing the size of the goal may help students focus on learning a particular aspect of the game. Narrowing the court restricts space and can thus facilitate the performance of drop and lob shots.

■ *Equipment*. Modifying the playing equipment makes the students feel safer, which allows for more successful executions of skills and movements. For example, students have more time to think about ball placement when the ball travels more slowly, or may attempt the forearm pass or dig when trainer volleyballs are used.

■ *Scoring or modifying the goal*. Modifying scoring rules shapes the game to reinforce practice. For example, in a volleyball lesson, teams may earn points for containing the first pass on their side of the court.

■ *Modification by adaptation*. Constraints on space, rules, scoring, and the number of players can be set up prior to the game to make outcome close. For example, a 2v2 volleyball game might be played on one fourth each side of the net, of a badminton court (Hopper, 2011) starting with a free ball toss for serve. After one team scores 2 points, the other team increases the opponents' playing area by adding a quadrant of the badminton court. Or more simply, more able players can be challenged by having to use the tram lines while the opponent uses the single court.

ASSESSMENT OF LEARNING OUTCOMES

The final pedagogical principle is assessment of learning outcomes. Assessment in the act of playing games is the most authentic and meaningful way for students to receive formative feedback and develop skillfulness and competence (Corbin, 2002). Most physical education teachers believe that assessment should be an ongoing part of instruction, so that students have feedback that helps them to reflect on and manage their learning. Games teaching is dramatically enriched through the use of assessment, particularly when that assessment is aligned with instructional objectives (Mitchell, Oslin, & Griffin, 2013). The Game Performance Assessment Instrument (Mitchell, Oslin, & Griffin, 2013) and the Team Sport Assessment Procedure (TSAP; Richard, Godbout, & Griffin, 2002) measure outcomes during game play. The reciprocal assessment model in figure 5.1 is similar to the TGfU model, in that the learner is placed in the center. The three interacting components of the model are the teacher, the task, and the assessment. The reciprocal aspect is indicated by the dual-direction arrows.

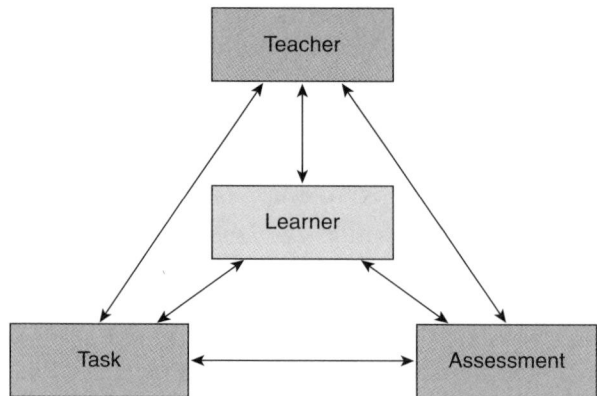

FIGURE 5.1 Reciprocal assessment model.

SUMMARY

In this chapter, we have presented four pedagogical principles: teaching as facilitating, understanding tactical complexity, offering appropriate modifications through representation, exaggeration, and adaptation, and finally, assessment of learning outcomes. The emergent learning focused teacher uses these to plan and design games lessons that help students become more reflective and self-directed.

A game-centered approach with an emphasis on authentic performance creates an active in-depth learning setting for students. One of the primary goals of this approach is to stimulate students' interest in games so that they value the need to work toward improved game knowledge. Improving game knowledge, we hope, leads to greater enjoyment, interest, and perceived competence in students who then become lifelong game players (Mitchell, Oslin, & Griffin, 2013).

Inventing Unopposed Target Games

Tony, the largest student in the class, has just finished throwing a small rubber ball at his partner, Sukh, who agreed to be the target first and is now rubbing his chest. Tony thinks he might suggest changing the distance for the thrower before being a target himself—clearly that ball hurt!

Their teacher, Mr. Berning, comes to check on the inventing games process, and is perplexed.

Mr. Berning: What on earth's happening here, boys?

Tony: But sir, you said we could use anything as a target. If we use a person, it'll improve our accuracy skills even more, because the target'll be moving too.

Mr. Berning (taking a deep breath): OK. Let's consider the instructions for the activity before we talk about using humans as targets. What does your card say?

The boys look at it and read together.

Both boys: Choose a target from the equipment area labeled Targets.

Mr. Berning: So what did you decide to use?

Tony: We've already got a hoop taped to the wall. See?

Mr. Berning: OK. So how did Sukh get to be hit by the ball?

Tony: Well, we thought we could make it more challenging by having one person run in front of the hoop and get double points if they hit him in front of the target.

Mr. Berning: How did it feel being hit in the chest, Sukh?

Sukh (shrugging): It was OK.

Mr. Berning: Really? It looked like a hard throw. Can you think of any other game that allows a ball to be deliberately thrown at a player?

Both boys: Ummm, no.

Mr. Berning: What's the message that you are sending by throwing a ball hard at someone?

Both boys shrug.

Mr. Berning: OK. We'll come back to this after you've had a chance to think about it, but for now, let's use only inanimate objects as targets!

The target games category is fundamental in the Teaching Games for Understanding (TGfU) process, because it is the category in which the key concepts and skills of sending are learned. In the same way, gymnastics is fundamental to all movement because students learn body management skills through the use of functional movement. Students can then apply this understanding to all other movements. The key concepts and actions involved in sending an object include applying the correct force to achieve the necessary direction, distance, and level required to reach the target. Such abilities are central to success in all the other game categories. In softball, for instance, players send the ball into an open space away from players, giving them enough time to run the bases. In net games, sending the object away makes it difficult for the opponent to retrieve, and in invasion games, sending the ball to a target is crucial in scoring and passing.

Target games are the least structurally complex of all the categories of the TGfU system in terms of the developmental domains (see chapter 4). They are also highly popular with adults: bowling and golf, for instance, are among the top 10 most popular activities for adults in Canada (Cragg et al., 1999). Because of their simplicity and popularity, and because they provide an ideal context in which to introduce TGfU principles, target games should be part of a games curriculum.

In both unopposed and opposed forms of target games, teachers have additional time to observe and diagnose student performances before and during game play and thus to create habits and decision-making routines that can be transferred to all other game categories. In unopposed target games, participants perform independently of each other while sharing the same space. This simple structure allows teachers and coaches to emphasize the setup and preshot routines and help learners make decisions that result in effective skill execution. These strategic concepts are covered later in this chapter. Opposed target games (covered in chapter 7) are more complex because players must decide whether to attempt to score or block opponent(s) from scoring. They are thus a step beyond unopposed target games in the complexity progression.

This chapter describes the inventing games process for unopposed target games using seven stages. Each stage includes suggestions for teaching democracy in action. An outline for both processes can be found in table 6.1. While students

Commentary on Human Targets

The TGfU classification system has no games in which the intent is to hit another person. Inadvertent collisions with the ball sometimes occur, such as while running to second base or as a result of a poorly executed or rushed passing shot in an invasion game. At times, teachers or coaches may deliberately direct players to aim at a teammate's body part, such as an outreached hand when passing (Mendez, Fernandez, & Casey, 2012). However, the intent is never to throw so hard that the ball cannot be caught, or to see the hand as a target for harm. Balls sent with an intent to harm (such as when bowlers aim at the batter rather than the wicket) raise questions of ethics, or fair (or fun) play. When a player's intent is to intimidate another player, this is a form of bullying. In cricket, the umpire has the discretion to call it intimidating bowling. Teachers and coaches have even more responsibility to protect those in their care.

Table 6.1 Inventing Target Games: Stages and Democracy-in-Action Focuses

	Stages for inventing unopposed target games	Democracy-in-action focus
1	Setting the learning environment.	**Decision making:** Establishing notions of fairness and cooperation to achieve a common goal
2	Developing target game constructs by observing a partner (competitive games).	**Free inquiry:** Making observations and reflecting; sharing opinions
3	Inventing and playing a new target game.	**Social justice:** Exhibiting respectful behavior and etiquette
4	Refining the invented game.	**Social justice:** Showing empathy
5	Refining the skills required in the invented game.	**Free inquiry:** Giving constructive feedback and exhibiting game etiquette
6	Challenging everyone by adapting rules.	**Social justice:** Creating adaptations; considering what is fair
7	Showcasing the game.	**Group process:** Honoring one's own work and that of others (fairness and equality)

Table 6.2 Strategic Concepts and Tactical Decisions in Unopposed Target Games

Object: To send an object away and make contact with a stationary target in fewer attempts than opponents **Unopposed:** The player performs independently of the opponent (e.g., archery, bowling, darts, golf)			
Strategic concepts	Tactical questions	Tactics (preshot decisions)	Skill execution (sending)
Accuracy to target	How to get closer to the target than the opponent	Determine a starting point, target line, immediate target, release point, and point of contact.	
Direction and level	How to send the object most effectively	Determine step length, approach speed, and backswing length.	Setup, stance, grip Object position
Distance	How to apply the correct amount of force to reach the target		Approach, backswing, release, follow-through
Variations in scoring (e.g., in bowling, the first attempt is to make a strike to knock down all the pins)			

create their own unopposed target games, the teacher introduces strategic concepts for understanding tactical decisions for these simple target games (see table 6.2). Neither table is designed to be followed in a linear fashion; they are, rather, resources to draw from in planning for specific classes and developmental levels.

It is worth taking time to establish the conditions of play, or set up the learning environment, in the first stage. Students need to be able to communicate effectively to make shared decisions in the inventing games process. Developing a new game requires trial and error: Students must be patient with both themselves and others as they learn to communicate and negotiate. Before taking even one shot, they need to make some tactical decisions and establish setup and preshot routines. This takes time. As with all the other inventing games processes, the stages in table 6.1 do not represent distinct lessons. One stage may require one to three lessons, or students may move through several stages in one lesson, depending on class time and student progress. The same inventing games process used in this chapter for unopposed games can be applied to opposed target games. Chapter 7, and in particular lessons 1 and 2, can also be used in tandem with this chapter to develop the concepts of unopposed games.

Following are some pedagogical hints and modifications to consider:

- Change only one element at a time (e.g., setup, target line, intermediate target, release point, point of contact, length of backswing and step, speed of approach) to increase or decrease task complexity.
- Students can work in pairs, threes, or fours.
- Change ball size, ball density, object speed, object color, distance from target, size of target, or scoring systems.
- Use cooperative structures first, followed by competitive ones.

Key Concept: Democracy in Action

In this book, the term *democracy in action* is used to describe principles, skills, and attributes that can be developed in authentic situations in a participatory, adaptive learning culture. For the purposes of this book, the democracy-in-action principles are as follows:

- *Group process:* The ability to negotiate, decide on, and adhere to group structures, including how to reach consensus, work together, and resolve conflicts.
- *Personal and social responsibility:* Balancing the needs of the individual and those of the group, and exploring how each can serve and support the other.
- *Free inquiry:* The ability, right, and responsibility to articulate and communicate ideas in the expectation that they will be heard and respected, and equally, to listen carefully to the ideas of others.
- *Decision making:* Using the structures negotiated and agreed on to make decisions (in both game play and game design) that best serve the needs of individuals and the group.
- *Social justice:* Creating ways of being and playing that are inclusive, fair, and attentive to issues of power, privilege, and difference.

By emphasizing the connection between content and life experience, teachers help learners make connections in all other arenas. The inventing games experience offers students the opportunity to learn about democracy in action as they negotiate, debate, overcome conflict, and navigate their way through a series of problem-solving activities that lead to their invented games.

STAGE 1:
Setting the Learning Environment

Focus: Creating safe conditions for discussions and decision making; setting up expectations for respectful supportive behaviors

Skill focus: Rolling the ball in the intended direction

Learner focus:

- Considering self as part of the community and creating a safe and respectful environment by contributing ideas and listening to those of others (affective)
- Working respectfully with a partner and agreeing on ways to make decisions about the game (affective)
- Creating and playing a cooperative bowling game with a partner (cognitive and psychomotor)
- Identifying a starting spot for releasing the object to ensure fairness (cognitive and affective)
- Taking turns sending the ball as part of respectful behavior and game etiquette (cognitive)

Equipment: Pens, paper, three pins, one 4 in. (10 cm) ball, and one line marker per pair

Setup: Students are in fours, and then pairs. Consider using a classroom for the discussion and the gym for the bowling games.

Learner Experiences

Setting Conditions for Decision Making and Cooperating

- In groups of four, students discuss what makes a classroom safe for learning. Each group writes down three to five ideas.
- Gather the whole class together and have groups share the best one or two ideas from their lists. Create a class list. (Post in the classroom or the gym for the duration of the unit at least.)
- The key focal points are respect, listening, and respectful behavior.
- In pairs, students discuss how they will make decisions such as rules for a game. Each group writes down three to five ideas. Following are possible ideas for how decisions will be made:
  - ▶ Take turns speaking.
  - ▶ Talk through decisions and decide jointly.
  - ▶ If both don't agree, reject the idea.
  - ▶ Use a talking stick; the student holding it cannot be interrupted.
  - ▶ Limit the time each person speaks.
  - ▶ Allow no interruptions.
  - ▶ Don't make rules unless they are necessary.

Inventing a Cooperative Bowling Game

Test the decision-making policy by having students create a simple cooperative bowling game using six pins and a small ball.

One person is designated the equipment manager (EM) and collects the equipment, and the other is the recorder (R) and writes notes. Learners then decide on the following:

- Arrangement of the pins (targets)
- Distance of the pins from the starting point
- Starting point
- How to release the ball
- Three rules
- Scoring system

Possible rules:

- Toes must be behind the line.
- Players may not cross the line until after the ball reaches the pins.
- The ball must be rolled, not thrown.
- Each person may bowl twice, unless all the pins are knocked down in one bowl (in which case, the player has an extra go at the end, or the bowl is worth a certain number of points).

Refining Bowling Skills

Students should practice bowling skills in the context of their invented games as much as possible. They should work on each of the following points separately:

- Identify the starting spot and take up the stance (i.e., still and focused on the target). Consider the questions from table 6.3 to help bring awareness of the concepts of direction and distance.
- Establish a comfortable grip.
- Swing back, step forward, swing forward, follow through toward the target, and release the ball low (Mitchell et al., 2006).
- Repeat this action for smooth and consistent form and rhythm.

Debrief

1. Debrief the decision-making process. Invite students to refine their agreements for making decisions.
2. Introduce the routine of thanking the partner for the game to develop a sense of respectful behavior and game etiquette. Remind students that we need other players to help us achieve our goals.

Table 6.3   Tactical Framework for Bowling Step and Arm Swing

Tactical concepts for accuracy	Preshot decisions	Skill execution
Direction	What part of the target am I aiming at? Where is my starting spot? How do I grip the object?	Stance: Still and focused on the target Comfortable grip
Distance	How far away is the target? How much backswing do I need to reach the target?	Swing back, step forward, swing forward, follow through toward the target, and release low

Modifications

- Modify balls and pins: smaller to challenge students and larger to provide greater success.
- Modify the distance: farther for challenge and closer for greater success.

Democracy in Action

Decision making: Establishing notions of fairness and cooperation to achieve a common goal

Because this game is cooperative, learners can work together to achieve a negotiated goal. Time can be spent helping learners establish rules that create fairness; for example, turn taking, starting from the same spot, suggesting ideas, listening to ideas. Students also need time to establish a decision-making agreement that can be recorded and revisited as needed. Review the decision-making process by asking questions such as the following:

- How did you remember to take turns?
- What does it mean to have respectful behavior in this game?
- Did your decision-making agreement work? How do you know?
- How did you decide on the scoring system?
- Why is it important to thank other players for playing?

Check for Learning

- What made this a cooperative game?
- What were the targets in the game?
- Why is it important to establish a consistent starting spot?
- How did you release the ball (bowl, roll, throw)?
- Could you repeat the way you sent the ball?

STAGE 2:
Developing Target Game Constructs by Observing a Partner

Focus: Learning by observing
Skill focus: Tossing
Learner focus:

- Defining the target game category (cognitive)
- Creating and playing a competitive tossing game with a partner (cognitive and psychomotor)
- Observing a partner's actions to create a sequence of actions (cognitive)

Equipment: For each pair, two hoops of different sizes, two sets of three bean-bags (each set is a different color), tape to attach hoops to the floor
Setup: Pairs toss beanbags toward the wall across the width of the gym.

Learner Experiences

Setting Conditions for Learning

- Invite students to reexamine their decision-making agreements.
- Define cooperative activity (through guided dialogue with teacher).
- One person is the equipment manager (EM) and collects the equipment, and the other is the recorder (R) and writes notes.

Inventing a Competitive Tossing Target Game (Hoop Game)

1. With two hoops of different sizes and three beanbags, students create a simple tossing game in pairs. They must decide on the following:

   - Arrangement of the targets (hoops). These can be on the floor or taped to the wall (see figure 6.1).

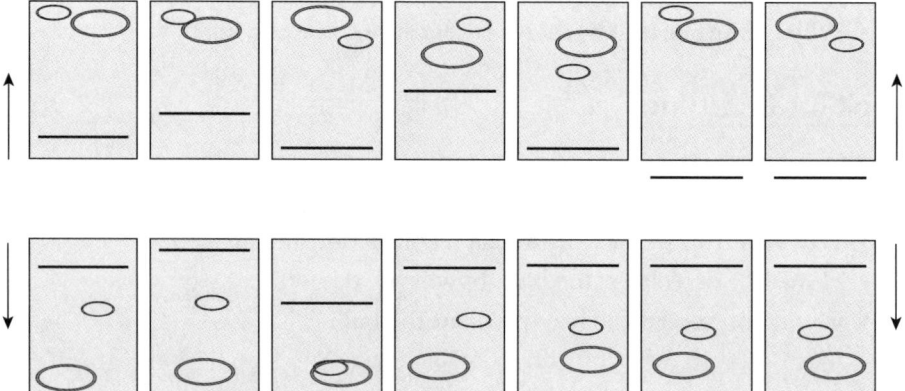

Figure 6.1 Starting lines and hoop arrangements.

- Distance of the hoops from the line
- Starting spot
- How to release the beanbags
- Three rules for fair play

2. Students play the game until they are comfortable with it.
3. In pairs, students discuss what they have to think about to get the beanbag into the hoop.

Possible decisions:

- How far is the hoop? How much force will I need to get it there?
- When do I let it go?
- How do I stand?
- Do I need to step into the action?

Refining Tossing Skills

1. One student observes the partner toss the beanbag (from the side). After watching about five tosses, the observer answers the following questions:

   - How does the partner hold the beanbag?
   - Does the partner stand in the same spot?
   - What is the partner doing to create force or power to get the beanbag to the hoop?
   - How high is the partner's hand when the beanbag is released?
   - Does the partner take a step toward the target?

2. Students reverse roles.
3. Students identify a sequence of steps from their observations:

   i. Setup
   ii. Stance
   iii. Grip
   iv. Approach backswing
   v. Release
   vi. Follow-through

4. Students repeat the actions and take note of each step. The partner can act as a coach to talk through each step and give feedback.

Table 6.4 shows a tactical framework for tossing in target games.

Developing a Competitive Game

1. Students create scoring systems.
2. Students modify the scoring rules as needed.

Table 6.4 Tactical Framework for Tossing in Target Games

Tactical concepts for accuracy	Preshot decisions	Skill execution
Direction	Determine the starting point, target line, immediate target, release point, and point of contact.	Setup, stance grip, ball position
Distance	Determine step length, approach speed, and backswing length.	Approach, backswing release, follow-through

Debrief

1. Reestablish the etiquette of thanking the opponent.
2. Students debrief the observation and feedback processes.

Modifications

- Hoops could be placed on the wall or on the floor.
- Bonus points could be awarded for near misses, or bigger targets could be drawn around the existing hoop.
- Adapt according to the age group in terms of the depth of observations, steps covered in the toss sequence, and feedback.

Democracy in Action

Free inquiry: Making observations and reflecting; encouraging voice and sharing opinions

Teachers who encourage students to share their observations take their learning seriously. Asking about their interpretations of their learning and valuing their ideas signals to children that what they say and what they are learning are important. This ongoing process of valuing and respecting opinions is fundamental to developing democratic citizens. Here are some suggested questions:

- How did you explain how your partner made the toss? Did you explain it in an encouraging way? In a matter-of-fact way?
- How did your partner describe your toss action? Was it helpful?
- Did you thank your partner for the feedback and the game? Why is that important?

Check for Learning

- What did you notice about your partner's toss?
- How did that help you in your toss?
- Why is it important to think about the action before you toss?
- What was your approach before you tossed?
- What did it feel like? Did it feel right? What made it right?
- What part of the sequence helped you the most? What will you remember to do next time?
- Did the feedback help you with your performance?

STAGE 3:
Inventing and Playing a New Target Game

Focus: Creating rules through negotiation

Skill focus: Using intermediate targets to improve accuracy

Learner focus:

- Defining the game by creating basic regulations and minimal rules (cognitive)
- Sharing ideas, negotiating, and establishing a decision-making process (cognitive)
- Testing the game through trial and error (psychomotor and cognitive)

Equipment:

- Target possibilities: Buckets, hoops, pins, cones, poly spots, boxes, bins, plastic milk bottles (1 gal [4 L] or 1/2 gal [2 L] sizes). The target can be raised or flattened to the ground. See figure 6.2 for examples of objects per pair.
- Line markers for a sending line
- Objects to send: Balls of various sizes and densities, beanbags, quoits
- Area boundaries: Line markers, benches, cones

Setup: See figure 6.2.

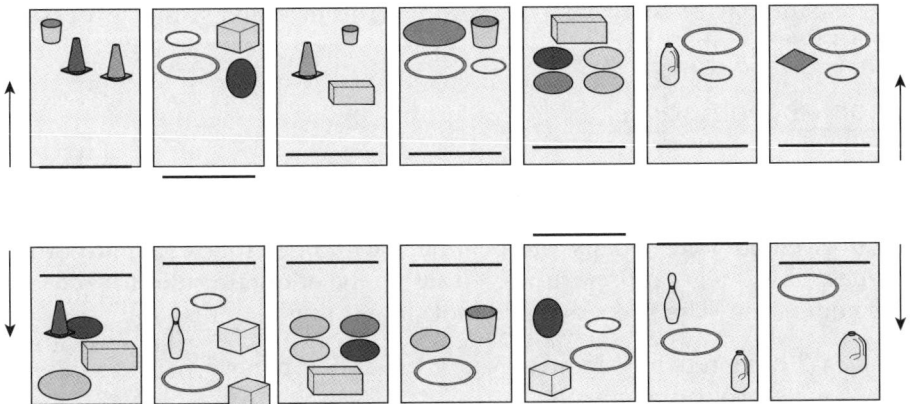

Figure 6.2 A variety of target arrangements.

Learner Experiences

Setting Conditions for Learning

- Students revisit their decision-making processes.
- Establish class rules and etiquette for interrupting games in progress.
- Identify one person as the equipment manager and the other as the recorder.

Inventing a Target Game

1. Students now have an opportunity to choose a game that is either cooperative or competitive. They need to decide on the following:

   - Five rules for the game (including one safety rule)
   - Playing area boundaries and how loose balls will be collected
   - Target arrangement (high or low)
   - Distance of targets from the line (can be moved)
   - Starting spot
   - How to release the object

2. Students play the game.

3. After the game has been established, pairs consider the following questions. If the answer to any of the questions is no, students need to change the rules until they can answer yes.

   - Is the game fun?
   - Is it safe?
   - Is it fair?
   - Is everyone involved equally?
   - Is it challenging?

Debrief

Students summarize their understanding of the invented games process and respectful behavior.

Democracy in Action

Social justice: Exhibiting respectful behavior and etiquette

Respectfulness is central to good communication. As learners work on their invented games, balls and beanbags will inevitably stray into other games. This is a great opportunity to set up the etiquette rules for retrieving equipment. The process could look something like this:

1. Without moving, look to see what is happening in the place where your object went.
2. Wait until the players have finished their turn.
3. Ask if you can collect your object, and wait for the answer.
4. Collect your object and apologize to the players for the intrusion.

Check for Learning

- What rules did you create for your game?
- Does your game work?
- Is it fun?
- What are etiquette rules?
- What is the purpose of the intermediate target? How did that help?

STAGE 4:
Refining the Invented Game

Focus: Improving invented games

Skill focus: Observation

Learner focus:

- Refining their game structures as they continue to play and discuss the game (psychomotor and cognitive)
- Giving partners constructive and respectful feedback on their sending actions (cognitive)

Equipment: The EM collects the same game equipment that was used in stage 3.

Setup: Students continue playing their invented games in pairs and then share them with other pairs of students.

Learner Experiences

Setting Conditions for Learning

Each pair chooses another pair.

1. The two pairs form a group to revisit the decision-making process.
2. One person is chosen as the equipment manager (EM) and another is the recorder (R).
3. Discuss the importance of constructive feedback (through guided dialogue by teacher).

Playing and Refining Invented Games

After reestablishing their invented games in pairs, students share their games with other pairs, as follows:

1. The R explains the games to the other pair's EM.
2. The EM says why she likes the game and offers some suggestions.
3. The EM then explains her game to the other pair's R.
4. The R says why he likes the games and offers some suggestions.
5. Each original pair discusses revisions to their game.

Debrief

The activities themselves constitute the debrief for this learner experience.

Democracy in Action

Social justice: Showing empathy

Students can consider these questions:

- Did the feedback help you with your game?
- How did playing the other pair's game help you think about your own game?
- Can you think of other examples in which taking part in somebody else's activity helps you to understand the game more?

You can then discuss empathy and its part in democracy.

STAGE 5:
Refining the Skills Required in the Invented Game

Focus: Improving sending accuracy
Skill focus: Sending
Learner focus:

- Using an intermediate target to improve accuracy and consistency in hitting the target (psychomotor and cognitive)
- Using an intermediate target in their own invented games (psychomotor and cognitive)

Equipment: For each group of four, four beanbags, four golf clubs, eight indoor golf balls, various sizes of balls (four of each), four Frisbees, two hoops, two pylons
Setup: Students are in fours and then in pairs for the continued invented game.

Learner Experiences

This stage could take several lessons to cover key components of the skills.

Setting Conditions for Learning

Invite students to stand in their first invented games pairs; then ask each student to leave that pair and pair up with someone else.

1. Students revisit the decision-making process as a group.
2. One person is chosen to be the EM; and another, to be the R.
3. Discuss the importance of constructive feedback.
4. Set up the aim and accuracy game shown in figure 6.3.

Playing the Aim and Accuracy Game

Players earn points by sending an object into a hoop.

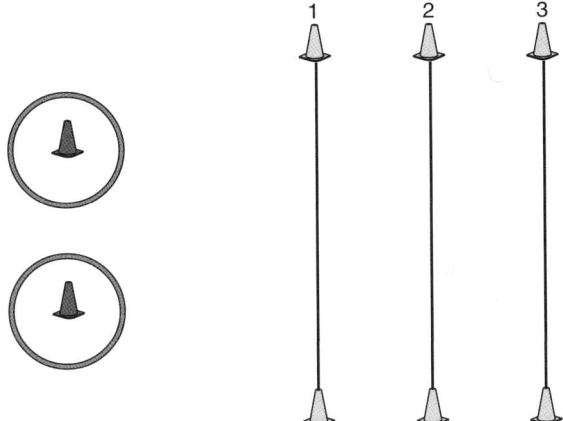

Figure 6.3 Aim and accuracy game.
Based on Sheppard 2007.

- If they send from the first line, they score 1 point; from the second line, 2 points; and from the third line, 3 points. Players can double their scores if they hit a pin or pylon in the middle of the hoop.
- Teams of two decide which object to send.
- The goal is to be the first team to earn 20 points or more.

Skill Development

1. Focus on the setup (starting spot, target, and intermediate target).
2. Once the game is established, introduce the concept of an intermediate target.
3. Place a sticker or marker at a closer target in line with the target for easier focus.
4. Experiment with the placement of the intermediate target.
5. Think and discuss the order of preparation before taking the shot.
6. Students write down the order of preparation.
7. After several shots, students ask their partners for feedback.
8. Students should provide helpful feedback to their partners.

Debrief

Students consider these questions:

- How does the intermediate target help your accuracy in reaching the target?
- How does thinking about the sequence for preparing your shot help you?

Democracy in Action

Free inquiry: Giving constructive feedback and exhibiting game etiquette

It is helpful to define what we mean by constructive feedback. Help students to focus on relevant content, such as the preparation of the shot and the intermediate target. How the feedback is delivered is often more important than what is said. Help students to be supportive without being meaningless, direct without being critical. Nonverbal feedback is also worth mentioning. Ridicule in the form of peer eye rolling, giggles, and sighs can be as devastating as direct insults. Ask students these questions:

- What is helpful feedback? What is unhelpful feedback?
- What part of the feedback is nonverbal?
- Did the feedback you received help you with your performance?
- Did you thank your partner for the feedback?
- What does feedback have to do with democracy?

Check for Learning

- What two things did you learn in the aim and accuracy game?
- Did the use of the intermediate target help with accuracy? How?
- Did it help with consistency? How?

STAGE 6:
Challenging Everyone by Adapting Rules

Focus: Engaging and challenging all players by adapting rules

Skill focus: Sending

Learner focus:

- Creating a scoring system democratically (cognitive)
- Manipulating game constraints such as space, scoring, and rules (cognitive and psychomotor)
- Appreciating the value of close games in terms of individual challenges (affective)

Equipment: Two hoops of equal size, two sets of three beanbags (each set is a different color)

Setup: See figure 6.4.

Figure 6.4 Adaptations of a game to help students of different abilities to play competitively.

Learner Experiences

1. Set up the game as in stage 2; both players use only one hoop initially (figure 6.4*a*).
2. Add a new rule requiring players to take one step toward the target if the shot misses and one step backward if the shot is successful. Students play until one person has hit the target a certain number of times.
3. Students replay the game with the winner using a smaller hoop as the target and the opponent using a larger hoop (figure 6.4*b*).
4. Students consider these questions: What makes a game fair? What can you change to make the game harder or easier for one player?
5. Students set up the invented games. The EMs collect the equipment.
6. Students consider how they would make the game fair if they have opponents who are more accurate or less accurate than they are.

Debrief

Students can answer the following questions:

- What did you learn from the adaptations game that you tried using in your invented game?
- When would you use these changes in the rules?

Democracy in Action

Social justice: Creating adaptations; considering what is fair

Adaptations to game structures allow players of different abilities to play together, while still providing individual challenge. Players of various disabilities may need modified equipment and adaptations to the rules to allow engagement. Students can consider the following questions:

- What makes a game fair?
- Is it fair to adapt the game structures to make the game more equal? Why?
- How does this help people of different abilities play together?
- How does this help us to engage with our opponents?

Check for Learning

How did moving forward or backward change the way you had to think about your shot?

STAGE 7:
Showcasing the Game

Focus: Game appreciation

Skill focus: Demonstrating the game; listening and playing the game

Learner focus:

- Demonstrating their game and rules clearly and concisely (psychomotor)
- Defining and articulating what is fun about their games (cognitive)
- Offering and receiving suggestions without being defensive or hurtful (affective)

Equipment: EMs collect game equipment for their invented game

Setup: Students are in pairs.

Learner Experiences

Following are some of the many ways to carry out showcasing:

- The simplest way is to group students in fours. One pair demonstrates a game and the other pair plays it (under the guidance of the first pair). Pairs then switch. This can be repeated until pairs have sampled as many games as time allows.
- One pair demonstrates its game to half the class, and this half plays the game in one half of the gym. Another pair demonstrates its game to the

other half of the class in the other half of the gym and those students play that game. The pair explaining the game steps into the role of coach.

- All pairs explain and demonstrate their games with no class participation.

Make note of the following instructional tips:

- Whichever showcasing version is chosen, adapt the rules to encourage fairness.
- Provide recording sheets to help observing students focus on listening and providing feedback.
- Emphasize respectful behavior through supportive feedback (comments, helpful suggestions, and applause).

Democracy in Action

Group process: Honoring one's own work and that of others (fairness and equality)

Students are usually very proud and enthusiastic when they demonstrate their games to others. They need encouragement and help to listen and honor the work of their peers as they wait for their turn.

Check for Learning

- What did you learn from watching other games?
- What suggestions did you accept?
- What do you think of your game now?
- What did you like about playing the other games?
- What can get in the way of receiving constructive feedback?

The activities in this chapter help students understand the cooperative and competitive constructs of unopposed target games. Once these are established, teaching can focus largely on accuracy skills. Teachers can use table 6.5 to

Table 6.5   Tactical Framework for Target Games

Tactical concepts for accuracy	Preshot decisions	Skill execution
Direction		
Distance		

organize their skills teaching. One skill can be broken down into direction and distance concepts and sequenced into thinking about preshot decisions for each concept. Finally, teachers might add descriptions of the skill execution required. Examples are given in table 6.3 (bowling step and arm swing) and table 6.4 (tossing).

By focusing on one part of the sending motion (e.g., setup, stance, grip, approach, backswing, release, follow-through), teachers create a mini skills focus for part of a lesson. When increasing or decreasing task complexity, it's important to remember that only one element should be changed at a time so that students can focus on what is important.

SUMMARY

This chapter has described the inventing games process as it applies to unopposed target games. Democracy in action is a crucial part of this process. All too often, group or partner work is offered to students without sufficient attention or advice as to how they will negotiate the business of making, re-evaluating, and refining decisions. Even in a multicultural world, certain skills, values, and attributes are to be universally encouraged. These include respect, careful listening, clear communication, empathy, fair play and equity. Hopefully, this chapter has shown how these can be encouraged through the processes of democracy in action, rather than handed down as dictates by teachers.

Innovative Approaches to Opposed Target Games

James Mandigo

Freddy and Ricky are trying to score points by tossing beanbags into hoops set across the gym. The farther they throw from, the more points they score if they succeed. The first one to reach 21 is the winner, and Freddy is getting pretty excited.

Freddy: I'm on 20! One more to go! What are you up to again?

Ricky is somewhat shy and easily demoralized in competition, especially if there is a chance of getting bumped, outrun, or overpowered. However, Mr. Sanders has been impressed with his progress in target games. He's been much more enthusiastic and determined, and he has developed quite a knack for hitting the hoops dead center. But now, his shoulders slump.

Ricky: I'm only on 15. I missed that last throw. I guess you win.

Freddy (looking puzzled): But it's your turn. You could score 6!

Ricky: I've never scored a 6. I've only gone for 4s.

Freddy: What've you got to lose? It's your best chance. If you hit it, you win. If you only score a 4, I'll probably win. I only need 1 point. Go for it!

Mr. Sanders makes a mental note of Freddy's generosity and watches as Ricky figures out the odds, walks to the farthest pylon, and makes his throw. As the beanbag sails into the center of the hoop, Freddy whoops; then runs at Ricky, hands outstretched. Mr. Sanders can't restrain a smile at the look on Ricky's face. At first it shows pure alarm as Freddy lumbers toward him; then he figures it out, and his face cracks into a huge smile. His high-five technique might be awkward, but, hey, that will improve too!

Target games share a common primary rule (intent) of "propelling an object, preferably with a high degree of accuracy, at a target" (Mitchell, Oslin, & Griffin, 2006, p. 7). In some cases, the pathway to the target is unobstructed (e.g., archery, bowling). In other cases, the pathway to the target contains fixed obstacles (e.g., trees, water, or sand traps in golf) or obstacles that are placed in the playing area during the course of play by other players (e.g., placing a guard in curling or shuffleboard). The offensive decisions made during opposed target games (i.e., trying to reach the target) are somewhat static, and other objects or obstacles, rather than people, influence defensive decisions. For example, curlers use their stones to try to defend a rock in a scoring position, whereas in archery, nobody defends the archery board (thank goodness!).

This chapter provides activities for learning strategic concepts for opposed target games and extending learners' knowledge of the overall structures of unopposed target games (i.e., direction, level, and distance). These are summarized in table 7.1 and listed in a suggested block plan sequence in table 7.2.

Target games are ideally positioned from a developmental perspective to foster situated learning not only of how to play games confidently and competently, but also of other life skills such as democracy in action in the context of playing. These skills include principles such as sharing, taking turns, etiquette, respect for others, critical thinking, and problem solving. By emphasizing these principles as part of the learning process, teachers can create a climate of compassion and cooperation to counteract negative social behaviors such as bullying, aggression, and violence.

The purpose of the unit plan shown in table 7.2 is to demonstrate the following:

- How to foster an understanding of the structure of target games
- How to foster an understanding of the strategic questions and tactics in target games
- How to use a Teaching Games for Understanding (TGfU) approach to teach target games to develop game literacy
- A progression of purposeful and sequential lessons that enhance awareness and skills related to democracy in action and social justice

To illustrate these concepts, an online resource developed by the Ontario Physical and Health Education Association (Ophea) called PlaySport is used throughout the unit. According to the Ophea website: "PlaySport is focused upon the development of the whole child. The developmental games . . . have been designed to help students develop an understanding and competence of the skills and tactics associated with playing sports while at the same time, developing important skills that can be transferred to other aspects of their lives" (Ophea, 2014).

Table 7.1 Strategic Concepts and Tactical Decisions in Opposed Target Games

Object: To send an object and make contact with a stationary target in fewer attempts than opponents

Opposed: Players can counterattack (e.g., in billiards, horseshoes, bocce, croquet, curling, horseshoes, pool, and shuffleboard)

Strategic concepts	Tactical questions	Tactics (preshot decisions)	Skill execution (sending)
Avoiding obstacles: Send the object in fewer attempts than the opponent while avoiding obstacles Concepts: Angles, direction, distance, level	• Is it possible to manipulate the object with spins or turns to avoid obstacles? • Is there another route to the target, other than the obvious direct route? • Is it possible to use other objects to get around obstacles?	• Determine a starting point, target line, release point, and point of contact • Determine an alternative-line around an obstacle • Determine angles for bank shots and routes for sending the object to the target	• Setup, stance, grip, object position • Examine possible shots from different viewpoints before applying setup, stance, grip, object position
Preventing scoring (offense): Remove opponent's objects that are in scoring positions Concepts: Force and spin	• How much force is required to remove an opponent's object? • What is the dynamic reaction required to remove an opponent's object?	• Determine a starting point, target line, immediate target, release point, and point of contact • Determine the correct spot on the object and the force needed to create a dynamic reaction between objects to gain an offensive advantage (e.g., raise)	• Setup, stance, grip, object position • Approach, backswing, release for spin, follow-through
Preventing scoring (defense): Block pathways to keep opponents from reaching the target directly Concepts: Force, direction, and distance	How can the object be used to defend an object that is in a scoring position?	Determine the amount of force needed to reach and cover the object without displacing it	• Setup, stance, grip object position • Approach, backswing, release for spin, follow through

Table 7.2 Block Plan for Unopposed Target Games Unit

Lesson number and topic	Learner experiences	Democracy-in-action focus
Lesson 1 **Accuracy to target**		**Personal and social responsibility:** Consequences of risk taking
Introduction	Target 21	
Skill development	Underarm throw	
Culmination	Beanbag golf	
Lesson 2 **Avoiding obstacles**		**Free inquiry:** Critical thinking
Introduction	Call ball	
Skill development	Sending a stationary object with an implement	
Culmination	Pylon croquet	
Lesson 3 **Using obstacles to get closer to a target**		**Free inquiry:** Communication and negotiation
Introduction	Push it	
Skill development	Push it back	
Culmination	Shuffleboard	
Lesson 4 **Preventing scoring (offense)**		**Personal and social responsibility:** Focus and concentration
Introduction	I like to move it	
Skill development	Sending an object toward a small target	
Culmination	Five-pin bowling	
Lesson 5 **Preventing scoring (offense)**		**Personal and social responsibility:** Roles and responsibilities
Introduction	Chips ahoy	
Skill development	Sending an object with accuracy and force to remove an opponent's object from a scoring opportunity	
Culmination	Floor curling	
Lesson 6 **Preventing scoring (defense)**		**Social justice:** Prevention and protection
Introduction	Defensive knockdown	
Skill development	Sending an object using various amounts of force	
Culmination	Paralympic boccia	

LESSON 1:
Accuracy to Target

Focus: Sending an object away accurately by using the most effective direction and level

Learner focus:

- Sending an object from different distances and with different amounts of force (psychomotor)
- Sending an object away under pressure (psychomotor)

Learner Experiences

Introduction: Target 21

Adapted from Ophea 2014

Equipment: Three pylons, beanbags (one per participant), one hula hoop, one poly spot

Setup: Participants place a hula hoop at one end of the playing area and a poly spot or floor marker in the center of the hula hoop. They then set three pylons at a range of distances from the hula hoop. Each participant selects a beanbag.

How to Play

- Divide the class into pairs.
- Each person receives one beanbag (preferably different colors).
- Alternating turns, players attempt to throw the beanbag into the hula hoop or onto the poly spot from one of the three distances. Players can choose the distances to throw from.
- If the beanbag lands in the hula hoop but not on the poly spot, multiply the distance by 1. For example, if thrown from the second pylon, the score would be 2×1 (2 points).
- If the beanbag lands on the poly spot, multiple the distance by 2. For example, if thrown from the farthest pylon, the score is 3×2 (6 points).
- The first person to 21 points wins the game.

Decision Making

Suggested questions for student interaction:

- What influenced where you stood? Your confidence level? Your score compared to your partner's score?
- At what distances were you most successful? Least successful?
- What can you do to improve your aim and accuracy?

Modifications

- Roll a ball along the ground.
- Timed 21: Count the number of points a person can score in two minutes.
- Send a different piece of equipment (e.g., Frisbee).
- Increase the number of pylons and the required score.

Skill Development: Underarm Throw

Equipment: Beanbag (one per pair), two pylons

Setup: Partners stand about 10 paces apart (the distance is determined by developmental age rather than set distance) along a line (use gym floor lines, floor tape, or ropes). Pylons could be used to mark the distance.

How to Play

- Partners practice sending the beanbag along the line or between the pylons using an underarm throw.
- Encourage students to work toward using a proficient throwing technique.
- Once students have improved their proficiency, encourage them to increase the distance.

Culmination: Beanbag Golf

Adapted from Ophea 2014.

Equipment: Beanbags (one per participant), hula hoops (one per pair)

Setup: Scatter hula hoops around the gym (one per pair). Vary the location of the hoops in terms of distances and obstacles between them. Label each hoop with a number.

How to Play

- In pairs, students alternate shots (with different-colored beanbags) as they try to get a beanbag in the hoop in as few throws as possible.
- Pairs proceed to the next hoop when the team in front has finished.
- The class continues until the first students return back to the hoops they started from.

Democracy in Action

Personal and social responsibility: Consequences of risk taking

Understanding risk and how to manage it strategically is a common feature of target games. For instance, does a player take a risk by trying to hit the ball over the water hazard in golf to put the ball into the hole in fewer strokes, or take a smaller risk by hitting the ball away from the water hazard, decreasing the chance of a stroke penalty?

Check for Learning

- What distance did you choose to throw the object from in the target 21 game? What influenced your decision?
- Did you ever attempt to take a riskier shot when you had fewer points than your partner? What were some of the consequences of taking a risk?
- Can you think of risky behaviors outside of the game environment? What are some of the consequences of these, to yourself and others?

LESSON 2:
Avoiding Obstacles

Focus: Sending an object and avoiding obstacles by adding spins or turns

Learner focus:

- Sending an object using a spin or turn (psychomotor)
- Avoiding obstacles in the path of the intended target (cognitive)

Learner Experiences

Introduction: Call Ball

Equipment: Tennis balls (enough for each person on one team)

Setup: Divide the class into four equal teams, and assign each team a letter (A, B, C, or D). Everyone gathers in one spot to begin.

How to Play

- Call out one of the letters, and throw out enough tennis balls for each member of that team to have one.
- Everyone begins to run inside the grid, but the team with the letter that is called must try to obtain one tennis ball each.
- The first person to retrieve a tennis ball yells "Stop," and members of the other teams must freeze in their positions while the rest of the members of the team of the letter that was called retrieve balls.
- Call out a second letter.
- The members of the team that collected the balls must attempt to roll their tennis balls along the ground and through the legs of another players from the second team that is called.
- A point is scored for each pair of legs a tennis ball goes through.

Modifications

- Players roll the ball between feet that are close together for more difficulty and further apart for greater ease.
- The members that freeze must do leg squats while standing.

- Throwers must use their nondominant hands.
- Players must roll the ball so that it stops rolling at someone's foot.
- Players have to bank the ball off another foot before it reaches the intended target.
- Balls must pass through two sets of legs.

Decision Making

- What influenced what target you were aiming for? Distance? Pathway? Obstacles?
- Did anyone try to score 2 points by rolling the ball between two sets of legs? Why or why not?

Skill Development: Sending a Stationary Object With an Implement

Equipment: Tennis ball (one per pair), pylon (one per pair)

Setup: Partners face each other about 15 paces apart with a line on the floor between them and a pylon placed in the middle of the line.

How to Play

- Each pair gets a tennis ball and finds a line on the floor (a line can also be drawn with sidewalk chalk outside on the pavement).
- Using good technique, one player tries to roll the ball along the line to a partner.
- By spinning the ball, players try to curve the ball along the ground so that it avoids the pylon in the middle.
- Remove the pylon along the line and put a floor marker in front of each player.
- Each player then attempts to put backspin on the ball so that it stops rolling on the floor marker.

Culmination: Pylon Croquet

Adapted from Ophea 2014.

Equipment: Floor hockey sticks, golf clubs, or croquet mallets (one per player); tennis balls (one per player); pylons (two for each gate); numerous obstacles (e.g., water bottles, boxes, skittles)

Setup: Set up a croquet course with multiple gates marked by pylons. Number each gate. (See figure 7.1.)

How to Play

- Play is in groups of two to four. Each player gets an implement (e.g., croquet mallet, hockey stick, golf club) and one tennis ball.
- Each group starts at its own gate.

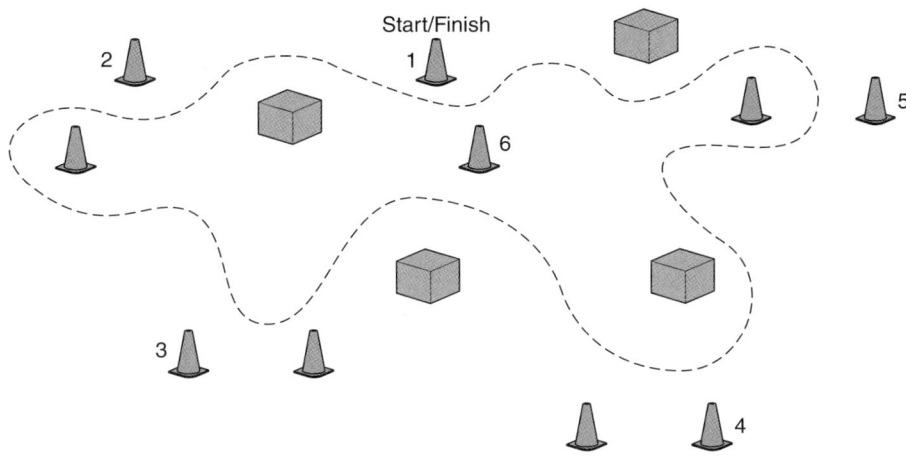

Figure 7.1 Setup for pylon croquet.

- Players alternate trying to project a ball through each gate in numerical sequence.
- The ball must go through the front of the gate to be successful.
- Players can hit an opponent's ball out of the way with their own ball if they wish.
- The ball must travel along the ground at all times (players may not raise their balls).
- Keep track of how many shots it takes players to complete the course.

Democracy in Action

Free inquiry: Critical thinking

In this lesson students must use critical thinking and plan ahead to avoid obstacles. They must also evaluate environmental conditions, such as slope and distance, before planning their routes.

Check for Learning

- How were you able to avoid and get around obstacles to reach your targets?
- What kind of planning did you have to do before you released your shot?
- What are some potential obstacles that you face each day? Do you have strategies to overcome them? What are some of these?
- Why is making a plan an effective way to solve problems? Can you think of situations in your everyday life in which having a plan is important? For example, what is your plan if you see someone else being bullied? Or if you are bullied?

LESSON 3:
Using Obstacles to Get Closer to a Target

Focus: Using other objects and obstacles to get closer to a target
Learner focus:

- Using other objects and obstacles to increase scoring chances (cognitive)
- Understanding how to contact another object to move it closer to a target (cognitive)

Learner Experiences

Introduction: Push It

Equipment: Two different-colored balls and one hula hoop or floor marker per group
Setup: Divide students into groups of three or four. Each group has two balls and a hoop or floor marker as a target.

How to Play

- Players work together to place one of their balls into a hoop or onto a floor marker by hitting it with their other ball. Teammates take turns projecting ball A to move ball B.
- Players must send ball A from the spot where it stopped rolling from the previous shot.
- The goal is to knock ball B into the hoop in as few tries as possible.
- Players attempt this several times.

Modifications

- Increase or decrease the size of ball A or ball B, or both.
- Add obstacles en route to the hoop.
- Players must send ball A with different body parts (e.g., nondominant hand or foot).
- Teams can compete against other teams to see who can put ball B into the hoop first.

Decision Making

- What part of ball B did you have to strike with ball A to make it go straight?
- What part of ball B did you have to strike with ball A to make it move to either side?
- How much effort did you need to use to make ball B move farther?

Skill Development: Push It Back

Equipment: Two tennis balls for each pair of participants

Setup: Partners stand about 15 paces from each other along a line.

How to Play

- With a partner, players choose a line on the ground and obtain two different-colored balls.
- Partners stand about 15 paces away along the line.
- Place one of the balls (ball A) about halfway on the line between the students.
- Partner A rolls a ball toward ball A and attempts to knock ball A to the partner.
- Partners alternate back and forth.

Culmination: Shuffleboard

Equipment: One shuffleboard stick for each participant and two discs for each participant (or ringette sticks and rings; floor hockey sticks and indoor pucks; golf clubs and tennis balls)

Setup: Using floor tape or sidewalk chalk outside, set up a shuffleboard court like that shown in figure 7.2.

How to Play

- Students are in groups of eight (4v4).
- Give all players the same number of objects (each team has a color).
- Teams alternate shots.
- Play continues until all of the objects have been projected by both teams.
- To score points, the object must be completely inside one of the five scoring areas. If the object touches one of the lines, it does not score.
- The exception to this is the 10-off area. If an object touches one of these lines, subtract 5 points. If the object is completely inside this area, subtract 10 points.
- The team with the most points at the end of the game wins.

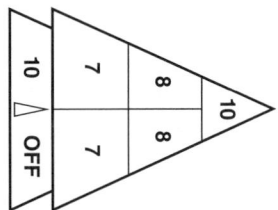 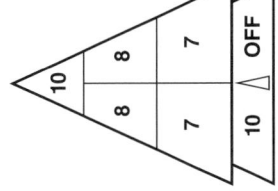

Figure 7.2   Shuffleboard court setup.

Democracy in Action

Free inquiry: Communication and negotiation

In both of these games, teamwork is important because players must work together to move an object close to a target. This requires communication and negotiation skills.

Check for Learning

- Why was it important to work with your teammates?
- How did you communicate about the kind of shot that would be most effective? How did you resolve any differences in opinion?
- Can you think of other situations outside of games in which you have to negotiate with someone to solve a problem? How do you eventually reach a decision?

LESSON 4:
Preventing Scoring (Offense)

Focus: Hitting a target or another object at the correct spot and with the correct amount of force to create a dynamic reaction between objects

Learner focus:

- Hitting a target to create a dynamic reaction with other obstacles or targets (psychomotor)
- Hitting another object so that it travels to a particular location (psychomotor and cognitive)

Introduction: I Like to Move It

Adapted from Ophea 2014.

Equipment: Six beanbags, one ball (e.g., tennis ball, gator skin ball)

Setup: Two teams of three to five players each stand facing each other behind designated lines for each team. A ball is placed midway between the teams.

How to Play

- Each team has three beanbags.
- Team members stand behind a designated line facing the other team.
- Using only underarm throws, team A tries to knock the ball across team B's line by projecting the beanbags at the ball, and vice versa.
- Only the instructor is allowed to enter the playing area to retrieve beanbags.
- A team that moves the ball across the other team's line scores a point.

Modifications

- Increase or decrease the size of the playing area.
- Increase or decrease the size of the ball.
- Deflate the ball to make it more difficult to roll.

Decision Making

- How does the placement of the beanbag on the ball affect the direction in which the ball travels?
- What happens to the beanbag after it hits the ball?
- How did the amount of force you use affect your accuracy in hitting the ball?

Skill Development: Sending an Object Toward a Small Target

Equipment: Four hoops or floor markers and two tennis balls for each pair of students

Setup: See figure 7.3.

How to Play

- Players in pairs choose a line on the ground and place a tennis ball halfway along it.
- Hoops are placed to the right and left of both players.
- Starting with an underarm roll, player 1 rolls a tennis ball to try to hit the center tennis ball into hoop A.
- Place the center tennis ball back in the middle, and have player 2 attempt to knock the center tennis ball into hoop A.
- Play continues until each player has knocked the center tennis ball into each of the hoops.

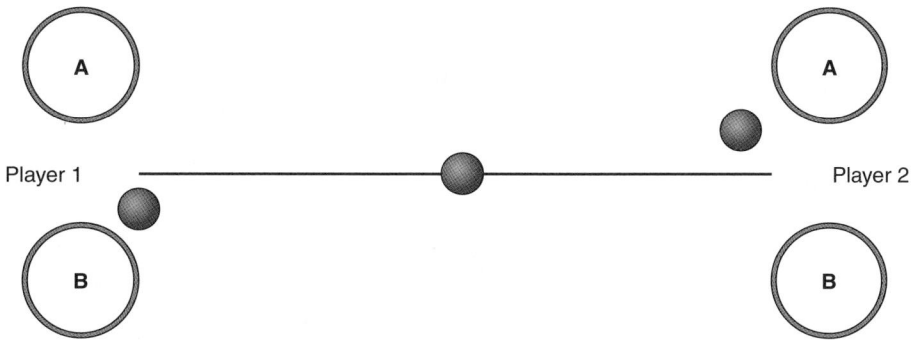

Figure 7.3 Setup for knocking a ball into hoops with a partner.

Culmination: Five-Pin Bowling

Equipment: Five pins (e.g., bowling pins, pylons, water bottles), one ball
Setup: See figure 7.4.

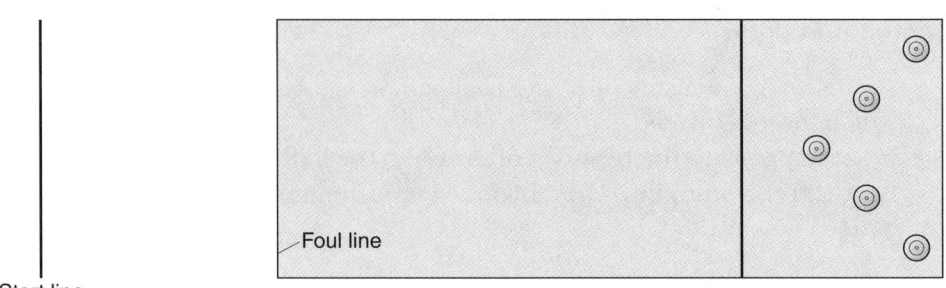

Start line

Foul line

Figure 7.4 Setup for five-pin bowling.

How to Play

- Players may use only an underarm roll.
- Each person has a maximum of three throws per frame.
- If all the pins are knocked down with the first ball, a strike is called—15 points.
- If all the pins are knocked over with the second ball, a spare is called—10 points.
- Knocking down all the pins with the third ball scores 5 points.

Democracy in Action

Personal and social responsibility: Focus and concentration

To create the type of dynamic reaction needed to succeed, students must focus on where they want to contact the intended target. Sometimes, they must hit the target straight on to move it straight back. Other times, they must hit the target to the left or to the right to create a dynamic reaction.

Check for Learning

- Which pin do you want to hit on your first throw to try to get a strike? Do you want to hit the center pin straight on or just slightly off to the side?
- Why is concentrating on where to hit the pin important? What happens if you lose your focus?
- Can you think of situations either at school or at home in which you need to focus and concentrate? What strategies help you refocus?

LESSON 5:
Preventing Scoring (Offense)

Focus: Removing an opponent's object when it is in a scoring position or a strategic area

Learner focus: Sending an object with enough force and precision that it moves an opponent's object from a scoring area (psychomotor and cognitive)

Learner Experiences

Introduction: Chips Ahoy

Adapted from Ophea 2014.

Equipment: Three hula hoops, twelve Wiffle balls in two colors (six balls of each), and eight tennis balls per group of four

Setup: See figure 7.5.

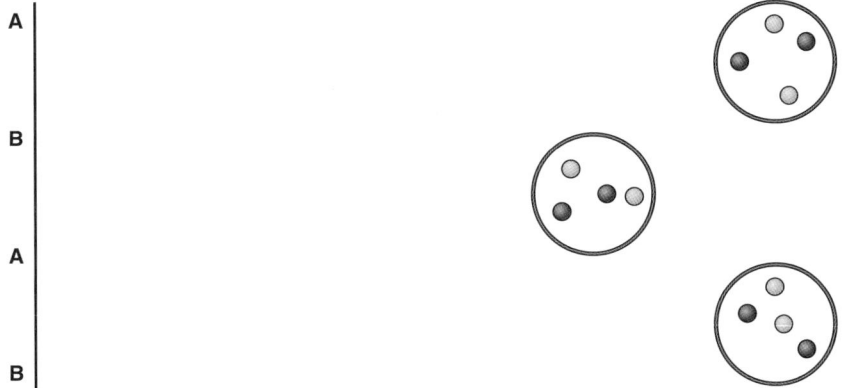

Figure 7.5 Chips ahoy setup.

How to Play

- Tape three hoops in a triangular shape to the floor.
- Place four balls in each of the hoops (two of each color).
- Students play 2v2 (team A vs. team B).
- Each person receives two tennis balls.
- All players stand 10 paces behind a line.
- Players alternate throws from behind the line to try to knock the other team's balls from the hoop.
- The team with the most balls remaining in the hoops after each person has thrown two tennis balls is the winning team.

Modifications

- Increase or decrease the distance to the hoop.
- Increase or decrease the size of the ball inside the hoop.
- Increase or decrease the size of the hoop.
- Students must knock out only the balls of one color.

Guiding Questions

- What makes a good takeout (to remove the balls from the hoop)?
- How do you generate enough force to remove an object?
- If you want to move an opponent's object to the right, where do you have to hit it? What about if you want to move it to the left? Straight back?
- If an object that you want to take out is blocked, can you deflect off other objects?
- How can you take out more than one object at a time?

Skill Development: Sending an Object With Accuracy and Force to Remove an Opponent's Object From a Scoring Opportunity

Equipment: Ten tennis balls and four pylons per pair

Setup: Using pylons, set up a grid with a partner. Player B places five tennis balls anywhere inside the grid.

How to Play

- Player A receives five tennis balls.
- Player A attempts to remove all five balls from the grid by hitting them with a tennis ball.
- Only underarm throws are permitted.
- Partners switch rolls after five throws.

Culmination: Floor Curling

Equipment: Indoor curling rocks, if available. Substitutions could include beanbags, Wiffle balls, scooter boards, indoor bocce balls or pylons (10 per group), floor tape, or one poly spot per group.

Setup: Use the pylons to create a large circle to represent the "house" and create a large X using floor tape or a poly spot to create the "button" in the middle of the "house." Use two pylons or a line on the floor to represent the toe line (i.e., the line from which the rocks must be released). Use two pylons or a line on the floor to represent the hog line, which is set up about 10 paces away from the toe line. See figure 7.6.

How to Play

- Each team has four players.
- Each team receives eight curling rocks of different colors.
- Each player on each team throws two rocks.

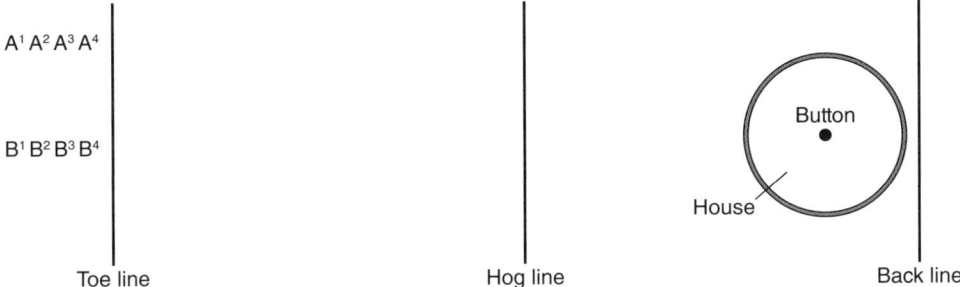

Figure 7.6 Floor curling setup.

- The rocks must remain in contact with the ground at all times.
- Players and teams alternate turns throwing a rock.
- All rocks must be released before the toe line.
- Only rocks that are between the hog line and the back line are considered in play. All other rocks are removed from play.
- Teams score a point for each rock that is closer than the opposing team's closest rock to the button.
- The team that scores 1 or more points in an end delivers the first rock in the next end.

Democracy in Action

Personal and social responsibility: Roles and responsibilities

In target games such as floor curling, teammates must communicate both before and during an end. Often, each teammate has a unique role. For example, the first person to throw might be good at setting up guards. The person who throws second might be good at takeouts. The third person to shoot might be good at placing the rock close to the button and getting around obstacles. The last person to throw might be good at all kinds of throws. Teammates have to discuss the roles they would like to play during a game and then stick to the plan.

Check for Learning

- What are some roles you had to play in this game?
- Were there roles you performed better than others?
- How did you decide who was going to play what role?
- What happened if you were in a role that you did not want to play?
- Can you think of situations in your daily life in which you were given a responsibility that you did not like? How did you deal with this?
- Why is it important in both sports and daily life to take on different types of responsibilities even if you might not enjoy them?

LESSON 6:
Preventing Scoring (Defense)

Focus: Defending space using objects or obstacles to take out an opponent's object, removing an obstacle, or guarding an important space or object

Skill focus: Underarm throwing, striking with an implement

Learner focus:

- Determining how best to position objects to guard space (cognitive)
- Determining the correct amount of force required to remove opponents' objects (cognitive)

Learner Experiences

Introduction: Defensive Knockdown

Based on Ophea 2014.

Equipment: Four pylons, four tennis ball, and one floor marker for each pair

Setup: See figure 7.7.

Figure 7.7 Defensive knockdown setup.

How to Play

- Player 2 sets up four pylons about 10 paces from a floor marker.
- Player 2 places three tennis balls as guards anywhere between player 1 and the pylons.
- Player 1 stands at the floor marker; player 2 stands behind the pylons.
- For each throw, player 2 tells player 1 which pylon to hit with the tennis ball and how to hit it (e.g., knock down pylon C, or roll the ball so that it stops at pylon C).
- Player 1 may not hit any of the other tennis balls in front of the pylons.
- Player 1 makes five throws, and then player 2 takes a turn.

Modifications

- Player 2 adds more than three tennis balls as obstacles.
- Player 1 banks the tennis ball off one of the obstacle tennis balls to hit the intended pylon.
- Player 1 gets five throws to hit the target, but must remove the three guards before throwing.

Debrief

- What makes a good guard?
- How close should a guard be to the object being guarded?
- What other target games use guards?

Skill Development: Sending an Object Using Various Amounts of Force

Activity and illustration adapted from J.L. Mandigo, 2003, Using problem based learning to enhance tactical awareness in target games. In *Teaching games for understanding in physical education and sport: An international perspective,* edited by J. Butler, L. Griffin, B. Lombardo & R. Nastasi (Oxon Hill, MD: National Association for Sport and Physical Education), 15-28. By permission of J. Butler.

Equipment: Nine beanbags, three pylons per game

Setup: Two players per team (2v2); see figure 7.8.

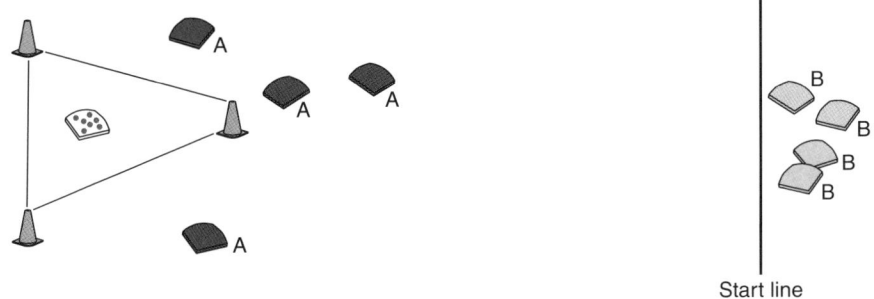

Figure 7.8 Setup for skill development activity for preventing scoring (defense).

How to Play

- Place a beanbag inside a triangle made of pylons.
- Team A uses underhand throws to deliver four beanbags as guards to protect the beanbag inside the triangle. The beanbags should remain outside of the triangle to be effective guards.
- Team B then gets four shots to try to knock the beanbag out of the triangle.
- If team B knocks the beanbag completely outside the triangle without knocking over any of the pylons, it scores 1 point.
- If team B does not knock the beanbag out of the triangle, team A scores 1 point.
- Teams play four to six ends, alternating between offense and defense.

Culmination: Paralympic Boccia

Activity and illustration adapted from J.L. Mandigo, 2003, Using problem based learning to enhance tactical awareness in target games. In *Teaching games for understanding in physical education and sport: An international perspective,* edited by J. Butler, L. Griffin, B. Lombardo & R. Nastasi (Oxon Hill, MD: National Association for Sport and Physical Education), 15-28. By permission of J. Butler.

Equipment: Twelve indoor boccia balls (or substitute with beanbags or Wiffle balls), six chairs or floor scooters per game

Setup: See figure 7.9.

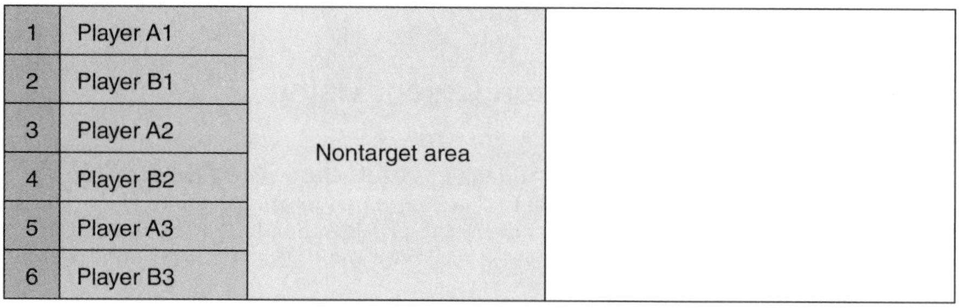

1	Player A1	
2	Player B1	
3	Player A2	Nontarget area
4	Player B2	
5	Player A3	
6	Player B3	

Figure 7.9 Setup for Paralympic boccia.

How to Play

- Play is 3v3.
- Team A occupies throwing boxes 1, 3, and 5, and team B occupies throwing boxes 2, 4, and 6.
- Each player sits in a chair in the box and must stay in that box throughout the game.
- Each player gets two balls corresponding to the team color.
- Each player initiates one end with the control of the jack (a different-colored ball).
- The jack must be thrown into the playing area beyond the nontarget area (shaded).
- The player who throws the jack also throws the first colored ball.
- The player to the right of the player who threw the jack and the first ball then throws the second colored ball.
- When throwing a ball, the player must have at least one buttock in contact with the chair.
- A ball is out of play if it touches or crosses the playing lines.
- The team to throw next is the team that does not have the closest colored ball to the jack.
- Once both teams have thrown all their balls, the team with the ball closest to the jack scores 1 point for each ball closer to the jack than the opponent's closest ball.

Democracy in Action

Social justice: Prevention and protection

Setting up guards to protect objects that are in a scoring position is an effective way to succeed in target games such as curling, bocce, and shuffleboard. Guards are a lot like prevention. They prevent threats from harming something. Learning about using guards to protect a scoring object is important in target games. Learning about prevention to protect oneself and one's community is important in life.

Check for Learning

- Why are guards important in target games?
- When is the best time to put up a guard?
- Can you think of situations in your daily life in which you have to protect something? What are things that are important to protect?
- Is it easier to protect something before or after something happens to it? What types of protection can you think of to help you and others stay healthy?

SUMMARY

Target games provide excellent opportunities for even shy and uncoordinated students to develop confidence and competence, as well as to learn some of the basic skills and attitudes required for democracy in action. This chapter provides activities for learning strategic concepts for opposed target games and extending learners' knowledge of the overall structures of unopposed target games (i.e., direction, level, and distance). It also shows how this learning can be transferred into democracy in action.

Inventing Striking Games:
Danish Longball

The atmosphere in the gym is tense. Jocelyn's up to bat, there are two outs, the score is even, and only a few minutes are left. Jocelyn belts the ball with everything she has. Unfortunately, she catches the edge of the flat-sided bat, and a fielder gleefully catches the ball. Side out. There is still about a minute left, but the members of the batting team seem resigned to their fate as they move out to field.

Norman (to Jocelyn): What's wrong with you? We're all out now because of your stupid hit, and now the others are going to score and win.

Ms. Taylor calls a time-out. She asks Jocelyn's team to gather in and directs the other team to discuss its closing game tactics.

Ms. Taylor: OK, Norman, we all heard your comment to Jocelyn. I can guess that you are feeling frustrated. It's a close game! But your comment to Jocelyn just now was uncalled for on so many levels. Can you tell me why that comment was so unfair?

Long pause.

Sim: Yeah, Norman. Jocelyn was doing her best!

Ms. Taylor: I believe I asked Norman.

Norman: Well . . . yeah. She did try, I suppose.

Ms. Taylor: May I remind you that there were two other outs before the third?

Ms. Taylor's look reminds Norman that he had been the first out.

Norman: Yeah. I suppose.

Ms. Taylor: We have to support everyone on our team, even when we make choices that don't pan out. If Jocelyn had hit a winner, she'd be a hero right now! Your team needs everyone to focus on defense in this last minute. How can you help Jocelyn get back into the game?

The number of striking games in the Teaching Games for Understanding (TGfU) classification is small, compared with the list of invasion games, for instance. Striking games include baseball, kickball, softball, cricket, and rounders. The small number of striking games may be because of their pedagogical challenges; for example, students spend a lot of time sitting out or barely moving, and teachers need to come up with modifications to create more student participation. That said, one game that demonstrates the educational potential of striking games is Danish longball (DLB; Bailey, 1983). It is packed with action and, although simple in structure, can be developed to increase the challenge, both tactically and technically. It can be played equally well both indoors and out, and it requires minimal equipment. Since it is a novel game and thus new to all players, everyone starts on a relatively even footing and learns a good deal in a short curriculum unit. DLB is an excellent starting place for students to learn how to manipulate rules and regulations without having to invent a game from scratch.

As the second category in the TGfU classification, striking games build on the constructs and sending skills of target games by emphasizing the ability to strike an object into open space away from opponents to create time and opportunity to run bases. The team playing defense learns how to field and reduce open space by reading, anticipating, and reacting to the striking actions of the batters. Once the ball has been retrieved and is back with the bowler or pitcher, both teams have time to regroup. Striking games are most closely related to target games in the sense that the batters on one team take turns striking the ball. The offensive players include only those running the bases and the batter. However, the entire team works together in defense. A number of decision-making and manipulative skills are required in both defense and offense.

This chapter is organized into two sections: how to play DLB (regulations and rules), and a guide for teaching and learning stages (including a framework of strategic concepts and tactical decisions, suggested stages, reflections, and assessment).

HOW TO PLAY DLB: REGULATIONS AND RULES

Regulations address the playing area, equipment, and players. Modifications can be made to all game regulations to increase or decrease difficulty. Figure 8.1 shows a diagram of the playing area.

Equipment consists of the following:

- Striking implement (in descending surface area and hence difficulty): tennis racket; racquet ball racquet; pickle ball bat; wide, short bat; wide, long bat; baseball bat
- Ball (in descending level of difficulty from larger size to smaller, high-low density): playground ball (4 in [10 cm]), Wiffle ball, small gator ball, tennis ball, racquet ball
- Eight cones to mark the batter's box and first base
- Poly spot to mark the pitcher's spot
- Tape to mark front and back lines

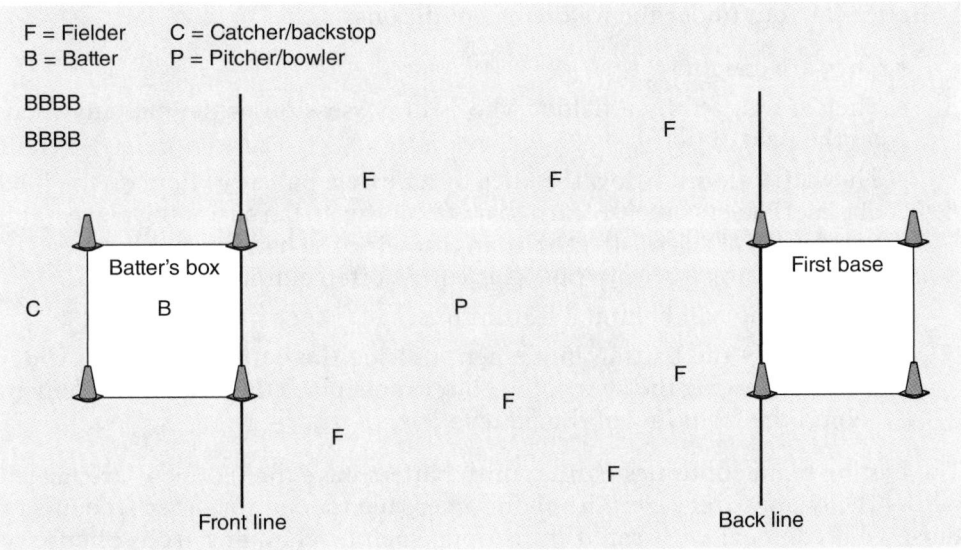

FIGURE 8.1   DLB playing area.

There are four to nine players per team (depending on the size of the playing area). The batting team is numbered to maintain the batting order. The fielding team consists of a pitcher, a catcher, and fielders.

The primary rule, or intent, of striking games is to place the ball away from fielders to provide an opportunity to run the bases and score more runs than opponents. The batting team attempts to create more time to score, while the fielding team attempts to decrease this time.

Following are the rules for DLB:

1. One batter stands behind the front line of the batter's box.
2. The pitcher or a fielder lobs the ball underarm to the batter. Each batter receives one pitch only unless it's a no-ball (i.e., higher than the shoulders and lower than the knees or outside arm's length).
3. The batter must run, regardless of whether the ball is struck.
4. Once the batting implement has been swung and dropped inside the batting box, the batter must run to the base, crossing the base's front line.
5. Batters may stay on base until they deem that another hit will provide an opportunity to return to the batter's box, or if a rule determines that the permissible number of players on first base has been exceeded.
6. Runners attempting to run home are allowed to return to first base if they have not crossed the halfway line. If they have crossed the halfway line, they must continue through the field until they are tagged out or have crossed the front line of the batting box.
7. Batters score by crossing the front line of the batting box.
8. Runners may not run once the pitcher has the ball, which is then considered dead. However, a runner who is between first and home base may continue running home.
9. Fielders may not run with the ball. One step from the pivot foot is permissible.

Batters are out under the following conditions:

- They are caught.
- They are tagged by a fielder who is in possession of the ball anywhere on the field of play.
- They are touched below the knee by a thrown ball anywhere on the field of play. (Players quickly learn that attempting to tag a running player with a thrown ball is less effective than throwing the ball to a fielder ahead of the runner for a certain tag. This rule is often eliminated.)
- They hit the ball behind the front line.
- They throw the batting implement outside the batter's box, or it slides there. Following the swing, the batter must place the batting implement behind the front line of the batter's box.

The batting team continues batting until batters have three outs or are tagged out by the changeover rule. The changeover rule (added for older students or those who can deal with rapid transitions such as changing from offense to defense, and vice versa) goes into effect when a fielder catches a pop fly.

- Fielders who catch a ball must immediately place the ball down by their feet.
- All the fielding players must run to cross the front line of the batting box to be safe.
- The batting team (including those in the box) run onto the field, attempting to pick up the ball.
- The batting team can stay at bat if a member of the fielding team who has yet to cross the front line is tagged out (Butler et al., 2007).

GUIDE FOR TEACHING STAGES

The primary rule for DLB can be divided into three offensive and three defensive concepts that have intertask transferability (see chapter 3). In other words, once learned in one striking game, these key concepts can be transferred quickly to other striking games. Table 8.1 identifies six main concepts (not an exhaustive list) and their corresponding tactics and skills that become the major structure for the inventing games stages shown in table 8.2. These six concepts need to be considered in the context of the game situation, remaining innings or time, score, and so forth. As with chapter 6, or inventing target games, stages are not intended to represent individual lessons. Time to complete a stage will be dependent on students' age, ability, and experience.

Table 8.1   Main Offensive and Defensive Strategic Concepts for All Striking Games

	Strategic concepts	Tactics	Skills needed
Offense (scoring)			
1	Hit the ball into open space in the field by determining where to send it and the degree of force needed to get it there.	Hitting low and hard into open space away from first base (to get onto first base).	Observing fielders, striking, body positioning, grip
2	Get onto the next base (or home base) by using both temporal awareness and anticipation. (Do I have enough time to get to the base? Should I go?)	Stealing bases, forcing plays (to get onto bases beyond first base).	Reading the game, such as anticipating the pitch (batter), decision making, sprinting
3	Help runners get from base(s) to home base.	Hitting hard and beyond the infield (to help runners get to the next base).	Striking and placing shots
Defense (preventing scoring)			
1	Prevent opponents from scoring by reducing the batting team's time.	Positioning fielders in areas to which the batter wants to hit. For example, in baseball and softball, with no runners on base, the batter is likely to hit away from first base and between second and third base. Fielders then move toward that space.	Decision making, ready position, locomotor skills, temporal skills, receiving and sending skills
2	Defend the bases.	Fielding and throwing to first base. Organization of short and long fielders and decision as to who will serve as cut offs.	Reading, decision making, ready position, locomotor skills, temporal skills, receiving and sending skills
3	Get the base runner out.	Fielding and throwing to the nearest base with an approaching runner.	Catching and throwing (short and long), decision making

Data from Singapore Ministry of Education 2003; Butler 2007.

Table 8.2 Inventing Striking Games: Stages and Democracy-in-Action Focuses

	Stages for inventing DLB	Democracy-in-action focus
1	Setting the learning environment Setting conditions for democracy in action	**Personal and social responsibility:** Teamwork and responsibilities
2	Changeover rule: Transitioning from offense to defense, and vice versa	**Decision making:** Implementing a team tactic; team support and tolerance of mistakes and decisions that don't work out
3	Refining rules and establishing the role of the referee	**Group process:** Majority rule (democracy requires minority rights for balance)
4	Strategic offense concept 1 and coach and observer roles: Hitting into open space to create time to run to first base and receiving feedback	**Free inquiry:** Awareness of and sensitivity to communication style (coach)
5	Strategic offense concept 2: Getting the runner to home base; communication	**Personal and social responsibility:** Team play for the good of others and the team
6	Strategic defense concept 1: Preventing opponents from scoring	**Free inquiry:** Quick thinking and communication
7	Strategic defense concept 2: Fielding to first base or home base	**Social justice:** Social power and opening up participation
8	Showcasing all games and standardizing one through the democratic process	**Free inquiry:** Giving and receiving feedback and feedforward
9	Playful DLB competition tournament	**Social justice:** Fair, even, and honest competition; respect for and acknowledgment of play and organization

STAGE 1:
Setting the Learning Environment

Focus: Playing and appreciating the rules and regulations of DLB. Following the TGfU model and the sequence of learning, students start with a small-sided game to learn the rules.

Learner focus:

- Differentiating rules for offensive (batting) and defensive (fielding) play (cognitive)
- Identifying DLB regulations (cognitive)
- Implementing a team strategy for involving all team members in team decision making (cognitive)
- Establishing the roles of equipment manager (EM) and recorder (R) (cognitive)

Equipment: Eight cones, one poly spot, one ball, four or five varied-size bats per game

Setup: No more than 6v6 for maximal involvement. For a class of 24, create two offensive (batting) teams and two defensive (fielding) teams. See figure 8.2 for an example of setup for two parallel games.

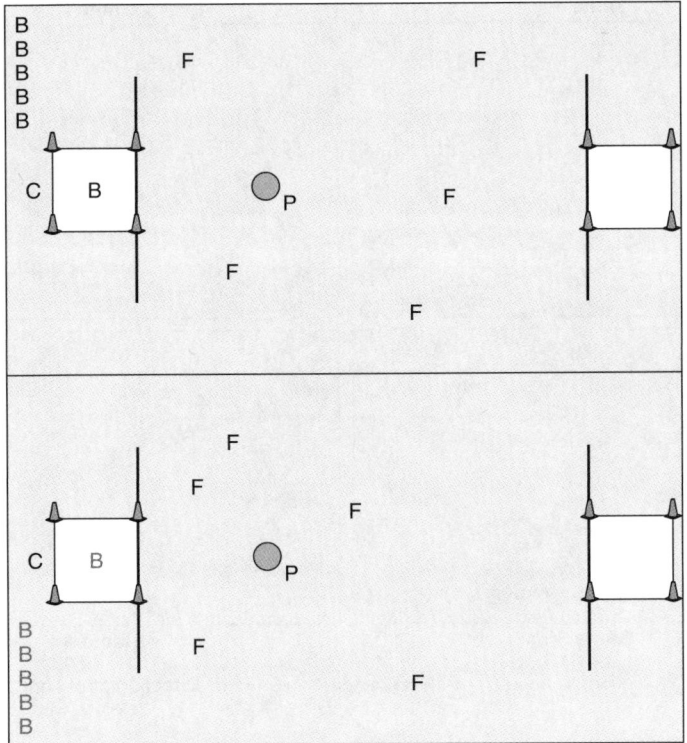

Figure 8.2. Parallel 6v6 DLB games.

Learner Experiences

Set up small-sided games of 6v6. Students play a game to understand the game structure and, in particular, the rules governing game play.

Ideally, the game is played outside, because grass and gravel fields provide more distance between bases, a larger field to cover, and more space to gather in groups and discuss tactics. Smaller games set up in the gym (using three sections) have significantly reduced distances between the bases. With shorter running distances, older students are tempted to throw the ball at the running player rather than pass it to tag the runner out. Therefore, consideration should be given to rotating groups or setting up the game on a diagonal (see figure 8.3) rather than straight across the gym floor. The size of the playing area should take into account the needs of the students, rather than the most readily available space. For example, for grade 3 students playing on a large field, the bases should be approximately 10 yards apart, whereas grade 6 students could have up to 30 yards between the bases, still only taking up a small proportion of the field. Refer to rule changes for further modifications (see stage 3).

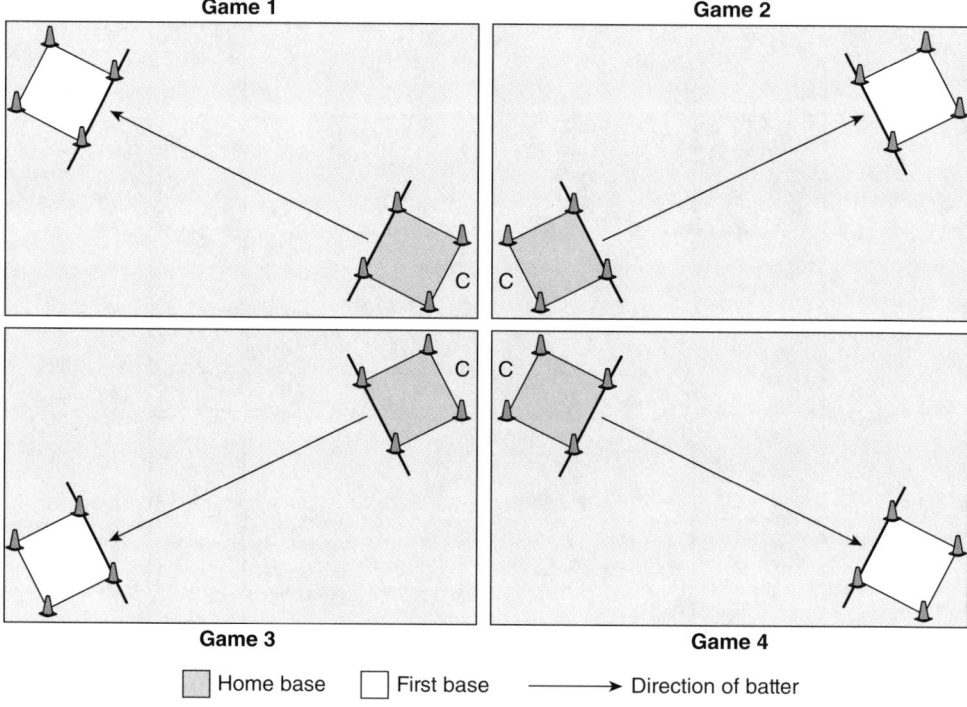

Figure 8.3 Setup for four concurrent games.

1. Create strategies for involving all team members in team decision making.
2. Teams share their ideas for team decision making.
3. Discuss the differences between regulations and rules.
4. Invite two players from each team to form temporary demonstration teams—one offensive and one defensive team. After the demonstrations, these students go back to their original teams in leadership roles.
5. Demonstrate the game using the two teams. Introduce the defensive rules to one team and the offensive rules to the other.
6. Observing teams are designated as defense or offense so they can observe one team demonstrating.
7. Allow time for student questions and review of rules.
8. Demonstrating team members go back to their original teams to review the rules of batting or fielding.
9. Set up two roles in each team: equipment manager (EM) and recorder (R).
10. The EMs (one from each team) collect equipment for the game. One collects playing equipment; the other collects boundary markers. The Rs write down the names of team members on a worksheet or an iPad.

11. Teams play two or three simultaneous games.
12. Start all students, regardless of age, with the basic rules, adding rules such as the changeover rule only once they have mastered the basic rules.
13. Switch the teams from offense to defense, and vice versa.

Decision Making

Offer time-outs to give students the opportunity to discuss the rules and how they can be used to their teams' advantage. Ask students the following questions:

- How can you use offense or defense rules to your team's advantage?
- Defense: To get a player out, the defense can either tag or throw at the runner. When would you use each? Which is more effective? How does this affect the team's tactics?
- Offense: Batters must run regardless of whether they hit the ball. When would you choose not to hit the ball and run? When would you try to hit the ball and where?

Democracy in Action

Personal and social responsibility: Teamwork and responsibilities

Encourage teams to create and write decision-making agreements that include all students in team decisions. Remind students of the following:

- Students do not have to contribute, but they do need the space or opportunity to do so, and they must understand that there are consequences for not contributing.
- There are both individual and team responsibilities (the individual to the team and the team to the individual).
- All members have an influence on the well-being and effectiveness of the team.
- The agreement must include time to discuss the content of the decision and how the decision will be made. The teams' first decisions are to elect the EM and R. The roles of the EM and R are to help the game setup run smoothly.

Check for Learning

- What are some examples of rules that address offense or defense parts of the game? Answers could be verbal or written.
- Can you identify some of the DLB regulations? Can you describe the playing area or equipment?
- What was your team strategy for team decision making? How has it worked out?

STAGE 2:
Changeover Rule (Transitions)

Focus: Transitioning from offense to defense, and vice versa. Leave this lesson out for younger students, because it requires that they be quick off the mark and aware of game situations and progress.

Learner focus:

- Explaining how the changeover rule comes into effect (cognitive)
- Discussing, organizing, and implementing a transitional strategy in teams (affective and psychomotor)

Equipment: Eight cones, one poly spot, one ball, four or five varied-size bats per game. One team wears pinnies.

Setup: No more than 6v6 for maximal involvement. For a class of 36, create three offensive (batting) teams and three defensive (fielding) teams.

Learner Experiences

1. If they haven't already, students play the game with teams switching from offense to defense, and vice versa.
2. Once students understand the rules, introduce the changeover rule. Demonstrate with one game how a pop fly catch initiates the implementation of the changeover rule. Simulate several trials of the changeover rule by sending up fly balls to be caught. The following constitutes one changeover: Team B hits a fly ball, which is caught by a player on Team A. The team A member places the ball where she caught it and runs with her teammates back to home base. If all team A members get back to home base without being tagged or hit below the knee, they are safe.
3. Students play the game.
4. Discuss and organize the transitions from offense to defense.
5. Simulate two changeovers. Repeat the previous scenario, but have a member of team A be tagged before getting back to home base. Team A is out. Team B now has to get back to home base without being tagged.
6. Students play the game.
7. Discuss and organize the transitions from defense to offense.
8. Implement the plans during game play using time-outs to modify.
9. Each team explains its strategies at the end of class.

Modifications

The easiest modification is not to use the changeover rule!

- Allow just one changeover in one play. One team must wear pinnies so the referee can see tags or outs more easily.

- Introduce multiple changeovers in one play once students understand the single changeover (e.g., allowing the batters to tag out the fielders, who then tag out the batters before either team has had time to get safely into the batter's box).

Democracy in Action

Decision making: Implementing a team tactic; team support and tolerance of mistakes and decisions that don't work out

Emphasize the use of the team decision-making agreement created in stage 1 to decide on a transitional tactic and how to implement it. The changeover rule can generate frustration, and action is fast. These can be contentious situations, ripe for moments of aporia, emotional eruption, paralysis, uncertainty, and failed communications (see chapter 2).

Check for Learning

Possibilities for checking for student learning include discussions, organization, and implementing transitional tactics in teams through student-written plans, observations of student play, and team explanations at the end of class.

Offense

- How will you prevent the fielding team from getting into the batter's box safely when your team has to retrieve the ball from the field?
- Can you create a system for runners in the first base box? When should they run?
- What options do you have for getting someone out (tagging or throwing the ball at the opponent below the knee)?

Defense

- How will you organize yourselves if the changeover rule is used while your team is fielding?
- What considerations can be made for those who have to run farther to be safely back in the batter's box?

STAGE 3:
Refining Rules and Establishing the Role of the Referee

Focus: Understanding striking game constructs (through refinement of DLB rules) and how to enforce them as a referee

Learner focus:

- Considering and negotiating rules that need changing, deleting, or adding with teammates (affective and cognitive)

- Exploring and appreciating the purposes of rules for players and referees (cognitive, affective, and psychomotor)
- Manipulating game constraints such as space, scoring, rules, or number of players (to even up the game) (cognitive and psychomotor)

Equipment: Eight cones, one poly spot, one ball, four or five varied-size bats per game

Setup: Students are in groups of six. If the class has an odd number of students, one can be a referee and the role can be rotated through all players.

Learner Experiences

1. Both teams share and discuss their decision-making agreements. Majority vote decides which agreement is used by both teams.
2. Revisit current DLB rules. Changes can be made to the following:
   a. Regulations

   - Size of box
   - Distance between boxes
   - Ball
   - Bats
   - Placement of pitcher's spot

   b. Rules

   - How is a player out? Consider existing rules and refine, add, or delete.
   - How does a team member score?
   - How many players can be on first base at once?
   - How does the pitcher have to release the ball (height, width)?
   - What are the limitations on the batter?
   - What adaptations can be made for one team to make the game even?
   - What adaptations can be made for individuals to make the game even?

3. Once the rules have been revised, groups rename their games to distinguish them from those of other groups and to establish ownership.
4. Establish the role of the referee. Start by giving the referee two rules (e.g., the ball must be pitched within defined parameters and the batter must hit the ball forwards of the home line). All other rules can initially be self-regulated until the referees feel more confident. Rotate roles at given times.
5. Add the referee responsibilities.
6. Students play the game with a time-out at the end of one inning to consider further refinements of the rules and regulations.

Democracy in Action

Group process: Majority rule (democracy requires minority rights for balance)

Decision-making agreements are tested as two teams come together to decide on changes to the rules and regulations. Most people understand that democracy is based on majority rule. However, it is important to have students discuss the basic and inalienable rights of the minority. Positions of power must be renegotiated and used responsibly. Rules should be evaluated and reconsidered. The emphasis needs to be on all groups and individuals having opportunities to speak and be heard. Be sure to point out links to friendship groups in school and to civil rights movements (race, ethnicity, sexual orientation, feminism), which needed allies to become successful.

What makes a team? Offer the following questions for discussion:

- How is a team different from a group of people? Answers might include the following: a common task, purpose, or intention; designated roles and tasks; the need to work together and support each other to be effective.
- What skills and attitudes are required for effective teamwork? Answers might include the following: clear communications and strategies, mutual support and encouragement, positive attitudes.

Check for Learning

This lesson could certainly be combined with a social studies lesson. Assessment might include a Q and A or written responses about the basic concepts of the following:

- Changeover rule
- Transition tactics
- How majority rule can marginalize minorities
- Democracy and minority rights

STAGE 4:
Strategic Offense Concept 1 and Coach and Observer Roles

Focus: Hitting into open space to create time to run to first base and receiving feedback (see offense strategy 1 in table 8.1). The entire class could learn one concept, or one team could learn offense concept 1 and one team could learn defense concept 1 in stage 6.

Learner focus:

- Explaining the batter's purpose in hitting into open space (cognitive)
- Hitting the ball to an unmarked target area (between two markers) in practice and game situations (psychomotor and cognitive)
- Observing fielders and attempting to hit into open space away from them (cognitive and psychomotor)
- Learning the role of the coach or observer

Equipment (for each group of four): Four markers or cones to represent fielders, a bat, four cones to mark first base

Setup: Groups of four—batter (B), fielder (F), pitcher (P), and batting coach (BC). See figure 8.4.

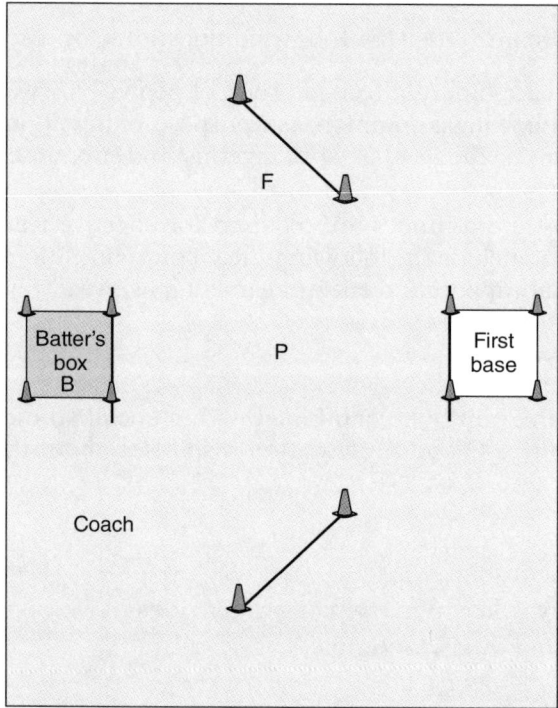

Figure 8.4 Setup for gates practice.

Learner Experiences

- Students consider how team members can get to first base quickly and successfully. Following are possibilities:
    - Hit the ball into space away from fielders.
    - Zigzag en route to first base.
    - Deliberately miss the ball to gain time to run.
- Students practice hitting the ball into open space.

Getting to First

1. The field is set up as shown in figure 8.4. The batter practices hitting hard and low between the gates (preparation, body position, backswing, follow-through, and run).
2. The fielder moves from the left to right gates at random and is stationary before the batter hits.
3. The batter reads the field (fielder positioning), decides on the placement of the hit, and then considers batting technique (e.g., body position, swing, ball contact, follow-through).
4. Repeat with the batter running to the base (ensuring that the bat is placed in the box).
5. Rotate the pitcher, batter, batting coach, and fielder.
6. The batting coaches use the Game Performance Assessment Instrument (GPAI), which identifies three components of batting—reading the field, positioning the body to hit the ball, and the actions of the swing—to give feedback to individual batters. (See table 8.3 for ideas.)
7. Students play small-sided games with an emphasis on offense (hitting the ball hard and low away from first base). Give bonus points for ball placement between the gates and away from the fielder to help shape game play.

Hitting Into Open Space

1. Students repeat the steps for gates practice using the ball placement zones as shown in figure 8.5. They focus on applying force to place the ball, as well as on the preparation, backswing, and follow-through.

Table 8.3   Sequences for Reading the Game by Player Role

Offense		Defense
Batter	**Runner on base**	**Fielder**
Read: Scan fielders and estimate the height, speed, and power of delivery. **Decisions:** Line of hit, power and force for hit. **Respond:** Change batting stance. **React:** Swing, drop the bat, and run. **Recover:** Back to base to observe the next pitch. **Reflection:** Observations by peers, video, GPAI.	**Read:** The force and direction of the ball in relation to the fielders. **Decisions:** Can I steal the base? When do I run? **Respond:** Decision to run. **React:** Run or stay. **Recover:** Base position to run again.	**Read:** The force and direction of the ball. **Decision:** Is it my ball, or do I support a teammate? **Respond:** Move to the ball or cover a teammate. **React:** Adjust to receive the ball or cover. **Decisions:** Where to throw, whether to throw the ball to the base. **Recover:** Return to base position. **Reflection:** Observations by peers, video, GPAI.

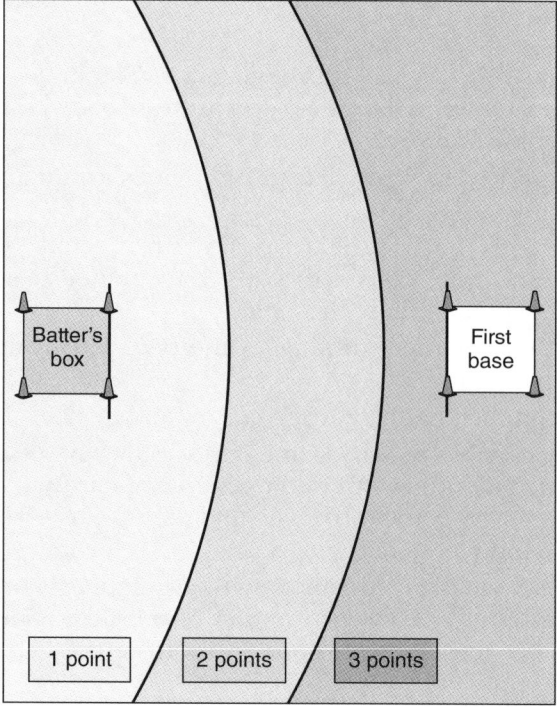

Figure 8.5 Setup for zone practice.

2. Add players in the field as in gates practice to encourage the batter to read the field.
3. Students switch roles.
4. Increase the coach's role from coaching batting technique to coaching getting onto first base.
5. Use time-outs to consider what-ifs and how to run to the base.

Modifications

- Hitting from a T stand
- Kicking the ball
- Having a teammate pitch
- Varying the distance from the batter to the markers
- Having a wider gap between markers
- Varying the size of the hitting implement and of the ball

Democracy in Action

Free inquiry: Awareness of and sensitivity to communication style (coach)

As students take turns playing the coach's role by observing both the hit and the run to base, they need to consider how to provide feedback. Ask them how they would like to receive information about their own performance. Encouraging students to speak about how they would like to receive feedback communicates the importance of considering not just what they say, but how they say it.

Check for Learning

Following are possibilities for identifying learning:

- The batting coach observes the batter using a techniques checklist or rating scale and provides verbal feedback.
- Repeat the at-bat so that the batter can use the observer's suggestions.
- The batting coach identifies what the batter is doing well and provide suggestions for improvement.
- Help students identify the batter's purpose in hitting into open space in a Q and A period during lesson closure.
- Have students hit the ball to an unmarked target area (between two markers), highlight successful attempts, and encourage peer assessment.
- Teammates observe and discuss together.

STAGE 5:
Strategic Offense Concept 2

Focus: Getting the runner back to home base (see table 8.1)

Learner focus:

- Creating strategies for helping teammates return from first base to home base, including establishing a communication system between the batter and the runner (cognitive)
- Anticipating when to run home by estimating how much time is created by the batter's placement of the ball (cognitive and psychomotor)

Learner Experiences

Have teams consider tactics for runners getting back to home base and scoring. Following are possibilities:

- Runners wait at first base until there is time to run.
- Teams appoint a guide or coach to get players home from first base.
- Runners zigzag en route to home base.
- Teams decide how many people can run at the same time (i.e., rush the defense).
- Batters sacrifice a fly hit.

- Players with a clear view of teammates running give feedback about when and if to run.
- Teams have a set number of time-outs.
- Teams have time to practice tactics.
- Players determine the best time to hit a fly ball.
- Players determine when the runner can leave the base.

Democracy in Action

Personal and social responsibility: Team play for the good of others and the team

Discuss team play in relation to how a player on first base can contribute to the success of other runners getting home. Because the focus in this stage is getting team members to home base to score runs, it would be a good opportunity to link this with a discussion of individual versus team responsibilities and to consider a balance between the two.

Check for Learning

- What were your tactics for getting runners home?
- Is there ever a time when a player must sacrifice his own play for the success of the team?
- Can this be related to our moral duty to act for the good of others?
- What are some of the responsibilities of individuals and the team?

STAGE 6:
Strategic Defense Concept 1

Focus: Preventing opponents from scoring by covering the field effectively (see table 8.1)

Learner focus:

- Learning the main strategies of fielding (cognitive)
- Employing defensive tactics as appropriate (cognitive)
- Using the ready position (body in motion) as the batter strikes the ball (psychomotor and cognitive)

Equipment: One bat, one racket, two balls, and seven poly spots for each group of six players

Setup: Each game has three fielders (defenders) and three attackers (two are batters and one is a feeder or pitcher).

Learner Experiences

1. Students play zones (see figure 8.5) with a focus on the defenders.
2. Students consider how best to defend the scoring zones.

   - How do you defend the space? (Spread out)
   - How do you spread out? (One front and two back, or two front and one back)
   - Where is it easiest to defend? (In the back, because you have more time to react and the ball has to go over the front fielders)

3. Students discuss the ready position by answering the following questions:

   - What do you read about the batter?
   - How does this help you anticipate where the batter might hit?
   - What body position makes it easier to catch?

4. Students discuss offense by answering the following questions:

   - Is it easier to score 1 point, 2 points, or 3 points?
   - Is it ever a good idea to risk being caught out in an attempt to score 3 points? When?
   - Can you place the ball into the gap or space?
   - Can you hit the ball high (or low) with more (or less) power? Which is more effective?
   - What body position makes it easier to strike?

5. Students go back to the 6v6 game, transferring defense concepts regarding reading batters, placing fielders (near and far), and keeping the body in motion in the ready position.

Modification

Give the batter a choice of a racket or a bat.

Democracy in Action

Free inquiry: Quick thinking and communication

Communication other than just how to place fielders is required during game play. As a player moves to field the ball, other fielders with clearer sight of the game play need to communicate to that player where to throw the ball.

Check for Learning

Possibilities for identifying learning include exploring the following through explanation or written responses:

- What is the main defensive strategy to prevent scoring?
- What is the rationale behind fielder placement?
- How do fielders need to communicate to get opponents out?

STAGE 7:
Strategic Defense Concept 2

Focus: Fielding to first base or home base ahead of runners (see table 8.1)

Learner focus:

- Sending the ball ahead of the runner to first base to get the runner out (psychomotor)
- Devising a defensive plan to deal with two situations: no runners on first base and one or more runners on first base (cognitive)
- Making tactical defensive decisions when first base is loaded (cognitive and psychomotor)

Equipment: Pinnies for one team in each game. EM collects equipment for their invented game.

Setup: One DLB court with a section on the long side set aside for skills practice.

Learner Experiences

1. Set up the game situation with no runners on first base. Teams devise a plan to get the ball to first base to get the runner out. Possible solutions include the following:

   - A fielder is placed at the front of first base to receive the ball to tag the runner.
   - The fielder closest to the ball runs to it and shouts "Mine!"
   - An intermediary fielder runs to the middle of the court as a cutoff and sends the ball to first base.
   - The catcher retrieves the ball after a no-hit and sends it to first base or to the cutoff.

2. Runners always return to home base whether they score or not. After a certain number of attempts, teams rotate.

3. Practice one tactic (decided by teams or by you depending on progress) with no offense. This creates time for refining the skills of throwing, catching, and moving in for the catch. For example, a practice can be set up in groups of three. Divide the court in two lengthwise to provide space for each team to practice. From an imaginary no-hit at home base, the catcher collects the ball and looks for the cutoff or first base fielder. Players should practice running from both sides and rotate positions. Emphasize calls, movement to the middle, turning, throwing, and catching.

4. Call time-outs to debrief.

5. Resume the first game (no runners on first base). Award teams 3 points for successful implementation of their defensive tactic and a bonus point for getting a player out.

6. Set up a game situation with runners on first base. Teams devise a second plan to get the ball to home base to prevent scoring. Create the following two scenarios for retrieving the ball:

   i. The catcher retrieves a miss-hit ball or a no-hit ball.
   ii. The batter hits the ball long past first base.

7. Teams decide their tactics for both situations. Plays are contrived and practiced for both situations.
8. Teams switch roles.
9. Call time-outs for team discussions.
10. Each team practices both of the preceding scenarios with no offense.
11. Set up the game situation mentioned in step 5.
12. Call time-outs to refine plans.
13. Award bonus points for successful implementation of defensive tactics.

Democracy in Action

Social justice: Social power and opening up participation

Students have different levels and kinds of social power. Some have patterns of assuming privileged positions (e.g., speaking on behalf of others or more than others). Some students feel less empowered because they are affected by the complications of race, gender, ethnicity, and sexual orientation. In collaborative groups, everyone has the right to speak and feel seen, acknowledged, and respected for their contributions.

Suggestions for opening up communication:

- Ask talkers to be conscious of others needing space to talk.
- Have the equipment manager or recorder ask once in every time-out, Can we hear from those who have not spoken yet?
- Give credit by acknowledging the person's name: "So as I understand it, Sophie's suggestion is to . . . ."

Check for Learning

How did your defense plan change with the two different situations: (a) no runners on first base and (b) one or more runners on first base?

STAGE 8:
Showcasing All Games and Standardizing One Through the Democratic Process

Focus: Showcasing variations of the DLB game and choosing one for standardization

Learner focus:

- Defining and articulating the changes they made to their games (cognitive)
- Demonstrating clearly and concisely their game rules (psychomotor)
- Explaining why they made the changes they did (affective)

Equipment: Each group's EM will collect equipment for the invented game made in stage 3. Pinnies for one team in each game.

Learner Experiences

1. Teams polish their games in preparation for the showcase.
2. Groups (two teams) elect one person to speak about the game. This person presents the rule changes and explains why they were made.
3. Each group showcases its game for two to three minutes.
4. Groups take questions and comments.
5. All groups play the showcased game.
6. Repeat steps 1 through 5 until all groups have showcased their games.
7. All students write down what they like and don't like about each game. A reporting sheet can be provided.
8. Students elect one person from each team to form a committee. The meeting could be conducted while play continues, or the class can observe the committee process. Comparisons can be made with how national organizations such as the NBA change or refine rules structures.
9. All students vote for their favorite game variations; the winner becomes the standardized game.
10. Once selected, the game can be furthered revised based on the feedback from the reporting sheets (see step 7).

Democracy in Action

Free inquiry: Giving and receiving feedback and feedforward

Feedback refers to information given about something that has happened. Feedforward is advice or suggestions offered to help groups move forward. Both need to be offered with sensitivity and respect. This usually occurs when the intention is to help and the information is specific. Receiving such information requires listening carefully and receiving it in the spirit in which it was given.

Check for Learning

- What did you learn from watching other groups' games?
- Were you surprised by the differences in the games? Why?
- Did you prefer to listen to feedback or feedforward, or to give it? Or did you find both equal?
- What do you need to improve about either listening or giving information?

STAGE 9:
Playful DLB Competition Tournament

Focus: Playful competition within the sport education model (Siedentop et al., 2011). See ideas for tournaments in chapter 12.

Learner focus: Good players make good decisions.

Learner Experiences

Once students are used to playing the game, they can begin to make better game play decisions. A strong thrower is only effective when throwing to the best place. Helping students learn the four Rs (see chapter 4) is fundamental in teaching how to make good decisions (Hopper, 2003).

Democracy in Action

Social justice: Fair, even, and honest competition; respect for and acknowledgment of play and organization

> At a time when there is a growing tendency for students to think that "stacking" teams, with imbalanced teams resulting in one sided scores, is OK, drawing attention to what is fair, even, and honest competition is critical, particularly if we want games to continue in schools as something educational and not the source of domination or bullying. One way to combat this trend is learning the merits of fair play and the skills required to organize games through inventing games.

> We can add another layer here by assessing effort and decisions, because the choices students make contribute to their overall performance. A scoring system could be implemented, perhaps using a high-medium-low ranking structure or rating scale, as shown in table 8.4.

It is essential to assess students in both the execution and selection of the skill. The following criteria can be used in rating:

Skill Execution

Executes chosen skills proficiently.

- Read and respond: Judges the pace and distance of the ball and moves to it.
- React: Is accurate and uses appropriate degree of force.
- Recover: Moves back to base.

Decision Making

Makes appropriate choices about which skill set to use: short or long throw, first or home base, depending on the location of the batter.

- Read: Observes the batter's location and action.
- Respond and react: Makes decision to send the ball toward the appropriate base.

Table 8.4 Fielding Assessment (Throwing Example Using the Four Rs)

		Skill execution (throwing)									Decision making					
		Read and respond			React			Recover (base)			Read			Respond and react		
	Attempts	1st	2nd	3rd	1st	2nd	3rd	1st	2nd	3rd	1st	2nd	3rd	1st	2nd	3rd
Players	William	4	4	3	5	5	5	3	3	5	1	3	3	4	5	5
	Betty	5	5	4	5	5	5	3	3	5	4	5	5	5	4	5
	Luke	3	3	4	3	3	3	5	5	5	5	5	5	4	4	4
	Paulo	1	1	2	3	3	4	3	3	3	3	4	4	5	4	4

Rating Scale

5 = Highly effective

3 = Moderately effective

1 = Not effective

Adapted from Mitchell, Oslin, and Tannehill 1999.

SUMMARY

DLB is a great game for introducing students to striking games. Because it is a novel game, it creates an almost equal footing (talent aside) for learners. While promoting the fundamental skills and techniques of catching, throwing, striking, bowling or pitching, and running, it also promotes decision making, at both the individual and team levels. DLB is a great game for exploring the TGfU approach in that the novelty of the game masks the newness of the teaching approach. It also provides further footing for exploring democracy in action.

CHAPTER

9

Striking Game: Cricket

Kevin Sandher

With only minutes left in class, voices are raised in the cricket game. When the teacher investigates, he finds two teammates in disagreement—the pair up at bat. He observes as the scorekeeper (one of the students from the batting team) yells out, "Three runs to win off the last ball." The batter is Todd, one of the best and fastest athletes in the school. His batting partner, Shane, is a little overweight and not nearly as fast as Todd.

As the bowler positions his fielders for this final ball of the game, the two batters get together to talk about tactics. Todd waves his hands emphatically, but Shane looks dejected. The ball is bowled, and Todd smacks it way into the outfield; they both complete one run and then turn back for another. Shane struggles toward his wicket as the wicketkeeper catches the long throw and takes off the bails.

Todd throws his bat into the air and screams, "Why did I get stuck with this guy?" There are nods and murmurs of agreement from the row of dejected batters at the bench. Some clap slowly and ironically as Shane walks from the field, head down, out of breath, and demoralized.

The teacher has a decision to make. Does he intervene? How? What should he say?

The main challenge in teaching cricket is its static nature and inherent difficulty. Striking games such as cricket don't allow maximal participation, and they require a high degree of eye–hand coordination to hit the ball squarely. The unit plan offered in this chapter tackles these issues by offering small-sided games that keep students active as they learn important tactics and skills incrementally to achieve success. Teaching Games for Understanding (TGfU) enables learners to appreciate the joy of game play, which in turn leads to a desire to learn techniques to play better. The main aim, or primary rule, of striking games such as cricket for the batting side is to create time to run; for the fielding side, it is to reduce this time.

This chapter provides a diverse range of activities in the hope that students will find their passion and thus engage in lifelong physical activity. In addition, students from countries in which cricket is popular, who may feel distant from traditional North American games, may become more engaged and empowered by having opportunities to teach their peers. This unit maximizes participation by modifying and adapting activities to fit a range of ability levels. The goal is not to develop elite-level cricket players; however, the activities can be modified to create optimal challenge for students who are particularly adept. The unit can be used for students ages 5 through 17, but could easily be used at the university level, with education students, for example.

UNIT PLAN STRUCTURE

This chapter presents an eight-lesson unit on how to teach cricket using a TGfU approach while introducing means to address social issues. The unit plan builds sequentially to help students understand the game as they move from one lesson to the next. Modified forms of cricket such as KWIK cricket (England and New Zealand) and MILO cricket (Australia) are used to introduce the sport. Plastic bats and balls are more suited to beginners than the traditional wood bat and leather ball. The scope and sequence of the unit allows for increasing complexity and tactical sequencing. That said, because teachers bring their unique perspectives to the class, lessons should always be fluid. Modifications can be added or removed to meet the needs and context of the class.

ASSESSMENT

Assessment follows a student-centered approach: the students themselves are involved in what and how learning is assessed. I work with students to create a rubric to assess their progress. I find the Game Performance Assessment Instrument (GPAI) useful in all game units. The GPAI rubric outlines the skills and tactics required in a game. These skills are not assessed in isolation; rather, peers or teachers use them while students play the game. These allow students to reflect on their own performances and discuss them with their peers. Examples of a GPAI are included at the end of this chapter. Teachers can use this template to include whatever skills or concepts they deem important.

Helpful assessments are 3-2-1 exit slips. At the end of class, students enter three things they learned, two things they want to learn, and one thing they want to improve. Not only do these allow students to reflect on the class, but they also help teachers plan the next lesson. The goal of assessment is to help students understand what they value and encourage them to enjoy and fully participate in the game.

Table 9.1 lists the fundamental aims of cricket, and table 9.2 shows a block plan that could be used for a cricket unit.

Table 9.1 Fundamental Aims of Cricket

Actions	Aims
Batting	• To score runs • To avoid getting out
Bowling	• To get the batter out • To prevent the batter from scoring runs
Fielding	• To dismiss the batter by effecting a dismissal through caught, run-out, or stumped • To prevent the batter from scoring runs

Table 9.2   Block Plan for Cricket Unit

Lesson number and topic	Learner experiences	Democracy-in-action focus
Lesson 1	Play the game: Learning basic rules	
	Offensive concept 1(a): Hitting to open space (vertical bat)	
Introduction	Continuous cricket; start with the game to introduce the basic rules	**Social justice:** Inclusion and empathy
Culmination	Line-up cricket game	
Lesson 2	Offensive concept 1(b): Hitting to open space (horizontal bat)	
	Defensive concept 1: Reducing the batter's time by fielding the ball quickly and returning it to the bowler or wicketkeeper	
Introduction	Crossfire fielding game	**Personal and social responsibility:** Teamwork and responsibilities
Development	Ground fielding: Technique and goal ball	
Culmination	Line-up cricket game	
Lesson 3	Offensive concept 1 (a and b): Hitting to open space	
	Defensive concept 2: Reducing batter time using throwing	
Introduction	Crossfire and replace	**Free inquiry:** Participation in community through voice
Development	Overarm throwing	
Culmination	Double chance continuous cricket	
Lesson 4	Offensive concept 2: Running between wickets	
	Defensive concept 3: Catching to get batters out	
Introduction	Crossfire and replace (catching)	**Decision making:** Using a preestablished plan
Development	Traffic lights: Running between wickets with a partner	
	Beat the catcher: Catching	
Culmination	Double chance pairs cricket	
Lesson 5	Combination skills	
Introduction	Catch volleyball	**Social justice:** Team play for the good of others
Development	Rapid-fire box batting	
Culmination	Double chance pairs cricket: 6 fielders vs. 2 batters	
Lesson 6	Defensive concept 4: Bowling to limit the batter's time	

(continued)

Table 9.2 *(continued)*

Lesson number and topic	Learner experiences	Democracy-in-action focus
Introduction	Catch soccer	**Decision making and free inquiry:** Democratically selecting a rule to add to the game; opening up participation
Development	Introduction to bowling (bombardment bowling)	
Culmination	Double chance pairs cricket: 6v6 with a new rule added	
Lesson 7	Using the GPAI for in-game assessments	
Introduction	Students democratically vote on their favorite warm-up game	**Social justice:** Giving and receiving feedback
Development	Students practice using the GPAI and have time for team tactic planning	
Culmination	Double chance pairs cricket game	
Lesson 8	Pairs cricket tournament	
Introduction	Teams invent a warm-up game based on warm-up games played	**Decision making:** Implementing a team tactic
Development	Students assess a partner from another team using the GPAI	
Culmination	Double chance pairs cricket tournament	

LESSON 1:
Play the Game—Learning Basic Rules

Focus: Offensive concept 1(a): Hitting to open space (vertical bat). Introduce the basic concept of batters hitting to open space to complete runs and fielders defending space to limit runs.

Learner focus:

- Understanding the basic rules of cricket to begin playing small-sided games (cognitive)
- Focusing on hitting to open space in small-sided games (cognitive)
- Batting with a vertical bat in practice conditions (psychomotor)
- Practicing ground fielding skills in gamelike situations (psychomotor)

Equipment: One bat and one ball per player

Setup: Players are in groups of five or six in a 10- by 10-yard grid.

Learner Experiences

Warm-Up

Students work on eye–hand coordination by hitting with the flat side of the bat.

1. Each student has a bat and a ball.
2. On your signal (if inside, you can use music to start and stop), students bounce their balls on their bats as they walk around the grid.
3. If the ball drops off, students safely retrieve it and start again.
4. Challenges: Add two balls, use the curved side of the bat, stop the ball on the bat.
5. Modifications: Use soft balls or simply have students catch balls.

Introduction: Continuous Cricket

Equipment: Two cones, one bat, one ball, one set of wickets per group of five to seven

Setup: Because batters in cricket can strike the ball anywhere in a 180-degree radius, the tee and the wickets should be placed toward the center of the space to allow batters to strike the ball forward and to the side (180 degrees), not backward (see figure 9.1). The cone the batters run to would normally be set 10 to 15 yards to both sides of where the batter stands. Another cone should mark where the bowler has to stand and where the batter stands and must touch his bat on a return run.

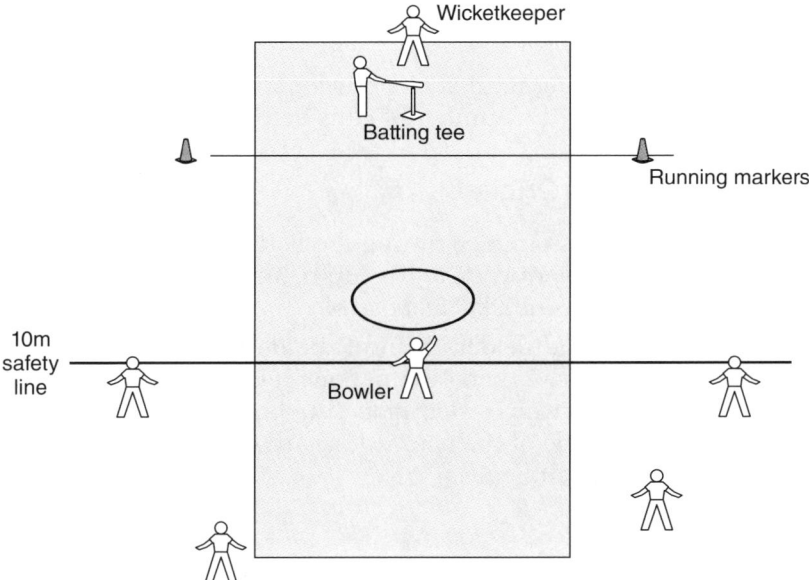

Figure 9.1 Continuous cricket off a tee.

- Players split into two teams: one batter versus four to six fielders.
- The fielding team spreads out in front of the batting tee and to the side of the batting tee, a minimum of 10 yards away from the batter for safety. No one except the wicketkeeper may be behind the batting tee.
- One fielder acts as wicketkeeper.

How to Play

Begin this game with a quick explanation of striking games (relating cricket to others in the category) and the basic premise of cricket. The primary aim of the game is for the batters to create as much time as possible to allow them to score as many runs as possible. This typically involves hitting the ball into space and away from the bowler, because the bowler can underarm-lob the ball toward the wickets as soon as she gets it from the fielders. The primary aim of the fielding side is to get the ball to the bowler as quickly as possible. This requires skill and tactics.

- A student serves the ball underarm with one bounce at the wicket (batting tee). The batter attempts to hit it. Whether she hits it or not, the batter has to run.
- A run is scored when the batter touches the bat on the ground past the cone and again when the bat is touched past the wicket (batting tee).
- The batter must not drop the bat as in baseball or softball, because no runs can be scored without the bat.
- Fielders must return the ball to the bowler as quickly as possible but may not run with the ball.
- Fielders return the ball every time to you or a designate (who continually serves).
- Each batter keeps going until she is bowled, caught, or hit wicket. Alternatively, you can limit the number of runs before students have to switch.

Culmination: Line-Up Cricket

In line-up cricket, students practice hitting the ball into scoring zones using a vertical bat. Fielders use teamwork to line up behind the ball to get it back to the hitting tee or wickets as quickly as possible.

Setup: Low batting tee and fielders behind the designated scoring zone line (2-point zone). You can have 2- and 4-point zones every 5 yards (see figure 9.2). Number each player in batting order. Place the ball on the tee. Position one running marker at each side of the wicket forward of the batter (near batter = easy; farther away = more difficult).

How to Play

Each batter in turn aims to hit the ball between the foul markers and then run between the running markers. A fielder collects the ball. All others run and line up behind the fielder. The ball is passed back until the last player in the line has it. The last player then runs to touch the wickets at the bowler's end with

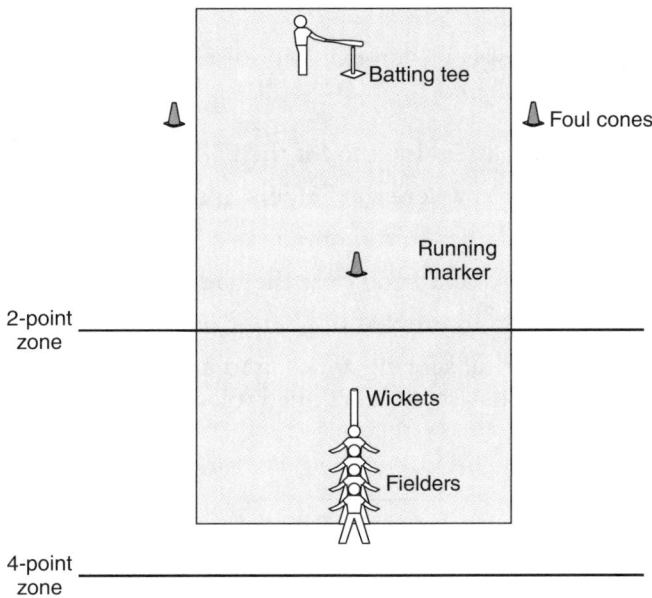

Figure 9.2 Line-up cricket off a tee.

the ball to stop the batter running. Repeat for each batter in turn. The batter with the most runs wins.

Modifications

- Increase the size of the neutral zone for batters (simplify).
- Use a bigger bat and softer ball (simplify).
- Change the distance of the side cones in each of the games.
- Change the distance of the hitting zones to widen the gap between the fielders.

Democracy in Action

Social justice: Inclusion and empathy

Students discuss how to make sure players of all ability levels can be included in the line-up cricket game. They consider how to make the game more inclusive of all ability levels and what adaptations can be made.

Check for Learning

Teacher Observations

- Are batters hitting to open spaces?
- Are fielders anticipating where the ball is going to be hit?
- Are batters using a vertical bat and hitting the ball into the hitting zones?

Student Self-Evaluations

Use the 3-2-1 evaluation sheet as an exit slip to see what students learned.

Questions

Q: Where should the batters look to hit the ball?

A: Into open spaces (i.e., where the fielders are not).

Q: What are important cues to remember as a batter?

A: Keep weight forward and head over the ball.

Q: What can fielders do to prevent the batter from scoring runs?

A: Spread out to cover all scoring zones, and anticipate where batters are going to hit the ball. Also, fielders need to cooperate to get to the ball as quickly as possible.

LESSON 2:
Offense Concept—Hitting to Open Space

Offensive concept 1(b): Hitting to open space (horizontal bat)

Defensive concept 1: Reducing the batter's time by fielding the ball quickly and returning it to the bowler or wicketkeeper

Focus: Introducing hitting the ball with a horizontal bat as well as the basics of ground fielding

Learner focus:

- Hitting to open space (cognitive)
- Batting with a horizontal bat in practice conditions (psychomotor)
- Using ground fielding skills in game and practice situations (psychomotor)

Sequence:

1. Warm-up: Crossfire and replace
2. Activity: Tee driving cricket horizontal bat hitting off tees
3. Activity: Goal ball
4. Game: Tee line cricket

Learner Experiences

Introduction: Crossfire

1. Have players grouped into pairs with one ball per pair.
2. Players form a circle with partners opposite each other and a set of stumps in the middle of the circle.
3. Players overarm throw at stumps between partners. Pairs score 1 point every time they hit the stumps. The pair with the most hits wins.

Development: Ground Fielding Technique and Goal Ball

Equipment: Bats, balls, wickets, cones

Setup: Two lines of equal teams facing each other 15 yards apart. Each team is just in front of its goal line.

How to Play

Students practice stopping a ground ball using two hands. Teams continually roll the ball underarm, attempting to cross the other team's goal line. A goal is scored each time a ball crosses the goal line. The first team to 10 goals wins. The ball must be rolled underarm from just in front of the goal line.

Culmination: Line-Up Cricket

Play line-up cricket as described in lesson 1.

Democracy in Action

Personal and social responsibility: Teamwork and responsibilities

Students uncover their roles on the team, initially through fielding. Where are the optimal positions to prevent runs? Encourage team discussions about fielding placements.

LESSON 3:
Defense Concept—Reducing Batter Time Using Throwing

Offensive concept 1: Hitting to open space

Defensive concept 2: Reducing batter time using throwing

Focus: Deciding when to use vertical and horizontal bat shots and learning basic throwing technique

Learner focus:

- Hitting to open space (cognitive)
- Deciding how much force to apply (cognitive)
- Refining basic throwing skills (psychomotor)
- Discussing and analyzing how rule changes affect the continuous cricket game (cognitive)

Sequence:

1. Warm-up: Crossfire and replace (throwing)
2. Activity: Hitting cricket ball off tee with a horizontal and vertical bat
3. Activity: Bombardment throwing overarm (move the ball)
4. Game: Double chance continuous cricket

Learner Experiences

Introduction: Crossfire and Replace

In this game, students experiment with throwing and review fielding from lesson 2. Group players into pairs with one ball per pair. Players form a circle with partners opposite each other and a set of stumps in the middle of the circle. Players overarm throw at the stumps between them. Pairs score 1 point every time they hit the stumps. The pair with the most hits wins.

Development: Overarm Throwing (Move the Ball)

Equipment: One large ball and one tennis ball per student

Setup: Two lines of equal teams face each other 15 yards apart. A big, soft ball is between the teams.

In this game, students practice throwing with proper technique at a target and practice fielding ground balls as in lesson 2. Teams stand in a straight line 15 yards apart facing each other. A soccer ball (or something similar) is placed in the middle. Once signaled, players throw balls at the soccer ball and attempt to roll it over their opponents' goal line to score a point. After each goal the soccer ball is returned to the middle. The team with the most points wins.

Culmination: Double Chance Continuous Cricket

This is the same as continuous cricket in lesson 1, with the exception that players have a batting tee next to them. If they miss the pitch, they can hit the ball off the tee.

Modification

Place the markers players have to run to closer to or farther from the wicket.

Democracy in Action

Free inquiry: Participation in community through voice

Students discuss the most effective ways to throw the ball to achieve accuracy and force. All members of the group have a right to be heard.

LESSON 4:
Running Between Wickets and Catching to Get Batters Out

Offensive concept 2: Running between wickets

Defensive concept 3: Catching to get batters out

Focus: Running between wickets, decision making and communication skills, and catching

Learner focus:

- Hitting to open space (cognitive)
- Running between wickets with a partner (cognitive)
- Being emphatic (clear) to the running partner (communication skills) to complete runs (affective)
- Deciding between horizontal and vertical bat shots (cognitive)
- Practicing basic catching skills (psychomotor)

Sequence:

1. Warm-up: Crossfire and replace (catching)
2. Activity: Traffic lights to introduce running between wickets
3. Skill enhancement: Basic catching skills
4. Game: Beat the catcher (combine catching and running between wickets)
5. Game: Double chance pairs cricket

Learner Experiences

Introduction: Crossfire and Replace

This is the same as in lesson 3, but it includes catching.

Development: Traffic Lights

Equipment: Bats, balls, cones, wickets

Setup: Place three cones on the floor to represent three traffic lights (see figure 9.3). The red light indicates no, the green light indicates yes, and the amber light indicates wait. Select two members of the class as batters and a third as a bowler. Spread four to six fielders in front of the wickets 180 degrees (no one behind the wickets).

How to Play

This game is an introduction to running between wickets with a partner. Explain to the class the key points to running between the wickets and the decision-making process involved in safely scoring runs.

Ask students to list tips for completing runs. Following are some examples:

- Making good emphatic calls of yes, no, or wait to notify the partner of one's intentions
- Understanding the partner's speed and quickness
- Knowing where the ball is hit in relation to the fielders
- Knowing how many runs to complete (i.e., how far the ball is in the outfield)
- Identifying slower fielders

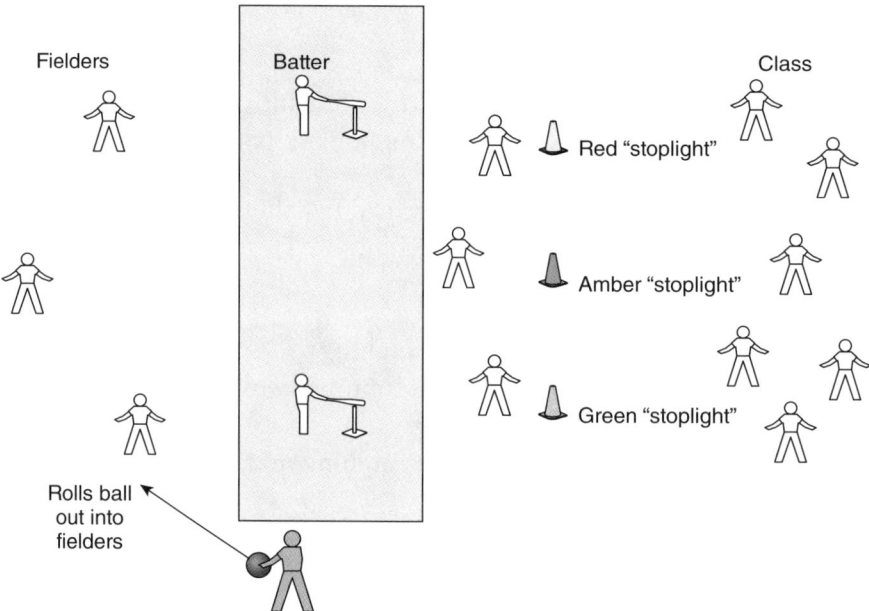

Figure 9.3 Setup for traffic lights.

Have the bowlers randomly roll the ball into the field. Each time the bowler rolls the ball into the field, the rest of the students decide what the batters should do. If they think they should run, they stand behind the green cone. If they think they shouldn't run, they stand behind the red cone. If they think they should wait to make a decision, they should stand behind the amber cone.

In each instance, students need to consider which of the batters should make the decision.

Beat the Catcher

Students use catching skills under pressure, while the other team practices running between the wickets and deciding how many runs to take. Students are in two teams with catchers (four to six) in a staggered line and batters (two) on each end of the wicket.

Catchers do the following:

- Throw the ball to each player who is diagonal from them in the staggered line.
- Start from the start of the line again every time they drop the ball.
- Try to send the ball from one end of the line and back.

Batters do the following:

- Communicate with each other to complete as many runs as possible before the catchers return the ball to the end of the line.
- In pairs, keep track of how many runs they get.

Culmination: Double Chance Pairs Cricket

Six fielders play against two batters. Batters practice running between the wickets, but they get a chance to hit the ball bowled to them. If they miss, they can hit it off the tee.

Modifications

- Add two or three balls to the catchers' line.
- Increase or decrease the distance between the wickets to make the game easier or harder.

Democracy in Action

Decision making: Using a preestablished plan

Using a preestablished plan, students institute tactics during game play to improve their chances of scoring runs. The decisions need to accommodate players of different speeds and abilities because, for a run to be scored, both runners must be safe.

LESSON 5:
Combination Skills

Focus: Running between wickets, making decisions and communicating, and catching

Learner focus:

- Hitting to open space (cognitive)
- Running between wickets with a partner (cognitive)
- Being emphatic with a running partner to complete runs (affective)
- Deciding between horizontal and vertical bat shots (cognitive)
- Practicing basic catching skills (psychomotor)
- Establishing a democratic decision-making policy (affective)

Sequence:

1. Warm-up: Catch volleyball (catching)
2. Activity: Rapid-fire box batting
3. Game: Double chance pairs cricket

Learner Experiences

Introduction: Catch Volleyball

Equipment: Balls and cones

Setup: Two teams of five to seven players start with one ball. Set cones in a rectangle (like a volleyball court) with cones down the middle splitting the court in half. Each court has a 5-yard no-go zone close to the net, and the ball has to make it over this zone.

How to Play

Players on one team underarm the ball into the other team's court. Players have to catch the ball in their court (modify by allowing the ball to bounce once). Every time the ball drops in the court, 1 point is awarded to the other team. Enforce a time limit of two seconds for holding the ball.

Development: Rapid-Fire Box Batting (6v1)

Setup: Six fielders face one batter. Set up two wickets (A and D) with five batting tees with balls on them between them (see figure 9.4). Fielders are 20 yards back (vary based on age and ability) guarding a 10-yard-wide goal. Fielders cannot move forward of the goals (safety zone) until the last ball is hit.

How to Play

The object of the game is for the batting team to hit the ball from the tees and through the goals, which are guarded by the fielding team. Each time the ball passes through the goals, the batter scores 10 points. Each batter has three to six hits. After the last ball is hit, the batter runs between wickets A and B (labeled as cones in figure 9.4), or between wickets C and D (i.e. side wickets and regular wickets), scoring single runs to be added to those acquired from hitting through the goals. To stop the batter from running, the fielders have to retrieve the balls and put them back on the tees. When all players from one team have batted, the teams reverse roles.

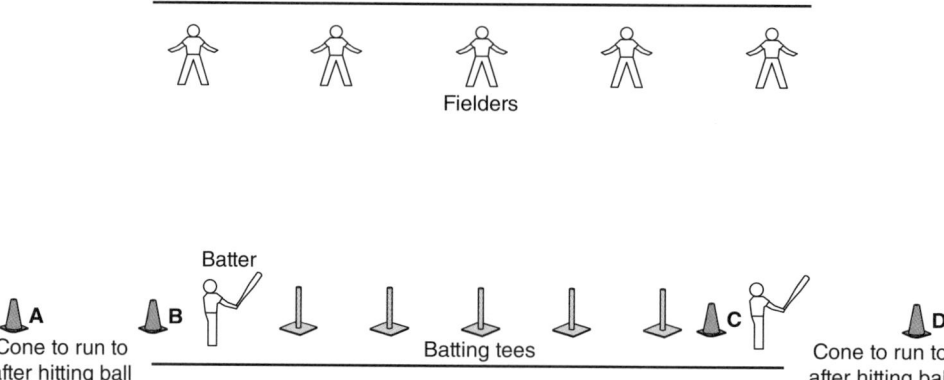

Figure 9.4 Setup for rapid-fire box batting game.

Culmination: Double Chance Pairs Cricket

Equipment: Two bats, two balls, two wickets, and two cones per game

Setup: Six fielders face two batters, or six on six with two games. This game can be played indoors (e.g., on an indoor basketball court) or outside in a space of any shape. Because batters in cricket can strike the ball anywhere in a 180-degree radius, the tee and the wickets should be placed toward the center of the space so they can strike the ball forward and to the side (180 degrees), not backward. The cone the batters run to is normally set 10 to 15 yards in front of the batter. The running partner is on the other wicket (this is the first time a running partner has been introduced). The cone should mark where the bowler stands and where the batter stands and must touch his bat on a return run. The nonstriker (running partner) is 10 yards away.

Modifications

- Make the cones closer to or farther from the batter to increase or decrease difficulty.
- Underarm-lob if students are not ready for this.
- Give students time to think and possibly write down their tactics about how to score and stop runs from being scored.

Democracy in Action

Social justice: Team play for the good of others

How can all team members help their teammates to increase the success of the team? During fielding and batting, circumstances arise in which more experienced players can sacrifice personal gain, such as a faster runner between the wickets adjusting his calling to help a slower runner he is paired with, to help the team.

Check for Learning

Teacher Observations

- Are batters hitting to open spaces?
- Are fielders anticipating where the ball is going to be hit?
- Are batters using a vertical bat and hitting the ball into the hitting zones?
- Are fielders getting to the ball as fast as possible?

Student Self-Evaluations

- Use the 3-2-1 evaluation sheet as an exit slip to see what students learned.
- Have students create a rule to add to a pairs game in the next class. Students can individually create rules and bring ideas to the next class. Allow time for groups to meet, negotiate, and democratically decide on the rule the group will add to the game. This should be done according to the policy the group has established.

Questions

Q: What are important cues to remember as a batter?

A: Keep weight forward and head over the ball.

Q: How should batters decide how much risk to take?

A: Batters should look at the score, where the fielders are, and how confident they are about hitting the ball in the air (i.e., risk vs. reward—hitting the ball in the air could result in more runs but could increase the risk of getting out!).

Q: What are the best ways to increase success while running between the wickets with a partner?

A: Good communication and cooperation with the batting partner. In addition, looking to hit to open spaces will help with quick runs.

LESSON 6:
Defense Concept—Bowling to Limit the Batter's Time

Focus: Building on concepts of batting (hitting to open space) and fielding (restricting open space) and adding the skill of bowling

Learner focus:

- Hitting to open space (cognitive and psychomotor)
- Running between wickets with a partner (cognitive and psychomotor)
- Discussing and practicing how to be emphatic (communication) with a running partner to complete runs (affective)
- Deciding between horizontal and vertical bat shots (cognitive)
- Practicing basic bowling skills (psychomotor)

Sequence:

1. Warm-up: Catch soccer (catching)
2. Skill enhancement: Bowling
3. Activity: Bombardment bowling
4. Game: Double chance pairs cricket

Learner Experiences

Introduction: Catch Soccer

Setup: Create two teams of five to seven players, who start with one ball. Set up a 15- by 15-yard rectangle with a set of wickets on each end. Set a semicircle about 5 yards from each wicket.

How to Play

Players must underarm the ball to each other as they work the ball up the field trying to hit the wickets to score a goal. Players are not allowed to run with the ball or hold the ball for longer than three seconds. If the ball is dropped or fumbled, or goes outside the marked area, the team loses possession.

Development: Discuss Bowling and Play Bombardment Bowling

Equipment: One soccer ball, one tennis ball per player

Setup: Teams of four to six players line up 10 yards from a soccer ball (facing each other), which is in the middle of the grid (see figure 9.5).

How to Play

The object of the bombardment bowling game is to practice bowling technique in a game situation while also working on accuracy. Once signaled, players bowl balls at the soccer ball and attempt to roll it over their opponents' goal to score a point. After each goal the soccer ball is returned to the middle.

In a class discussion, ask questions such as the following:

- Has anyone seen cricket players bowl before?
- How does bowling differ from pitching in baseball or softball? (The main differences are that players must keep their arms straight and are allowed to run up.)

Culmination: Double Chance Pairs Cricket

In this culmination game, students have an opportunity to combine the skills they learned in all of the preceding lessons. Six fielders face six batters, bowling

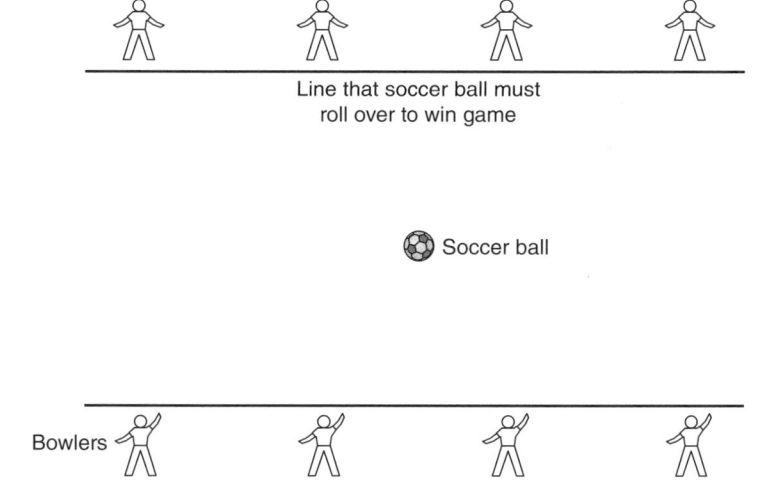

Line that soccer ball must roll over to win game

Soccer ball

Bowlers

Figure 9.5 Setup for bombardment bowling.

is allowed, and the setup is the same as single-pairs cricket. Allow bowling if students choose, because this will allow them to tie in what they learned from lesson 5.

Modifications

- Change the size of the field.
- Include more balls or allow overarm throws or both.
- Let balls bounce.
- Allow only left- or right-handed catching.
- Have players roll the ball to work on fielding.

Democracy in Action

Decision making and free inquiry: Democratically selecting a rule to add to the game; opening up participation

Students are free to contribute to a group discussion about whether the rule change positively affected the game.

Check for Learning

- Have each student create a rule to add to a pairs game and bring it to the next class. Allow time for groups to meet, negotiate, and democratically decide what rule to add to the game.
- Students self-assess (in groups) to see whether their rule made the game better according to the criteria.

LESSON 7:
Using the GPAI for Assessment

Focus: Building on the concepts of batting (hitting to open space) and fielding (restricting open space). Add the skill of bowling, and use all of these in game situations. Students use the GPAI to provide feedback on game play (skills and decisions).

Learner focus:

- Hitting to open space (cognitive and psychomotor)
- Running between wickets with a partner (cognitive and psychomotor)
- Giving feedback regarding game skills using the GPAI (cognitive)
- Constructing team tactics for how to score runs and stop runs from being scored for the next class tournament (cognitive)
- Providing ideas about and insights into the team plan (affective)

Sequence:

1. Warm-up: Class vote on the favorite warm-up game
2. GPAI: Introduction to using the GPAI for assessment
3. Team planning time: Tactics to use in pairs cricket
4. Game: Double chance pairs cricket

Introduction: Students' Choice

Students vote on their favorite warm-up game or invent a warm-up game.

Culmination: Double Chance Pairs Cricket

Equipment: Bats, balls, wickets, cones

Setup: Students are spread out around the gym in their groups. Partner each student with a student from another group, and then explain the GPAI.

How to Play

Students assess each other's skills in an authentic situation using the GPAI. Those who are assessing gain a deeper understanding of the skills necessary to succeed in the game.

Each student is paired with a student from the opposing team to practice using the GPAI. The students first assess their fielding skills. Limit the assessment to one skill the first time using the GPAI. Identify three or four cues for each skill so that observers are clear about what to assess.

1. Allow about five minutes for play and about four minutes for debriefing from the observer.
2. Partners switch roles from observer to player, and vice versa.
3. A second round of play occurs so that players can implement the suggestions made by the observers.
4. Students repeat steps 1 through 3, assessing batting skills.
5. Students post their offensive and defensive tactics so the team can stay focused on game play.

Democracy in Action

Social justice: Giving and receiving feedback

Students need to be fair and honest in their feedback to peers as well as be open to receiving feedback. Open dialogue and an emotionally safe environment are crucial.

Check for Learning

- Students hand in practice GPAIs for your feedback for the next class.
- Students hand in their tactical planning sheets for your feedback for the next class.

LESSON 8:
Pairs Cricket Tournament

Focus: Building on strategic concepts of batting (hitting to open space) and fielding (restricting open space). Add the skill of bowling, and use all of these skills in game situations. Use the GPAI to provide feedback on game play (skills and decisions). Allow students to apply team plans (tactics) in the tournament (spread over two to four lessons).

Learner focus:

- Demonstrating acquired skills (psychomotor)
- Applying tactics and plans to game situations (cognitive)
- Revising tactics and strategies as the game progresses (cognitive)

Sequence:

1. Warm-up: Teams invent warm-up activities.
2. GPAI: Review the use of the GPAI for assessment in games. Give students time to read your feedback.
3. Team planning time: Allow students to review, revise, and discuss strategies from the games they played in the last class.
4. Game: Double chance pairs cricket tournament

Equipment: Bats, balls, cones, wickets

Setup: Students are spread out around the gym in their groups. Partner each student with a student from another group.

Learner Experiences

Warm-Up: Students' Choice

Students vote on a warm-up game or invent one.

- Review the purpose of using the GPAI.
- Review the check mark system and the areas students are observing.
- Pair up students and assign playing and observing roles.
- Have students discuss the results with their partners.
- Students practice using the GPAI during a pairs game.

Development: Tactical Planning Session

Students are spread out around the gym in groups to review, revise, and discuss their plans from the last class. This exercise gives students a deeper understanding of the tactics needed for succeeding in the game—both offensive (batting) and defensive (fielding and bowling) tactics. Students use their group decision-making policy to establish their plans democratically; all students have an opportunity to voice their ideas.

Students in groups revise their tactical planning sheet for the pairs game. All group members are encouraged to participate, and groups use a democratic decision-making policy to establish tactical plans. Students submit copies of their plans to you for feedback.

Culmination: Double Chance Pairs Cricket

Students are in teams of 12, with 6 playing and 6 observing from each team. Students are paired with a person on their own team to use the GPAI. One team observes fielding skills, and the other team observes batting skills.

a. Team 1 (fielding): Groups A and B
b. Team 2 (batting): Groups C and D

Set up eight observational periods, as shown in table 9.3.

Table 9.3 Observational Pairings

	Batting	Fielding
1	A observes B	C observes D
2	B observes A	D observes C
3	A observes B	C observes D
4	B observes A	D observes C
	Teams switch from offense to defense, and from defense to offense.	
5	C observes D	A observes B
6	D observes C	B observes A
7	C observes D	A observes B
8	D observes C	B observes A

A round-robin tournament format can be used if time allows.

Democracy in Action

Decision making: Implementing a team tactic

It is one thing for students to process and make group decisions. It is another for students to observe the consequences of their decisions as they play out in real time. On the basis of these observations they take the next step, which is to adjust and refine their team tactics. This process of adaptation is essential to the sustainability of democratic systems.

Check for Learning

- Students hand in their GPAIs for your feedback for the next class.
- Students hand in their tactical planning sheets for your feedback for the next class.
- Students self- and group evaluate to gauge how well they adhered to their group decision-making policies.

Cricket Unit GPAI

Students should pay attention to the GPAI at the start of the unit; then, throughout the unit, they should watch for each of the criteria covered in this assessment. The criteria are short and concise to facilitate using the GPAI.

Batting (Tally Method)

Evaluate the batter's skill (front foot shots) and decision making. You can use the following chart to tally the player's success; place a check mark in the appropriate column when the player successfully fulfills the category.

On Ball (Striker)

- Skill: Does the batter transfer weight and follow through on ball contact?
- Decision making: Does the batter hit the ball into open areas?

Batting Assessment

Ball	Skill	Decision making
1		
2		
3		
4		
5		

Off Ball (Nonstriker)

Decision making: Does the player make the correct decision on whether to take the run?

Fielding (Subjective Method)

On Ball

- Skill (receiving): The player's knees are bent in the ready position; the head is over or behind the ball when the ball is in the air. The player absorbs force (cushions the ball) when it approaches or is in the air.
- Decision making: The player throws to the correct wicket to get the out (throws to the side where that batter is farther from the wicket).

Off Ball

- Base: The player is in and returns to the ready position between balls.
- Cover: The player gets into the correct position to cover for throws.

Fielding Assessment

		On ball		Off ball	
		Skill execution	Decision making	Base	Cover
Possession sequence	1				
	2				
	3				
	4				
	5				

* Excellent; always performed well.

✓ Usually effective; mostly did well.

+ Has potential; needs more work but is getting the idea.

X Not effective; rarely or never did well.

Bowling (Subjective Method)

- Skill: Does the player keep his arm high (brush his ear)? Does the player follow through to his opposite thigh?
- Adjust: Does the bowler adjust to the handedness of the batter (whether she is right- or left-handed)?
- Decision making: Does the bowler bowl to the plan that the captain has set up in terms of fielding positions?

Bowling Assessment

Ball	Skill	Adjust	Decision making
1			
2			
3			
4			
5			

* Excellent; always performed well.

✓ Usually effective; mostly did well.

+ Has potential; needs more work but is getting the idea.

X Not effective; rarely or never did well.

Cricket Unit Summary

- When observing your partner, what was the most difficult aspect to assess?
- What two aspects of your partner's fielding skills should he or she work on?
- Invent one activity or drill that your partner could do to improve.
- How did analyzing your partner help your own fielding?
- What aspects would you add or subtract to the GPAI? Why?
- Was this assessment instrument a valuable tool for analyzing your partner?

From J.I. Butler, 2016, *Playing fair* (Champaign, IL: Human Kinetics).

SUMMARY

As noted in the introduction to this chapter, cricket can be a challenging game for students in terms of their physical development and prowess. At the same time, it can put them in the spotlight as they try out their throwing, catching, and striking skills. This chapter has offered some practical ways to develop confidence and competence in small games and to give students a sense of ownership as they engage in observation and feedback, thus opening them up to the very real enjoyments that this game offers to students across the globe.

Inventing Net and Wall Games

Joy Butler and Tim Hopper

Way Lin: Why have one ball, when we could have two?

John: No way! No one uses two balls!

Sunita: Why not? It might be fun!

Jaqui: At least we can try. We can always change it later.

John: It's just lame. And this whole game is lame, and so is this stupid teacher. Doesn't Mr. Samuelson know it's hockey season?

John folds his arms. As far as he's concerned, it's game over. Ignoring his silence, the group carries on with the discussion.

The energy in the gym is high as the grade 6 groups showcase their games, in turn. Because inventing games is an experiment, a couple of other teachers have come to watch, including John's classroom teacher. There is a lot of cheering and applause as each group finishes up playing, with one exception.

One girl takes on the role of coach and another acts as the referee; John stands with his arms folded, and the other boys hang back, uncertain. Their game stops and starts; then peters to a close. In the debriefing session, they explode, and it takes a while for Mr. Samuelson to regain some calm.

Mr. Samuelson: There seemed to be some disagreement among you when it came to the presentation. What was the problem?

John: The game stank. I hated it. No one listened to me from day 1.

Way Lin: You just sulked 'cause we didn't take your idea *one time*. You had plenty of chances to speak up. But you didn't, and if you don't join in, you have to suck it up!

Sunita: You just sulked 'cause you didn't get your own way as usual. Our game rocked!

A teacher who observed the lesson noted that "there was more being learned than how to throw and catch a ball." So what exactly did the students learn?

The intent of the inventing games process for net and wall games is for students to create and own a game that flows and is fun, fair, and safe for everyone. To meet this intention, learners need to find out what it feels like to play net games such as tennis, badminton, table tennis, pickleball, and volleyball, and wall games such as squash, racquetball, handball, and Wallyball. They need to understand how all such games develop from the primary rule: to send an object to the opponent's half in net games or shared space in wall games so that the opponent is unable to return it or is forced to make an error. Students need to understand the back-and-forth exchange of an object as they send it over a net or a line on a wall. They need to figure out how to send the object into spaces to challenge their opponents' abilities to keep the ball in play. Also, they need to learn how to guard their own court spaces by anticipating where the object will land so they can prepare to send it back. Finally, as players work in groups, they need to learn how to create games that all players (of all abilities) can play with enjoyment and success.

This chapter explains how to build an inventing games process for students learning to play net and wall games for the first time. Chapter 11 shows how the strategies and tactics learned in the net and wall inventing games of this chapter can be transferred to the game of pickleball.

FRAMEWORK (STRATEGIC CONCEPTS AND TACTICAL DECISIONS)

Table 10.1 highlights the strategic concepts that extend from the primary rule in net and wall games as players anticipate where opponents will send the ball and recognize patterns of play that enable them to outmaneuver their opponents.

The first strategic concept is spatial awareness: Where should I go to receive the ball? Anticipatory positioning on the court then gives players time to execute on-ball tactics as they adjust to the flight of the ball and prepare a suitable response to the opponent's strike. Players usually mirror their opponents roughly on the other side of the court when covering the expected target area. The idea of spin develops as players gain the ability to be ready for the ball in the hitting zone. Cues for these skills can then be taught, such as "Strike the ball as it falls in front of your body" and "Strike the ball with a bat using a swing from low to high." The spin allows more controlled use of power because it controls the ball flight. Spin, power, consistency, and effective positioning then lead to more dynamic object placement as players learn to maneuver their opponents with depth and angle variations.

STAGES OF INVENTION AND DEMOCRACY IN ACTION

Table 10.2 indicates the stages in which skills associated with democracy in action are developed. These skills arise as players explore, experiment, and select ideas within the constraints of net and wall games. Gradually, the players build relationships with each other as they share ideas, build consensus, communicate, and develop tolerance and fairness. Empathy for other players grows as games develop based on adaptations that encourage, challenge, and include players of all ability levels. As players own their games, they help each

Table 10.1 Strategic Concepts, Skills, and Tactics for Net and Wall Games

Strategic concepts and skills	On-ball tactics	Off-ball tactics
1. Spatial awareness (consistency, placement) Skills: Throwing, catching on the bounce and volley, forehand and backhand, serving and receiving serve	• Return the object high (more time) and keep it in bounds. • Place the ball away from opponents and look for angles. • Apply spin to control ball flight. • Use power to attack space and reduce the opponent's time to respond.	• Move to base position (recover) behind the back line. • Base and cover as the opponent strikes the ball. • Adjust to send the ball to spaces. • Adjust as the ball lands. • Anticipate where opponents will return the ball.
2. Positioning on court and of the body in motion Skills: Running, stopping, sidestepping, changing direction, assuming a ready position, receiving serve	• Retreat to cover the court after striking. • Hold ground after striking. • After striking, move to a volley position at the net to limit the opponent's options and time.	• Move to the baseline to cover the court. • Be base ready (court positioning) and choose the target to guard. • Move to anticipate the ball's path. • Maintain forward momentum after hitting the ball. • Split step (cover) to set up for the next shot.
3. Anticipate trajectory (spin on the ball) Skills: Throwing and catching, topspin, slice, spike or smash, lob, drop shot, slice serve	• Use a spike, or smash, on a high ball. • Use a lob and topspin in the open backcourt with an opponent at the net. • Use a drop shot and underspin in the open frontcourt with an opponent who is back.	• Read to move forward to anticipate a high ball. • Read open space and set up with the weight on the back foot. • Read the opponent's position and set up for an early shot.
4. Depth and maneuvering (power firm and light) Skills: Hitting with specific force, lob shot, drop shot, serve, spin shot, volley, drive, dig	• To pressurize opponent, decide on force for length and ball speed with spin. • Return the ball deep with height, or lob to keep the ball in bounds or to create time to regroup. • Take the ball early for easy power and to reduce the opponent's time to recover.	• Read the opponent to attack high-percentage shots to open space. • Recover deep in the court behind the baseline. • Read a short ball, adjust to take the ball early, and attack reduced target space.
5. Angles and maneuvering (dynamic placement) Skills: Forehand and backhand drives, angle of racket or hand, volley, serve	• Use crosscourt drives to press the opponent. • Use spin and aim for angles to upcourt. • Aim at the opponent to crowd his or her shot.	• Move to base (recover) to set up behind the back line for the next shot. • Cover the opponent's target area. • Move forward across the baseline when anticipating a short ball.

Table 10.2 Inventing Net and Wall Games: Stages and Democracy-in-Action Focuses

Stage number	Inventing net or wall games	Democracy-in-action focus
1	Setting the learning environment for (A) democracy in action and (B) game constructs—defining net and wall games.	**Free inquiry:** Listening and talking as part of the democratic process
		Free inquiry: Appreciating the need to define intent as part of clear communications
2	Spatial awareness in net games—castle game.	**Social justice:** Developing tolerance of differences by noticing the inherent qualities of net games and competitive and cooperative activities
3	Spatial awareness in wall games. Identifying the role of the referee.	**Social justice:** Role of referees (arbitrators and advocates of fairness)
4	Creating net and wall games through the democratic process.	**Group process:** Democratic decision making and consensus building
5	Challenging everyone through adaptation.	**Social justice:** Adaptation and affirmative action
6	Refining games and identifying the role of the coach.	**Free inquiry:** Observations and the work of coaching
7	Showcasing games and revising (feedback).	**Free inquiry:** Giving and receiving advice
8	Competitive game: Thinking about tactics (offense and defense).	**Personal and social responsibility:** Playing a role to develop empathy and imagination

other develop the skills they need through observation, coaching, and giving and receiving advice. Finally, game play becomes competitive (but empathetic) through game structures that encourage tactical awareness without being overly exclusive in terms of technical skills.

In this unit, students work in pairs, threes, and fours. They need to communicate effectively to make shared decisions. We have found that having a game observer, at least some of the time, is critical. The first focus is on establishing a learning environment in which students feel safe to try out ideas without fear of being ridiculed and judged. This takes time. The stages do not represent distinct lessons; stage 1A may require one to three lessons, or one lesson may be enough for several stages, depending on class time, learner receptivity, and progress.

STAGE 1:
Setting the Learning Environment

Stage 1A: Setting the Environment for Democracy in Action

Focus: Creating safe, respectful, and supportive conditions for discussions and decision making through cooperative and competitive net and wall games

Learner focus:

- Demonstrating the skills necessary for clear communication: intentional talking and active listening (cognitive)
- Understanding that how we listen and talk contributes to respectful and supportive learning environments (affective)
- Establishing democratic policies for making decisions (cognitive)
- Creating and playing a game using three skills on their own and with a partner (psychomotor)
- Understanding competition and cooperation

Equipment: Pens, paper, one playground ball per student

Setup: Students are in pairs, spaced out across the gym.

Learner Experiences

1. Each person writes answers to these questions: How do you communicate ideas? What is meant by active listening? Partners then take turns sharing their ideas. The listener engages in active listening for content and emotion and then paraphrases what she heard and what emotions she sensed. The speaker then says whether she agrees with the summation and is invited to comment. Partners then switch roles. Pairs can then answer the following questions:

   - What was one thing you learned from this exercise?
   - What did you learn about yourself in terms of your listening skills?
   - What did you learn about your partner when he or she was listening or talking?

2. Students individually write down three important points they have learned about talking and listening, and then use these in a democratic decision-making policy.

3. Each student collects a playground ball. Introduce three net game skills that can be used in combination. Here are examples:

   - Toss, bounce, catch (grades 3 through 5)
   - Set, bounce, catch (grades 4 through 8)
   - Bump, bounce, catch (grades 4 through 8)

Students explore possibilities such as tossing a ball from a stationary position or while moving forward, tossing it sideways from a stationary position or in motion, or tossing it far enough away to have to run to catch it after a bounce or without a bounce.

4. Students create a solo game using all three skills.

5. Students observe the variations of the games and discuss their creativity, fun, and complexities.

6. In the same pairs as the listening exercise, students create a game using any of the examples from step 3.

7. The whole class observes a few of the games.

8. Students take a few minutes to refine their games and scoring systems.

9. Students showcase their games, asking observers in their pairs to decide whether they are competitive or cooperative.

10. Lead a discussion about what makes a game competitive or cooperative. Possible responses:

   • Trying to outwit each other to win
   • Trying to score more points than the opponent
   • Working with each other toward a goal

11. Ask learners to change their games from competitive to cooperative, or vice versa, and give them time to play.

12. Students discuss which of the two versions they preferred and why.

Modifications

■ Modify ball size to challenge (smaller and or higher-density) or simplify (beach balls).

■ Ask older students to identify what they had to manipulate to change the accessibility of the game.

Democracy in Action

Free inquiry: Listening and talking as part of the democratic process

Collaborative groups depend on complex communications and collaborative decisions. These require that every member contribute ideas, speak clearly, and listen actively. A hierarchical group has quicker and simpler paths of communication and decision making. One person usually makes a decision and then disseminates the information down the chain.

Review the listening and talking exercise through questions such as the following:

   ■ How did thinking about your intent to speak change the way you spoke?

   ■ Did having to summarize the other person's ideas help you to listen? How?

- How did this affect the way you approached your game creation?
- How vital are contributions and listening skills to the democratic process? Why?

Giving students opportunities to define what they enjoy about cooperative activities or competitive activities is a step toward helping them know themselves better. This can lead them to make good choices, including choices about activities for lifelong learning.

Check for Learning

- How did you contribute to inventing your game?
- Were you aware of your listening skills with your partner?
- What do you like about competitive activities? Cooperative activities?

Stage 1B: Game Constructs—Defining Net and Wall Games

Focus: Spatial awareness and how to win a point (offense)

Learner focus:

- Defining the net game category in the context of all games (cognitive)
- Creating and playing a game using three specific techniques on their own and with a partner (cognitive, psychomotor, and affective)
- Establishing a policy for making decisions (cognitive)
- Understanding spatial awareness in relationship to the intent of the game and competition (cognitive and psychomotor)

Equipment: One soft volleyball ball, training ball, or beach ball per pair (see figure 10.1), a high net (to increase thinking time)

Learner Experiences

1. Explore commonalities among net games (badminton, pickleball, table tennis, tennis, volleyball).
2. Establish the characteristics or structures of net games:
   - A net divides the court.
   - Teams or players are separated by the net.
   - Games can be played in pairs or in teams.
   - Scoring is achieved by sending the ball back to the opponent's half so that he is unable to return it or is forced to make an error. Serving is the only time the object is held.
   - Offense focuses on ball placement, power, and spin.

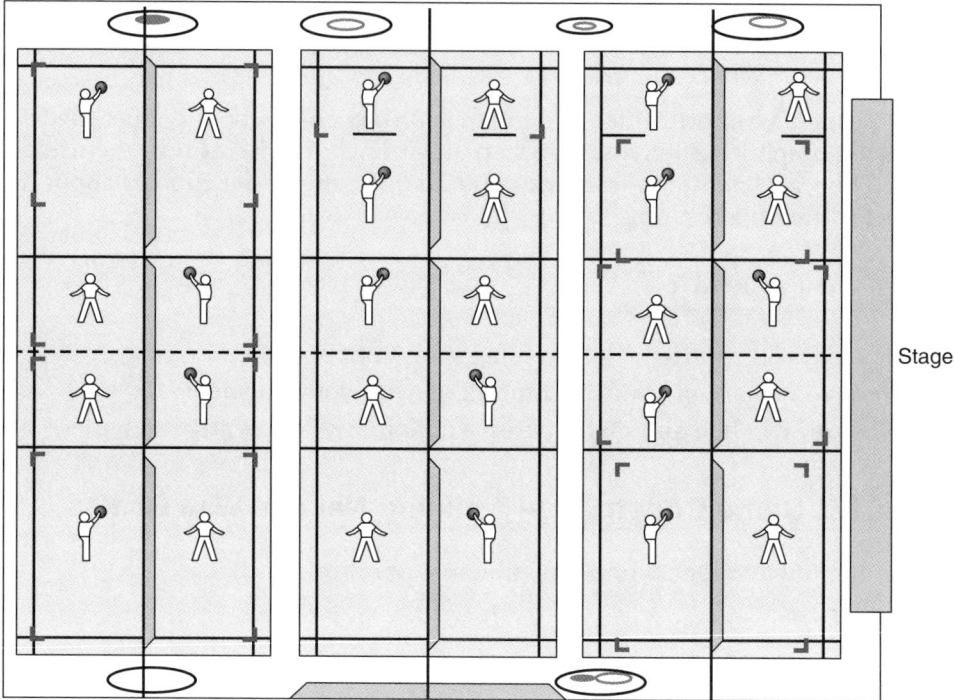

Figure 10.1 Setup for pairs facing across a high net.

- Defense focuses on positioning, anticipation, and interception.
- Transition involves getting back to the middle on the baseline or at the net.

3. Students use one hand to toss the ball back and forth to a partner across the net. They cooperate to work toward goals of 5, 10, and 15 passes without dropping the ball.
4. Define the differences between close-range and far-range passing.
5. Students invent a competitive game of one-handed tossing.
6. Define two rules:

- The ball can bounce, but only once.
- The ball cannot touch your side of the court before it is sent over the net.

7. Pairs establish two or three tactics for winning points.
8. Students choose different opponents, creating new pairs.
9. Students discuss player differences. What did they notice?

Modification

Increase or decrease the distance between players in cooperative passing.

Democracy in Action

Free inquiry: Appreciating the need to define intent as part of clear communications

Defining intent allows us to be clear in our communications. It helps focus our thoughts and provides purpose. Spending some time gathering our thoughts is helpful; we can even write them down first. Some students have more confidence speaking than others do; some carry more social power. Some of the reasons for lack of confidence might be lack of family support, peer bullying, or marginalization by dominant groups.

Ask the following questions:

- How does defining intent help in our democratic process?
- When would this skill be useful? Why?
- Are you comfortable speaking in pairs, small groups, large groups?
- What helps you feel comfortable?
- How do you help others feel more comfortable?

Check for Learning

- What are the characteristics of net games?
- How do they differ? How are they similar?
- What were the differences between the one-handed game at the start of the lesson and the one you just played?
- Which did you prefer? Why?

STAGE 2:
Spatial Awareness in Net Games—Castle Game

Focus: Scoring points, creating rules, identifying ways to enforce rules, and using a referee in cooperative net games

Learner focus:

- Creating rules for an invented net game (cognitive)
- Sending the ball to the intended space (psychomotor)
- Identifying strategies and applying these to track and catch a falling ball (cognitive and psychomotor)
- Exploring and appreciating the purposes of rules as players and referees (cognitive, affective, and psychomotor)

Equipment: One pylon between two players, one short-handled bat per player, one ball per pair

Setup: Students are in threes (see figure 10.2); one person acts as referee to remind players of key rules.

Figure 10.2 Setup for the castle game.

To help students get a sense of playing a net or wall game, you can introduce a simple game that exaggerates the idea of keeping the ball going. The intent is to give students a feel for the flow of playing in the rally of a net or wall game. To do this, focus on effective off-ball movements to encourage them to move to where the ball will bounce (see table 10.1). For example, as shown in the castle game (figure 10.2), if two players were trying to send the ball up in the air to come down and bounce on a small target (the castle), the player waiting to receive the ball should move to a space behind the target, opposite the partner as she sends the ball. A question such as Where do you go after sending the ball? can prompt this movement. Once players figure out this response, they can coordinate their actions to receive the ball and send it toward the target.

The basic rules of the castle game create a supportive relationship between the players because the actions of one player initiate the responses of the other. Assigning a third player to the role of referee to enforce the simple rules is helpful, because players often forget to toss the ball above their heads or to let it bounce once. The referee can help the players create additional rules about starting, keeping the ball in play, or scoring. Referees can later take up a coaching role, encouraging tactical ideas such as moving in anticipation of the ball's direction or setting up in a ready (base) position.

Learner Experiences

1. Students play the castle game in threes. The goal is to send the ball to hit the pylon (castle), which concludes the game. The game can be played firstly as a cooperative game in which players help each other to hit the target and secondly as a competitive game where points are earned by the player who hits the castle.

2. Rules:

   - Send the ball above head height.
   - The ball must bounce once.
   - Alternate hitting the ball with the partner.

3. The three students can create additional rules, such as the following:

- How to send the ball to keep it in play
- How to score a point if any one of the three rules is broken
- How many points are needed to win the game
- How to restart the game when a point is won

4. The skill focus is on catching a falling ball.

- Focus players' attention on tracking the ball trajectory.
- Encourage senders to use an underarm throw and to take a step toward the target with the opposite foot.

Modifications

- As the students learn to set up to send the ball to the target, they can gradually be shown how to hit the ball using their hands or a short-handled racket.
- Once the rules are understood and basic tactical responses applied, smaller balls and bats, and even boundaries (limiting the playing area), can be added to extend the game.

Democracy in Action

Social justice: Developing tolerance of differences by noticing the inherent qualities of net games and competitive and cooperative activities

The emphasis of flow in the back and forth of the ball motion helps students appreciate the inherent qualities of net and wall games. A discussion of what students enjoy, what they don't, and why can serve the following purposes:

- Students understand the intrinsic pleasure they derive from physical activity, helping to sustain lifelong activity.
- Students learn about their own preferences and those of others, inspiring greater tolerance for differences.

Check for Learning

- What do you like about net games so far?
- Did you experience the flow of net games? What does that mean?
- What changed when you tried to win a point over your opponent rather than trying to hit the castle?
- How does watching the trajectory of the ball help you catch it?
- Do you like competitive or cooperative games best? What do you like or dislike about each?
- What was your experience of being a referee?

STAGE 3:
Spatial Awareness in Wall Games and Identifying the Role of the Referee

Focus: Winning a point, creating rules, and identifying means to enforce rules in cooperative wall games

Learner focus:

- Using angles on the wall to place the ball on the court in a cooperative game (psychomotor and cognitive)
- Understanding the concept of matching angles as the ball hits the wall and moves away (cognitive)
- Learning and enforcing rules as a referee (cognitive)
- Applying basic off-ball strategies to cover the court effectively (cognitive and psychomotor)

Equipment: Tape for marking walls, spots, and lines; one short-handled bat per player; one ball per pair

Setup: Students are in threes (see figure 10.3): two players and one referee.

Learner Experiences

1. Set up games against the wall in threes. One person acts as referee. Rotate positions every five minutes.
2. Rules:

   - Send the ball over a line on the wall.
   - The ball must bounce once.
   - Alternate hitting the ball from where it is caught.

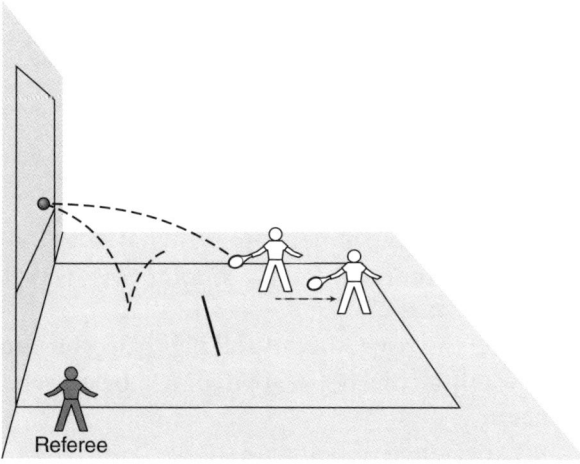

Figure 10.3 Setup for a cooperative wall game.

3. The three students can create additional rules, such as the following:

- How to send the ball to keep it in play
- How to score a point if any of the three rules are broken
- How many points are needed to win the game
- How to restart the game fairly when a point is won

4. Role of the referee:

- Watch the game with the three basic rules in mind.
- Stop the game when an infraction occurs. Explain the infraction quickly, and give possession to the other player.
- As rules are created by groups add other rules to the referee's repertoire.

Modification

Referees can later take up a coaching role, in which they encourage tactical ideas such as moving in anticipation of the ball's trajectory or setting up in a ready position to receive it.

Democracy in Action

Social justice: Role of referees (arbitrators and advocates of fairness)

With less emphasis on the structure of game making (because students have learned this process in net games), more emphasis can be placed on the role of the referee. Initially, the referee might offer frequent reminders of the rules to give players the benefit of the doubt (e.g., remind them to toss the ball above the head to create a fair start to the game). The intent is to restore fairness after a rule violation that gives an advantage to the other party. The referee must know the actions that are infractions and the consequences for each. Knocking a ball outside of the area results in a point awarded to the other player. Running into another player's space as he is about to hit the ball is a different type of violation. Students can sort through the types of violations and categorize them.

Check for Learning

- What skills do you think a referee needs to learn?
- What were some consequences for infractions in your game?
- What parallels can you make between rules for your game and rules governing student behavior in school?

These questions are specific to game construct understanding:

- How was the wall game different from or similar to the castle (net) game?
- Which game did you enjoy more? Why?
- What rules did you need to add that didn't seem obvious before you played the game?

STAGE 4:
Creating Net and Wall Games Through the Democratic Process

Focus: Constructing rules through the democratic process

Learner focus:

- Defining games by creating basic regulations and minimal rules (cognitive)
- Sharing ideas, negotiating, and establishing a decision-making process (cognitive)
- Testing games through trial and error (psychomotor and cognitive)

Equipment: For wall games, tape for marking walls, movable lines, poly spots for court marking, one short-handled bat per player; for net games, lines dividing the play area or a high net, one short-handled bat per player, choices of balls for net and wall games ranging from small to large and high to low density

Setup: The gym might be set up as depicted in figure 10.4. Each group of three or four moves to a small area of the gym once they have chosen to play a wall or net game. The groups are made up of two players, one observer (to record observations and give feedback), and one referee.

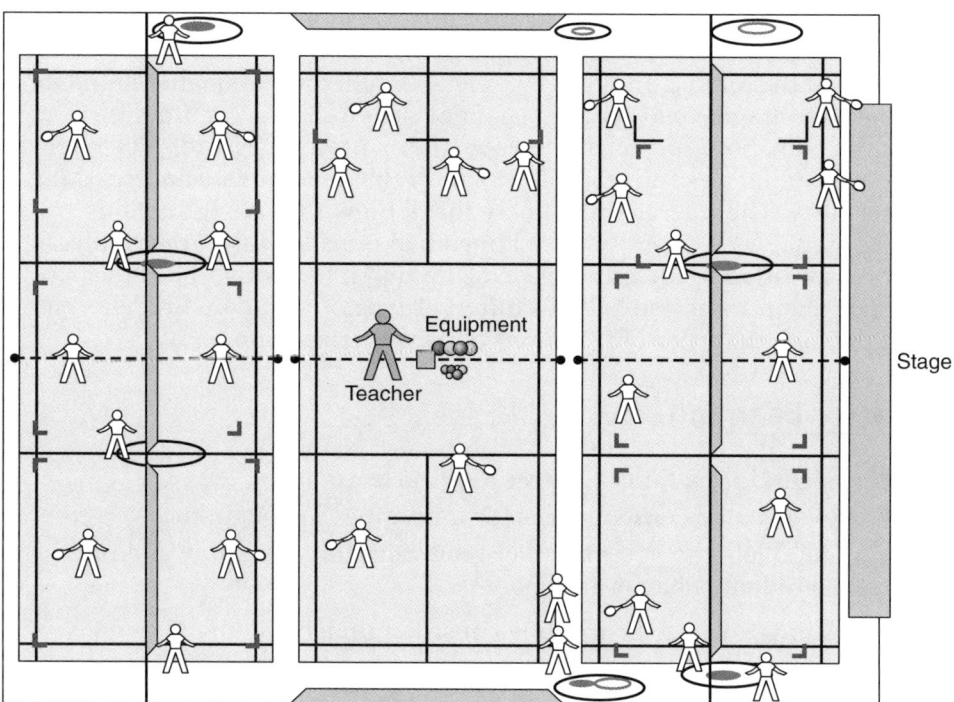

Figure 10.4 Setup of competitive games.

Learner Experiences

1. In groups of four, students do the following, in order:
   a. Create a decision-making process.
   b. Identify roles for the equipment manager (EM) and coach (C).
   c. Decide whether to create a wall or net game.
   d. Decide whether the game will be competitive or cooperative.

2. Groups create rules based on similar structures from stages 3 and 4, including a safety rule.

3. Discuss the purpose of rules, and emphasize the following:
   - Allow the game to flow.
   - Provide a structure to which all players can relate.
   - Provide a safe environment.
   - Establish fairness.
   - Involve everyone.
   - Help make the game fun.
   - Provide challenge.

4. The EMs collect equipment the group has agreed on, and groups move to their assigned areas to set up their games.

5. Students play the game 1v1 in two adjacent areas (all four in the group are active).

6. One pair then watches the other pair and then offers feedback about their game.

7. Then switch roles

8. The group of four then discusses the final shaping of their game, which is next played by both pairs to reinforce the changes (if any are made).

9. Allow time for students to discuss the development of the game and their observations of the other pair playing the game.

Modification

Advise groups on their choices of balls to speed up or slow down the game according to the ability of the group members, the size of the court, and so on.

Democracy in Action

Group process: Democratic decision making and consensus building

The groups form a collaborative learning system with roles assigned. They choose a democratic process that ensures that everyone has input into the decisions. It is important to establish the process (preferably in writing), so that you can refer to it if and when things break down.

Students often want a unanimous vote. This is possible in small friendship groups but more difficult in larger ones. Consensus building should be offered as a more effective structure for the inventing games processes. Time spent discussing the importance of accepting consensus is also valuable. Once a decision is made, everyone needs to get behind it. Sour grapes impede the work and create bad feelings (as illustrated in the vignette at the beginning of the chapter). Ask students the following:

- How did your group choose the process of making decisions?
- What is consensus building?
- What does this have to do with democracy?
- How did you resolve key decisions?

Check for Learning

- What type of game did your group choose—wall or net?
- How did the observing-and-playing process go? What did you learn from observing?

STAGE 5:
Challenging Everyone Through Adaptation

Focus: Engaging and challenging all players by adapting court space
Learner focus:

- Creating a scoring system democratically (cognitive)
- Manipulating game constraints, such as space, scoring, rules, and the number of players, to make the game even (cognitive and psychomotor)
- Appreciating the value of close games in terms of individual challenges (affective)

Equipment: For wall games, tape for marking walls, movable lines, poly spots for court marking, one short-handled bat per player; for net games, lines dividing the play area or a high net, one short-handled bat or racquet per player, choices of balls for net and wall games ranging from small to large and high to low density

Set-up: Groups of four: two players, one referee, and one observer (records adaptations and feedback of games).

Learner Experiences

1. Ask groups to devise a scoring system that challenges expert players while allowing players of all ability levels to play together by manipulating space, the scoring system, the rules, or the number of players. Following are possible solutions:

- The winner of the first net game has their side of the court increased to make it easier for the opponent to send the ball into open spaces.
- The winner of the first wall game has to hit the ball above a higher line to give the opponent more time to play a shot.

2. Students try out their adaptations through trial and error and agree on adaptations.

3. Students record adaptations.

4. Each pair observes the other pair's game to determine whether or not the game flows and to suggest improvements.

Democracy in Action

Social justice: Adaptation and affirmative action

The following key concepts and issues can be addressed in a discussion:

- People are different, but equal. Women and girls tend to be shorter. How does this play out in a game such as basketball? How can people who are differently abled engage in sport? (Examples include wheelchair basketball, sled hockey, and the Paralympics.)
- What is affirmative action, and why is it necessary (e.g., Brown vs. Board of Education)?
- A democratic process takes time. What are the upsides and downsides of discussing things in a group? Of revisiting decisions already made?

Check for Learning

- What did you change to make your game more even?
- How did that change the game?
- How did you feel about the game?
- Is it fair? Why?
- Could this idea be applied anywhere else in your life?
- How is this similar to affirmative action legislation?

STAGE 6:
Refining Games and Establishing the Role of the Coach

Focus: Flow in competitive games and coach observations

Learner focus:

- Considering and negotiating rules that need changing, deleting, or adding with teammates (affective and cognitive)
- Appreciating the role of a coach (affective)

- Revisiting adaptations and applying them to promote competition and challenge (cognitive and psychomotor)
- Appreciating a sense of flow through closely fought rallies (affective)
- Refocusing after sending the ball to position themselves on court to be ready to receive the next shot (psychomotor)

Equipment: For wall games, tape for marking walls, movable lines, poly spots for court marking, one short-handled bat per player; for net games, lines dividing the play area or a high net, one short-handled bat per player, choices of balls for net and wall games ranging from small to large and high to low density

Setup: Students are in fours (two to play, one to referee, and one to observe).

Learner Experiences

1. Give students three or four parts of an action (choosing from examples such as a forehand swing in tennis, a set in volleyball, or a serve in either tennis or volleyball) written separately on cards. Ask them to put the skills in order. The action can be performed by a student, by you, or on a video clip, but it should be one that students can repeat as they decide on the order.

2. Define the role of a coach.

3. Students form groups of four: two coaches observing two players. Each coach watches a player. As discussed in chapter 9, students use the Game Performance Assessment Instrument (GPAI) to observe on-ball skills, ball placement, off-ball skills, and where the player goes after sending the ball.

4. Students switch roles.

5. Students review all the rules and regulations to decide whether any need to be tweaked or deleted, or whether new ones are needed.

6. Students consider the following questions:

   - Does the game flow?
   - Is it structured?
   - Is it safe for everyone?
   - Is it fair?
   - Is everyone involved?
   - Is everyone challenged?
   - Is it fun?

These questions might be introduced as a package with older students, or one at a time with younger ones. As students work through these questions, they consider changes and improvements to their games. Changes in regulations involve changing court dimensions, ball size or type, goal size, and the scoring system. These can be manipulated to make the game more accessible or more challenging. Changes in rules usually influence the flow, fairness, and accessibility of games.

Democracy in Action

Free inquiry: Observations and the work of coaching

The process of observing and watching the small details helps coaches pay a particular kind of attention. This not only informs students about the actions of others, but also helps them improve their own performance.

Check for Learning

- Is the coach's role one you would like to pursue, or one that you are content to let someone else do?
- What did you learn from the observation exercise(s)?
- What are the responsibilities of a coach?
- How would a hierarchical coach operate?
- How would a collaborative, empowerment-type coach operate?
- How does the type of coach change how the group learns?
- How did the experience of playing change with the inclusion of the coach?

STAGE 7:
Showcasing Games and Revising

Focus: Identifying and celebrating what is fun in each game

Learner focus:

- Defining and articulating what is fun about the game (cognitive)
- Demonstrating clearly and concisely the game and its rules (psychomotor)
- Offering and receiving suggestions with clear intent (affective)

Equipment: Varies according to the games; EMs collect the equipment for their groups

Setup: Students move to each group's designated game space, or the class is seated in front of a net court or a wall court. Variations in the games may cause a short delay as players adjust their courts.

Learner Experiences

1. Allow time for groups to prepare their presentations.
2. In large classes, groups can be paired up to demonstrate to each other. In this way, several games can be showcased simultaneously. In smaller classes, each group can showcase its game to the whole class.
3. Each coach explains the game to the class.
4. The group then showcases the game.

5. After a few minutes of play, the rest of the class comments or suggests improvements.
6. Pair up groups.
7. Each group plays the other group's game. The coaches explain and guide the process.
8. Both groups choose which game they want to play.
9. If all students prefer one game, then both groups can play it (students almost always pick the game they invented).
10. Groups revise their games based on others' ideas.

Democracy in Action

Free inquiry: Giving and receiving advice

As groups proudly show their games to either other groups or the class, they need encouragement to honor the work of their peers by listening and considering ways to improve others' games. It takes practice to engage in the reciprocal process of receiving ideas or suggestions and giving advice.

Check for Learning

- What did you learn from watching other games?
- What suggestions did you accept?
- What did you like about playing other games?
- What ideas could your group include?
- What gets in the way of receiving constructive feedback?

Note: End the inventing games process here for younger or less experienced students.

STAGE 8:
Competitive Game—Thinking About Tactics

Focus: Playing attitude

Learner focus:

- Role playing four types of players to explore player attitudes
- Considering strategies for game play

Equipment: Tape for marking walls, one short-handled bat per player. Figure 10.4 shows how the court can be set up for up to 30 players.

Setup: Students are in groups of three or four. Two play while the other two take on the roles of referee and observer. Groups of three have no observer. Roles reverse every five minutes.

Learner Experiences

1. Using their own games, students take on one of the following four animal roles.

   - Rabbit: Scamper around the court covering the opponent's target area. Take no risks. Stay far behind the baseline. Hit the ball high, safe, and deep in the court until the opponent makes an error.
   - Monkey: Hit to space to make the opponent move around the court. Hit from side to side, short and deep and, if possible, with spin. Move to anticipate where the opponent will play the next shot.
   - Bull: Try to win points by rushing the net or wall when possible; use volleys, overheads, and drop shots to hit to spaces and force mistakes.
   - Bear: Use power from the back of the court to hit winners or force errors in timing; keep the opponent under pressure with hard, low shots.

2. Reinstate the role of coaches while two players play. Assign one coach to each player. Coach in terms of tactics and skills of the animal above. Students then switch roles.

3. Students consider offensive tactical decisions: How do they set up scoring opportunities? How do they score more points than their opponents? Following are possible solutions for offensive skills:

   - Use spaces on the court.
   - Attack the frontcourt (i.e., serve-volley).
   - Drop the ball short; then move into the frontcourt.
   - Use spin to send the ball deep and then short.
   - Send the ball from side to side.
   - Send with controlled power.
   - Reduce the opponent's time.
   - Volley the ball and send to open spaces.
   - Take the ball on the rise and move into the opponent's target area.

4. Students consider defensive tactical decisions, such as in the following contexts:

   - Having one player take one of the four animal roles without revealing it. The other player plays as himself.
   - The players play a game while the coach observes closely to determine which role the player is playing.
   - The coach and the player not in the role discuss tactics for playing against the opponent.
   - Players continue playing, with time-outs.
   - Players reverse roles.

Following are possible solutions for defensive tactical decisions:

• Move behind the expected target area.
• Send the ball high and take up a base position quickly.
• Lob the ball.

Democracy in Action

Personal and social responsibility: Playing a role to develop empathy and imagination

The exercise of playing a role is akin to putting oneself in someone else's shoes. Role-playing gives permission to step outside personal, cultural, and gendered constraints. Awareness comes from experiencing what it's like to play in a different way and recognizing the skills needed for taking on that role.

Check for Learning

▪ Which role did you enjoy playing the most?
▪ Which role was most like your own?
▪ What did you learn from each of the roles?
▪ What did this exercise help you understand about strategies?

SUMMARY

For learning to be sustainable and transferable, experiences need to be meaningful and thus memorable. Students are challenged when they have to work through their previous perceptions of what defines a game in order to create games that are safe, that flow, and that are fair and fun for everyone. The democracy-in-action process leads to a real sense of game play that develops from a sense of empathy for other players. As an eight-year-old student recently stated after completing an inventing games unit, "Democratic process is where you take a third from him, a third from me, and a third from her, put them together, and then make them make sense." Working together, students learn to create games that are close, exciting, and fair. The role of the teacher is to observe, offer ideas when students get stuck, show examples of students changing games to make them flow, and celebrate students' ability to create games that are fun for everyone.

Net and Wall Games: Pickleball

Tim Hopper

On a small island in Puget Sound in 1965, the Pritchard and Bell families needed something to amuse their children through the long summer holidays. They had an asphalt badminton court and badminton rackets, but no shuttlecocks, just a 3-inch (7.6 cm) plastic ball. So the two dads started improvising.

The first challenge was their dog, Pickles, who kept running off with the ball (hence the game's name). The second was that the kids found it hard to hit the ball with the lightweight badminton rackets. The dads created wooden rackets—which were something like large table tennis paddles. These were better, but now the players needed more time to adjust to the flight of the ball, so they agreed to allow the ball to bounce once to create longer and more engaging rallies. This worked well as the ball bounced high, giving them lots of time to keep the ball in play. However, after a while, they realized that the badminton net was too high to be able to attack open spaces. The game speeded up when they lowered the net from 5 feet to 3 feet (1.5 m to 1 m).

Realizing that if they rushed the net and volleyed, the point was over, they added a new rule that forbade volleying in the badminton service box. This worked well, but the serving player still had an advantage if she or he served then ran to volley the return. So the families concocted the double bounce rule: *A ball served across court has to bounce in the receiver's area beyond the service line, and then the returned shot has to bounce somewhere in the server's court before a volley can be played.* This new rule opened the game up to longer rallies. Points were contested as players responded to their opponents' deep, short, angled, volleyed, and lobbed shots.

From this recursive process of adjusting equipment, rules, and areas of play, the modern-day game of pickleball was invented.

Adapted from SportsKnowHow.com

The invention of pickleball mirrors the inventing games process described in the previous chapter, and indeed, throughout this book. Through democratic processes, these adults and children collectively explored, experimented with, selected, and then refined the rules of their new game. This chapter connects this process to my experiences with teaching pickleball using the Teaching

Games for Understanding (TGfU; Thorpe & Bunker, 1989) and sport education (Siedentop, 2002) approaches. It explores the ways purposefully designed games can progressively build skills and strategies through negotiation and collaborative problem solving.

By chapter's end, the reader should have an understanding of the ways in which learning might be sequentially developed through playing pickleball. This is not offered as a rigid and formulaic "unit plan," but as an organic conceptual development that might unfold in very different ways. Students are encouraged to use the four Rs (read, respond, react, recover) to initiate their off-the-ball movements and shot selection, as outlined in chapter 4, as they play challenging games (both the standard game of pickleball and games with the appropriate modifications and exaggerations). In so doing they begin to understand and apply key concepts and strategies. Students' attention to tactical concepts is enabled by tasks such as observation exercises and the use of feedback sheets, which are also described here.

Belonging in the net and wall games category, pickleball is a divided court game whose primary intent, as for all net and wall games, is to get the ball in the court area more often than the opponents do. As shown in figure 11.1, the game is played on the outside lines of a badminton court with paddle bats and a Wiffle ball. The ball is allowed to bounce once between hits and can be volleyed in the air outside of the no-volley zone. A point is conceded if the ball is (1) missed either in the air or after bouncing once in the court, (2) hit outside of the court (sideline or baseline) before bouncing, or (3) not hit over the net.

GAME UNDERSTANDING

The invention of pickleball highlights the following key insights about how players engage in net and wall games:

- Letting the ball bounce provides more time to play a shot.
- The higher the ball is hit, the more time players have to play a shot.

Our narrative demonstrates that players learned to move to the front of the court to volley the ball before it bounced, thus reducing their opponents' time to

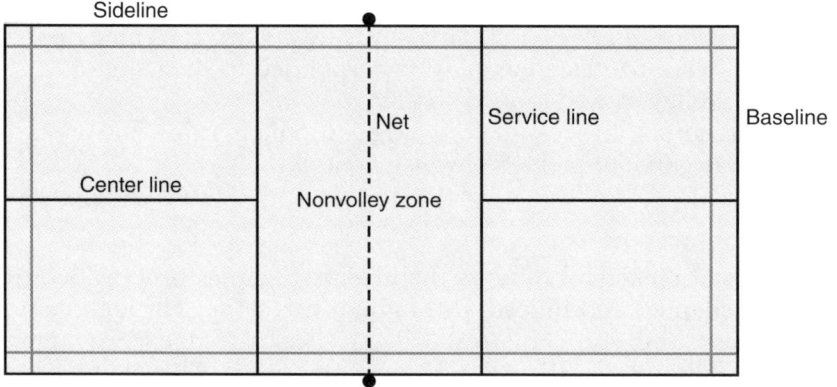

FIGURE 11.1 The pickleball court.

react. Through democratic dialogue, the players decided to add rules to reduce this advantage by introducing the no-volley zone and the double bounce rule. These experiments show how defending and attacking a space is critical to all net and wall games. Once they grasp this space idea, players find it easier to antici-pate where an opponent will send the ball. The earlier players can anticipate where the ball will be sent (and therefore where to position themselves to return it), the more time they have to set up and direct the ball to gain an advantage.

Both time and space depend on the concept of force. The holes in the Wiffle ball reduce the ability of power shots to dominate the game. However, these balls respond well to variations in force used to send the ball high, deep, low, and short, as well as to how the bat is used to apply spin and control the ball's flight and bounce. Once players become proficient in the use of time, space, and force, the game becomes a battle of wits as players make key decisions about strategies and tactics. Who will gamble and take a risk to coerce an error from an opponent, perhaps by running to the service line to force the person to hit a passing shot through a small space? Who will avoid taking a risk, perhaps by hitting high balls and covering the space to which the opponent will hit? Risk is another factor in the conceptual analyses players make as they decide what to do in game situations.

The four Rs model can help players apply the tactical concepts of time, space, force, and risk to net and wall games as they learn to read the game and move in preparation to play a shot (Hopper, 2003, 2007). See chapter 4 for more on the four Rs.

To use the four Rs model, the novice player needs to learn how to adapt to the constraints of the game to play with proficiency and intelligence. The strategic principles (ways of playing) shown in table 11.1 can be used to design modified games to help students learn to play pickleball.

The off-ball movements in table 11.1 refer to how players show tactical awareness by putting themselves in the right place in the court before the ball arrives, to execute successful shots.

- *Base* is the stable position a player returns to after playing a shot: knees bent and feet shoulder-width apart and slightly staggered, ready to push off in any direction.
- *Decision* actions reflect reading and anticipating; then choosing to stay in base position, move back to defend, or move in to attack an anticipated short ball.
- *Cover* actions refer to doing a little jump split step as the opponent strikes the ball to move to cover the opponent's target area.

Table 11.1 Strategic Principles of Net and Wall Games

Principle	Key off-ball movements
Consistency	*Base* and *cover* (as the opponent strikes the ball)
Ball placement	*Adjustment* (to send the ball to spaces)
Court positioning	*Base* and *decision* (where to guard on the target)
Spin on the ball	*Adjustment* (to the ball path to apply spin)
Controlled power	*Decision* (force needed for reaching the target: length and speed)

- *Adjustment* movements refer to players reacting to the arriving ball's trajectory with small push-off movements so that they can execute selected shots in the hitting zone in front of their bodies.

Off-ball movements can be assessed using the Game Performance Assessment Instrument (GPAI) with a peer assessment form such as that shown in figure 11.2 (Hopper, 2007). Asking students to watch and check off or cross off when peers use the appropriate off-ball movement helps focus their attention on how these movements not only facilitate skill development but also generate better play.

Observer:_____ Player: _____

Watch your assigned player(s). For each point, do the following:

1. Focus on skill execution and related off-ball movements.
2. Record a check mark for an appropriate response and an X for an inappropriate response for each movement skill as the point is displayed.
3. After 3 or 4 points, give the player feedback based on your observations.
4. Return to the game focusing on a new movement skill, or repeat the previous movement skill if improvement is needed.

Skill: Sending the ball efficiently into the court to hit the appropriate target area, or striking the ball in the hitting zone and setting up for recovery.

Base: Recover to a position to defend the expected target area and set up to attack the opponent's target area.

Decision: Read with anticipatory movement to decide to stay in base position, move back to defend, or move in to attack an expected short ball.

Cover: Respond with a quick little jump split step in the opponent's target area as the opponent strikes the ball; then move to cover where the ball is sent.

Adjustment: React to the ball with small push-off movements to set up to execute a shot in the hitting zone.

Person	Skill	Base (recover)	Decision (read)	Cover (respond)	Adjust (react)
Tim Hopper	✓✓✓	✓✓✓ X	✓✓✓✓ Good to move forward on short serve Anticipate	✓✓✓	✓ X ✓ ✓ Move back to give yourself time
Joy Butler	✓✓✓ Try pushing ball to deep corners	✓ X ✓✓ ✓ Remember to move back to base after each attack	XX ✓✓✓✓ Good read of drop shot	✓✓ X ✓ ✓	X ✓✓✓✓

FIGURE 11.2 Sample GPAI for pickleball.
From J.I. Butler, 2016, *Playing fair* (Champaign, IL: Human Kinetics).

TACTICAL FRAMEWORK FOR STRATEGIC PRINCIPLES

The rules, equipment, and structures of pickleball create constraints and challenges that influence how players engage. This section offers four tables that frame the tactical problems in pickleball. Table 11.2 focuses on the strategic principles of consistency and related court positioning. The focus here is on developing flowing games that focus student attention on where to go after playing a shot and what to do as the opponent strikes the ball. Skill cues focus on basic drive patterns and using the underarm serve to start the game.

Table 11.3 focuses on ball placement and the related notion of court positioning. Anticipation is critical as players consider where the opponent will place the next shot. Playing more offensively involves trying to move the opponent around the court and hitting to open spaces to force an error or a short ball. Table 11.3 assumes that players can keep the ball in play and thus focus on challenging opponents to return the ball. The where questions create the need to develop more refined on-ball placement skills such as the backhand drive, lob, volley, and smash.

Table 11.4 offers the final level of play: integrating consistency and placement principles with spin and power shots. To develop the use of topspin and slice, players must have learned to position themselves on the court effectively. They are now learning to control rallies by moving the opponent around the court both side to side and front to back. To apply spin, players need to be moving forward to play the shot as they strike the ball in the hitting zone approximately at knee to waist height, and just in front of the body.

Table 11.5 applies strategic principles to doubles play. Doubles play should happen only after all students are able to keep the ball in play (the worst experience for doubles players is being unable to contribute). The assumption here is that all the players have reached table 11.1 principles of play. The how and when questions focus on the doubles pair moving as a unit to cover the court area and control the volley area in the front part of the court. Key strategies are to create gaps in the opponents' court and to reduce the time they have to cover the court.

LESSONS AND LEARNING EXPERIENCES

The block plan in table 11.6 outlines how games in a pickleball unit can be sequenced with assessments woven throughout the unit; these include GPAI assessments (figure 11.2), team role assessments (figure 11.3), and then stations in which students record their progress in tasks related to the games played (figure 11.4). The games unit plan is based on a sequence of games developed in relation to the content analysis in tables 11.2 to 11.5.

Democracy-in-action ideas are then listed, based on table 10.2 in chapter 10. The unit culminates with a team tournament that fosters learning through interaction. The unit design is, of course, influenced by such factors as the length of lessons, the makeup of students in a class (ability, age, gender, prior experiences), and the opportunities to practice outside of class. Table 11.6 offers a suggested sequence that would be suitable for a class of eighth-graders.

Table 11.2 Pickleball Tactical Problems: Consistency and Court Positioning

Strategic principle	Tactical problems	On-ball skills	Off-ball movements
Consistency and court positioning	**How** do you play to be consistent and keep the ball in play? *Hit the ball high and into the center of the target area* **Where** do you position yourself after your shot? • *Behind the opponent's target area* • *Behind the back line of the court* **Where** do you send the ball to challenge the opponent? *To spaces wide (to the side), deep, and short within the area of the court*	Drives and footwork Underarm serve	Ready stance (base) Jump split step (cover) Push-off (adjust)

Table 11.3 Pickleball Tactical Problems: Ball Placement and Court Positioning

Strategic principle	Tactical problems	On-ball skills	Off-ball movements
Ball placement and court positioning	**Where** to place the ball to create spaces to attack? • *Send shots deep in the court.* • *Hit to open areas on the outside of the court.* • *Hit the ball short and then long.* • *Vary heights to get a short ball.* • *Attack the opponent's weaker side.* • *Hit deep at the opponent to crowd her shot.* **Where** do you position yourself based on ball placement and the anticipated response of the opponent? • *Move in to attack an anticipated short ball.* • *Approach the shot down line, move in to volley, or attack open space and gain midcourt area.* • *Hit the ball behind the opponent and coast in for a short ball.* • *Hit a drop shot or lob, and move in to gain the midcourt area.* • *Get behind lobs and then smash to spaces and move in to service line to attack response.* • *Counter opponent's attack with high balls for time and anticipate shot for surprise counter-attack.*	Backhand and forehand drives with contact in the hitting zone Basic topspin for depth on placement Serve to area Flat basic slice approach shot to keep ball low Volley punch action Lob Smash Passing shots	Anticipate target (decision) Recovery split step (base) Quick push-off movement (cover) Knee bend to split step (adjustment) Recovery split step (base) Anticipate target (decision)

Table 11.4 Pickleball Tactical Problems: Spin and Power

Strategic principle	Tactical problems	On-ball skills	Off-ball movements
Spin and power	**When** do you use spin in shots to press, defend, or attack spaces? • *Spin on serve for kick and ball movement to challenge the opponent on the return.* • *Rally with topspin or slice to pressing zones or spaces to move the opponent out of position.* • *Slice under the ball for low bounce and to approach the net.* • *If the opponent is deep in the court, use a drop shot with underspin so the ball bounces low.* **How** do you use spin and force in a stroke to set up or win a point or stay in the rally? • *Attack pressing zones to keep the opponent in a defensive role.* • *Hit an approach shot down the line and move to net.* • *Hit rising ball by taking the ball early as it bounces and then coasting into the net.* • *Volley the ball deep or drop it short.* • *Lob or passing shot when opponent attacks the net.* • *Use height to gain time and spin to control ball flight.* • *Serve with hard and soft strokes and then move to cover anticipated target spaces.* • *Smash with spin and power into spaces.*	Slice spin with short preparation bat action high to low on the ball Topspin to control power with bat action low to high on the ball Side slice on the serve to break the bounce Use topspin on the serve to kick the ball up Smash balls above the head	Recovery to baseline (base) Read as doing recovery, with split step (decision) Split-step as the ball is played (cover) React to the ball as it bounces to execute a shot (adjustment) Side-step recovery to the ready position (base)

Table 11.5 Pickleball Tactical Problems: Doubles Play

Strategic principles	Tactical problems	On-ball skills	Off-ball movements

Consistency
Placement
Positioning
Spin
Power
	How do you work as a pair to cover the space?
	
	• *Play as a pair: two up or two back.*
	• *Use height to create time to recover.*
	
	How do you create spaces to attack as a pair?
	• *Drop the ball short and move to the midcourt area.*
	• *Look for spaces to create open areas.*
	
	When does a pair move forward in the court, and when does a pair move back?
	• *Basic doubles positioning when a partner returns the serve is to have the partner in the midcourt area.*
	• *Use a backcourt setup when the partner serves.*
	• *Intercept the volley off the partner's shot with split step to cross and cut-off opponent's return.*
	• *Following a lob.*
	  · *Move back to cover the smash.*
	  · *Move forward as a pair when a lob is successful.*
		Hit the ball deep
		
		Use a drop shot
		
		Use angles to open up spaces
		
		Volley intercept
		
		Volley put away into spaces
		
		Lob
			Use a split step to push off the side to cover the court
			
			Recover to base
			
			Push forward as a pair
			
			Adjust step
			
			Pairs anticipate where ball will be sent by opponents

Table 11.6   Block Plan for Pickleball Unit

Lesson	Introductory game or task	Development game or tasks	Culminating focus game
1	Rally in full court	Spot-to-spot Wall ball game invention	Invented wall ball Spot-to-spot
2	Push-off game Wall-ball with partner from team	Spot-to-spot Win-racket game Short-court feed	Win-racket in full court
3	Short-court game Assign team roles	Space adapt Wall ball Partner feed	Space adapt
4	Team play Space adapt	Monarch Serve to target	Monarch GPAI
5	Team practice and assign roles	Short and in—volley Line game invention	Short and in—volley Monarch GPAI
6	Short and in	Volley dink Line game	Short and in Team monarch GPAI
7	Rally games	Stations	Team monarch
8	Stations	Doubles dink Line game Volley dink	Doubles dink 3 and win!
9	Short-court	Station re-assessment	Official practice with doubles
10	GPAI	Stations	Team practice with officials
11	Team role assessment	GPAI	Final rankings
12	Tournament event		

Team manager: _____ Group: _____

Class: _____

I was able to manage the team by...	Yes	How?	No	Why not?
Ensuring consensus building in any decision making				
Using a variety of strategies to encourage all team members to speak				
Using majority voting when needed				
Using a variety of strategies for conflict resolution				
Involving all players fairly when rotating subs and assigning positional play				

FIGURE 11.3   Sample assessment rubric for a team manager.
From J.I. Butler, 2016, *Playing fair* (Champaign, IL: Human Kinetics).

Team: _____

Player	1. Short game consistency				2. Service and monarch				3. Drives and space adapt				4. Officiating, singles, doubles, and GPAI			
	Longest rally (number of shots)	4R *Feed Tick Base Adjust*	Base *Spot Tick Hit to space*	Spot to spot	Won as monarch	Won point as server	Won as serves	Score out of 5 serves	Got to full court	Longest wall rally	BASE in with racket	Number of space adapt games	Officiated a game	Served a game in singles	Played a game in doubles	GPAI on game
Example *Tim Hopper*	12	✓	✓		✓	✓	✓	4	✓	14	✓	3	✓	✓		✓

FIGURE 11.4 Sample game station assessment form: team stats to mark progress.
From J.I. Butler, 2016, *Playing fair* (Champaign, IL: Human Kinetics).

187

In the next section, these strategic principles are applied to the three court areas created by the rules of pickleball. Modified games are suggested for each court area; they focus on cooperative games that exaggerate tactical problems and related skills and then competitive games that represent aspects of pickleball. Throughout all the lessons, connections are made to the democracy-in-action ideas highlighted in chapter 10.

COURT AREAS AND LEARNING TO PLAY PICKLEBALL

The rules of pickleball create three areas of play in a badminton court:

- A short-court area created by the rule that players cannot volley the ball in the service box area
- A full-length court for ground strokes area, generated because the serve and serve-return shots must bounce in the court (double bounce rule)
- A volley court in the midcourt area where players can volley the ball (hit it before it bounces)

Once novice players have struggled to keep the ball in play in the pickleball court, I usually direct them to play against the wall with a partner observing. As shown in figure 11.5, the intent here is to rally the ball (sponge or Wiffle) against the wall six times or more in a row to answer the tactical problem of being consistent and keeping the ball in play. The teacher models the setup of one partner observing to suggest the right equipment (hand, scoop, or bat), ball, and target placement on the wall. Once pairs have agreed on how to work in the relationship, the teacher adds a line marker on the ground to mark the area within which the ball must land and behind which the player must stand after playing a shot. This becomes the base between shots. Players who cannot hit the ball as it arrives can self-feed the ball by hitting it upward and then striking it

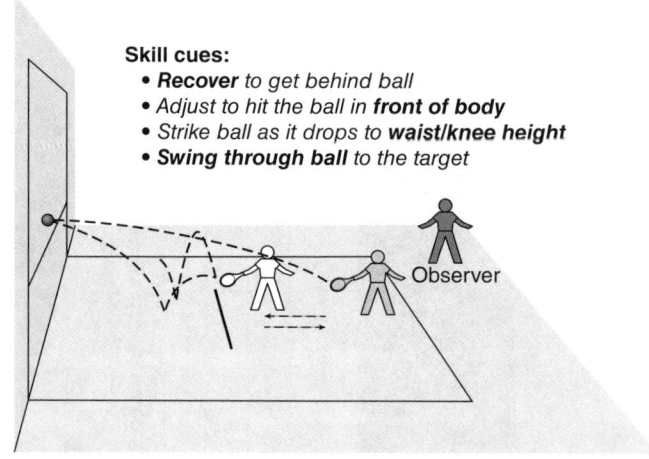

Skill cues:
- **Recover** to get behind ball
- Adjust to hit the ball in **front of body**
- Strike ball as it drops to **waist/knee height**
- **Swing through ball** to the target

Observer

FIGURE 11.5 Setup for wall ball to spots with observer.

to hit the wall. A key question is how to send the ball high on the wall to create time to recover to play the next shot. The critical question regarding tactical awareness is where to position oneself after a shot. The observer reminds the player to return behind the line marker on the ground (as shown in figure 11.5) in the base position to recover to play the next shot.

Once each player has played and chosen the optimal equipment, the two players work together to invent a game using the wall, the targets, and line markers. The game can be cooperative (e.g., players work to achieve a common goal such as 20 hits in row aiming at a wall target) or competitive (players score points when their opponents miss). The game should have three main rules addressing the following:

How to start and restart

How to keep ball in play

How to score points

At this point, players can be prompted by the tactical question Where do you send the ball to challenge your opponent? The answers (see table 11.2) suggest sending to spaces or back at the opponent if they have not recovered outside the area of play. Students learn to work democratically to structure the play environment, offer feedback, listen, adapt to the spatial demands of the game, and create a challenging game.

AREA 1: SHORT-COURT GAMES

The tactical focus of short-court games is consistency and court positioning. Variations of wall ball games can be played frequently throughout a unit to help players refine their technique of striking the ball and moving to relocate to the bounce. Modified games in the short-court area can focus on consistency (How do you keep the ball in play?) and positioning in relation to the opponents' target area in their court (Where do you position yourself after your shot?).

Spot-to-Spot Rally Game

The game in figure 11.6, spot-to-spot rally, focuses on returning to the base between strokes. The aim of the game is to rally the ball inside the service box area, aiming to hit the partner's spot. Following are the rules of play:

- Start by hitting the ball over the net into the partner's service box.
- Try for the longest rally with only one bounce between hits (self-hits allowed).
- Score a target point every time you hit a spot.

The tactical focus in the spot-to-spot rally game is sending the ball high enough to create time to recover and always returning to the spot behind the service line in order to move forward to the next shot. A task to help develop drive technique skill cues is for the players on their own to practice against the

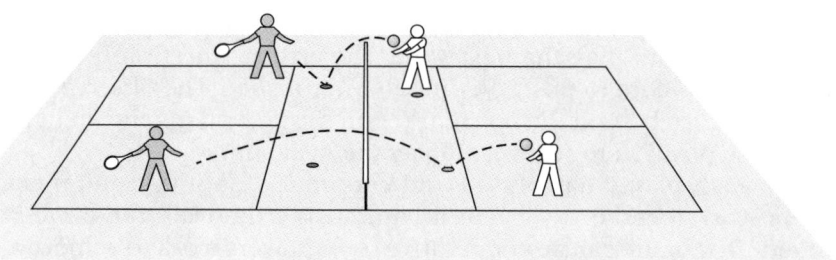

FIGURE 11.6 Setup for the spot-to-spot short-court rally game.

wall or to have one partner catch the ball at the net and feed it to the spot for the partner (see the far pair in figure 11.6). Following are key cues for partners to use:

- Use a V grip on the bat handle and keep the bat parallel to the ground.
- Bend your knees and keep your feet shoulder-width apart and staggered.
- Shift your weight from your back to front foot and strike the ball in front of your body.
- Keep the bat face parallel to the ground when striking the ball.
- Follow through to the target.

Observing and coaching as well as giving and receiving advice are key democracy-in-action elements here. When players return to the spot-to-spot rally game, they can extend the rules by inventing a scoring system and changing the space and spot placement. If the focus is now on competition, teachers can ask, Where do you send the ball to challenge your opponents?

Win the Bat Game

The tactical focus of the win the bat game (figure 11.7) is on placement and positioning. Initially, as the court size is increased, partners rally to figure out how to keep the ball in the court to achieve four shots in a row. The larger area often causes players to stand still and watch, rather than cover the court. The win the bat game allows one player to focus on movement while the other focuses on striking the ball. One player has the bat; the other is catching the ball and then sending it to the target. If the sender hits the target, she becomes the batter. The batter wins points if the sender makes a mistake. The game exaggerates positioning behind target area in order to send to open spaces by simplifying the idea of positioning for the bat player. The bat player knows where the catcher will send the ball so she can set up early to aim the ball to open spaces.

The intent of win the bat is to score points by sending the ball into the court so the catcher can't return it. Following are the rules:

- The ball must go over the net and must bounce once in the half-court.
- The batter gains a point if the thrower's ball lands out or bounces more than once before being caught.

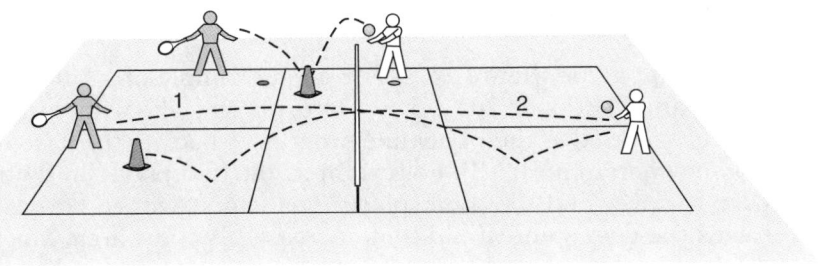

FIGURE 11.7 Setup for the win the bat game.

- Players restart the point from behind the back line.
- If the catcher hits the target, she gets the bat.

In this game, the teacher asks players to consider where to place the ball to create spaces to attack. As noted in table 11.3, batters can now explore ways to hit the ball deep and then short, high and then low, and from side to side. They can also combine these placements to cause the thrower to make a mistake. Both players can be asked to consider where to position themselves based on ball placement and the anticipated response of the opponent. For the batter, the answer is behind the target, but for the thrower, the answer depends on where the spaces are on his side of the court. Following are key cues for the batter:

- Set up your base early to receive the ball.
- Adjust your body as the ball arrives so that you can strike the ball in the hitting zone.
- Hit with a flat racket face and transfer your weight forward.

Win the bat is a game that demonstrates the challenges students have hitting with the backhand, especially if the target is on the receiver's backhand side. The key for the backhand is to shift the grip to feel the face of the bat on side of the thumb and the fleshy part of the hand. With this backhand grip, the player then practices striking a ball fed by a partner (see the far pair in figure 11.7), emphasizing bending the knees, stepping into the shot, and brushing the bat face up and through the ball as it drops (Hopper, 2007). This practice from a consistent feed with feedback from a partner can be extended to practicing against a wall and then back to the win the bat game in short court areas and then in full-length courts.

In terms of democracy in action, players learn to appreciate the need to define their intent as they adjust the game to work on skills, coach, and give feedback. The process helps them develop tolerance for their peer's playing abilities.

AREA 2: LONG-COURT GAMES

As players gain confidence in positioning and striking forehand and backhand drives, their play can extend into the full court. Now the focus is on learning to hit to the spaces of the court and to cover their opponents' target areas.

Space Adapt Game

The space adapt game (figure 11.8) is a good example of a "modification-by-adaptation game" (Hopper, 2011, p. 6). Here, players who win points have their court space increased as their backline progresses back to the baseline in three areas (as shown in figure 11.8). For example, the first player in figure 11.8 has one space to cover and the other player has two spaces to cover; whichever player wins the next point would then increase his court area. For the pair in the rear, the one player has three spaces to cover, and the other has two spaces. The game can be played in a half court or, if two players have a whole court, they can play gradually, adding up six areas as they win points. First person to cover six areas wins the game.

The intent of space adapt is to score points by keeping the ball in the court area more often than the opponent does. Following are the rules:

- The point starts after the serve has been returned into the court areas.
- Players lose a point if the ball bounces twice, is hit into the net, or is hit out of the court area.
- The first person to 2 points increases his court space by one area, and the score resets.
- The first person to win 2 points in the full-court area wins the game.

The space adapt game promotes tactical awareness in several areas. First, as students consider where to place the ball to create spaces to attack, they focus on using the spaces to create spaces. Where the zone is long and thin (see figure 11.8), sending the ball short and then long gives an advantage to the player on the right who has only one zone to cover. The game also makes players consider where to position themselves based on ball placement and the anticipated response of their opponents. As the target spaces increase, the answer to this question changes. For novice players playing on smaller courts, the answer becomes more apparent as they learn where more able opponents will send the ball and can thus set up early to hit to the increased spaces. Again, this reveals the important of hitting to spaces. Previous tasks (such as partner feeding drills and wall practice with spots to aim at) are ways to practice taking advantage of the spaces as they become available. Once players can play successfully in the full court, they can play games that develop consistency, such as hitting four shots in a row before a point can be won.

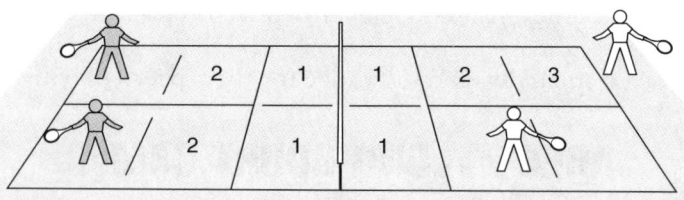

FIGURE 11.8 Setup for the space adapt game.

The democracy-in-action focus for the space adapt game is on developing empathy in a close game.

Monarch of the Court

The game monarch of the court (figure 11.9) focuses on the use of service and the return of serve. It involves players serving underarm from the back line in half- or full-court areas to opponents on the other side of the net. This game is a great way to engage many players and offers an ideal context for peer assessment.

The intent of the game is to be the receiver (the monarch) at the end of the game. Following are the rules:

- Servers send the ball into the opponent's service box from behind the baseline and from their hand.
- After the ball bounces once in the service court, the receiver sends it back to the server's court.
- Players play out the point from the service return using pickleball rules.
- Serving players rotate; waiting servers field a ball so they are ready to serve when their turn comes.
- The serving player who wins a point keeps tally. When the server has 2 points, he goes for 3 points. If the server wins, he becomes the monarch of the court; if he loses, he returns to 0 points.

Monarch games can be played in two half-court areas serving down the line, or on a full court serving across court. This game emphasizes serving the ball consistently over the net and then considering where to place the ball to create spaces to attack. Target areas from the serve create spaces in the opponents' court to aim at when the ball is returned. This can be practiced with targets set up on the court. Players rotate, aiming to hit a target as partners field the ball. The tactical concept from table 11.3 asks players to consider where to position themselves based on ball placement and the anticipated response of the opponent. After learning to set up with a base position behind the baseline, players can then explore the use of spin on the ball and appropriate positioning in response to opponents as they address the question of how to use spin and

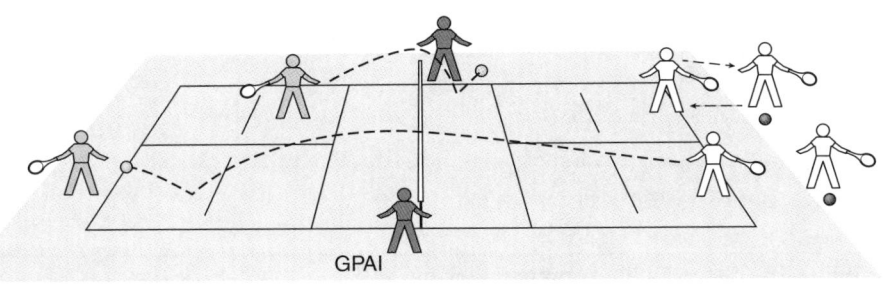

FIGURE 11.9 Setup for monarch of the court game.

force in a stroke to set up or win a point or stay in the rally. Following are key cues for the server:

- Stand sideways on.
- Step into the court area by shifting your weight forward.
- From ball in hand, strike the ball as it drops onto the bat.
- Angle the bat parallel to the ground and toward the target area (with the wrist cocked up).
- Add spin by brushing up on the ball for topspin, or cut across the ball for underspin and sidespin.

Monarch of the court highlights the democracy-in-action elements of observation and coaching as well as giving and receiving feedback in the context of a competitive game.

AREA 3: VOLLEY-COURT GAMES

The volley shot involves striking the ball before it bounces into open spaces. Essentially, volleys reduce the time opponents have to play the next shot.

Short and In Game

The short and in game (figure 11.10) creates the need to volley by exaggerating the use of the volley to win a point. When the ball is hit shorter than the dotted line, the player hits the ball and moves to the service line into a base position in preparation for the next shot.

The intent of the game is to be the first to win 4 points after playing a volley. Following are the rules:

- Players rally in pairs hitting the ball beyond the dotted line.
- If the ball is hit short, inside the dotted line, the player must hit a shot and approach the net.
- Players cannot volley the ball in the no-volley zone.

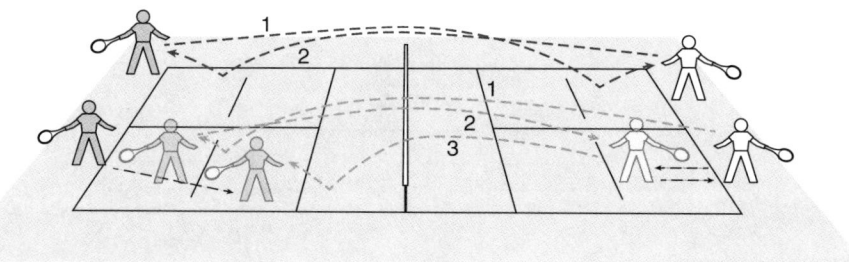

FIGURE 11.10 Setup for the short and in game.

The game exaggerates the idea of hitting down the line on short balls and creates the conditions for the player to consider where to position themselves based on ball placement and the anticipated response of the opponent. Often, shadow drills help students set up to volley as they practice the movement pattern of running forward, stopping in base, and volleying.

Line Game

Key to the effective volley is a punch action with minimal bat movement and a simple weight shift forward to attack the ball. The line game in figure 11.11 helps to address the key movement pattern as well as the punch action.

The intent of the game is to get the ball to bounce on the opponent's side of the line. Following are the rules:

- Send the ball down to bounce on your side of the line between two pylons or markers onto the opponent's side.
- Catch the ball before it bounces on your side of the line; then send it back from where you caught it.
- The ball must be sent from above head height and must bounce between the markers on your side of the line.
- Score points for opponent dropping catches, not sending between markers, and not bouncing the ball before the line.

In the line game, sending the ball down to bounce on one's own side of the line creates time for opponents to move to the flight trajectory of the ball as it bounces up and then falls on their side of the line. As players send the ball, their opponents can do a jump split step (cover) that allows them to push off to where the ball is sent and then adjust to catch the ball, or later to use a bat to strike the ball back by punching it down to the ground in front of the line. The punch action comes from (1) a wide base with the foot opposite the bat leading as the player's weight is shifted from the back to front foot, (2) the bat striking the ball in front with a flat face, and (3) the opposite hand up and tracking the ball and matching the bat hand as the ball is struck. A good progression here is to have one player with a bat (the other catching by hand) play up to 3 points and then swap. In addition, the spots can be used to create an adapted game

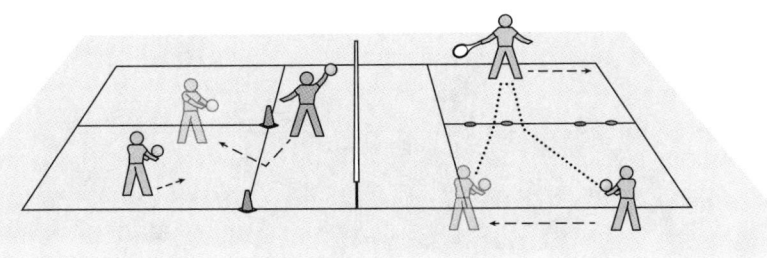

FIGURE 11.11   Setup for the line game.

in which the successful player is challenged by having the space between his spots decreased or increased.

Volley-Up Dink Game

The volley-up dink game (figure 11.12) enables players to learn to volley with time because the ball must be sent upwards. This creates time to play a volley with the player either hitting high and long or soft and short. Because the ball must be hit up players learn to consider where to position themselves after their shots. Volley-up dink allows time for the player to explore how to use spin to control the ball, such as under spin to do drop shots or topspin to control a lob shot of the ball, as players learn to aim the ball short and long within the constraint that the ball must be hit upward.

The intent of the game is to volley the ball in the court more often than the opponent does. Following are the rules:

- A point is scored when the ball lands in the opponent's court.
- A point is scored when the opponent's ball lands out or in the net.
- Players may only hit the ball upward with a volley.
- Players serve from behind the back line into the opponent's service box and move into the court.
- The returner sends the ball back with a volley and then moves into the court.

To practice, players can work in pairs. One player sends the ball by hand for the partner to volley with a punch action. Such games then progress to the short and in game, which transfers the volley to the full game of pickleball.

The combination of games encourages democracy in action as students develop tolerance for varying abilities, see the need for adaptations, and play different roles such as defending and attacking.

DOUBLES DINK TENNIS

This final section offers two doubles games that can be used to explore the strategic principles noted in table 11.5. Building from the previous sections, in these games players focus on the tactical questions of how to work as a pair

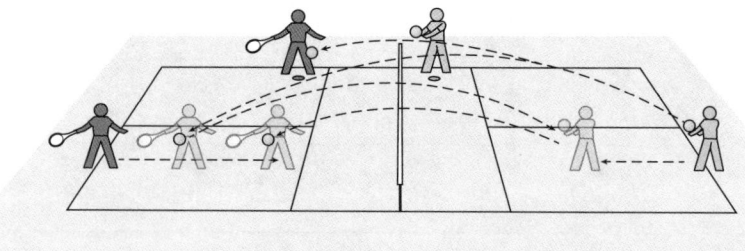

FIGURE 11.12 Setup for the volley-up dink game.

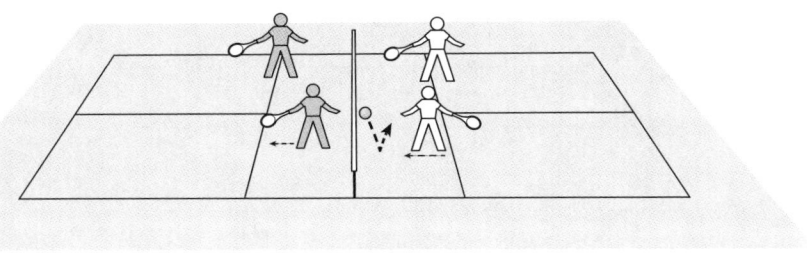

FIGURE 11.13 Setup for doubles dink tennis game.

to cover the space and how to create spaces to attack as a pair. Doubles dink in figure 11.13 emphasizes the short game of angles in which the ball cannot be volleyed, encouraging small ("dink") shots after the bounce, as well as lobbing to the backcourt, and setting up as a pair in the volley area just behind the service line.

The intent of the game is to outdink the opponents from a ball played from the net. Following are the rules:

- One player from a pair balances the ball on the net to start the game.
- As the ball falls on one side of the net, the point starts from the bounce.
- Players may not volley the ball into the no-volley zone; the rest of the pickleball rules apply.
- The first team to 4 points wins.

Doubles dink tennis really focuses on partners communicating to cover the frontcourt and backcourt as well as the sides of the court. After every shot, each player needs to cover the angles, setting up in a base position to be ready to adjust quickly to the shot.

This game addresses the democracy-in-action element of free inquiry. Working with a partner develops consensus-building skills and tolerance for the partner's contributions.

THREE FOR A WIN

The final game, three for a win (figure 11.14), helps pairs work from the serve into the point. This game is similar to pickleball doubles, except that the point starts after a serve is returned and the serving pair puts the ball into play. The game creates rallies that allows the pairs to consider when to move forward in the court and when to move back. The key here is to figure out how to attack with the volley in rallies to disrupt the opponents' coverage of the court.

The intent of the game is to win 3 points in a row as the serving team. Following are the rules:

- To start, one player from the serving pair serves the ball crosscourt to land in the service box.

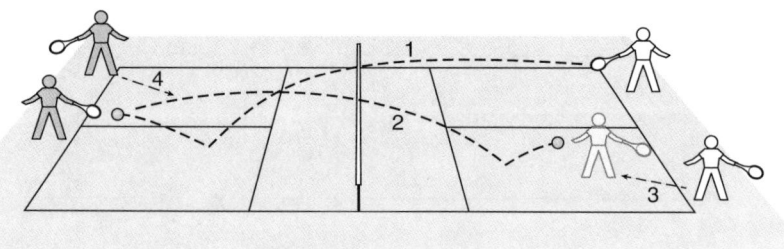

FIGURE 11.14   Setup for three for a win game.

- To start the point, the receiving player returns the ball into the serving pair's court.
- From the serving team playing the returned ball, the players on both teams may volley the ball to start the point.

SUMMARY

Modified games provide progressions that increase the challenge in environments initially shaped by the teacher and eventually by the students themselves, as they learn to play and practice in worthwhile games. The sport education model formalizes the idea that sport is learned as part of a growing commitment to a team, with associated consensus building, as players take on authentic team roles such as coach, manager, official, and equipment monitor, in preparation to play in formal team competition. Students are motivated by the prospect of a festival tournament, which gives them the opportunity to engage and contribute to their teams' scores. Team ranking ensures that players of similar ability play each other. A handicap scoring system (such as giving a point start to a player who loses the first game) with tennis scoring promotes close and exciting games. When a sport education model is used, units of instruction can be spread over a longer period to help students acquire skills through practice inside and outside of class.

Inventing
Invasion Games

From a distance, Ms. McGinley observes a group of students as they discuss the rules of their invented game. Three girls and a boy sit on a bench, side by side, looking at the floor. Two tall eighth-grade boys stand in front of them, talking animatedly, waving their arms and nodding as they speak over the heads of the other four. Ms. McGinley doesn't know what's going on, but she is speculating. Maybe inviting the students to choose their own groups wasn't such a good idea. These two are notoriously heavy-handed; some teachers have called them bullies. She wonders where to draw the line between allowing students to develop their natural social power and constraining it. After all, not all students are going to be leaders, but she is certain that making sure all students have a voice, or at least the opportunity to have a voice, is key in this process. As she gets close, she hears the two boys telling the others how the game is going to work.

After listening for a while, she interrupts.

Ms. McGinley: Can you remind me how you agreed to make decisions?

The four students on the bench look at her with visible relief.

Gurjita: We decided that we would take a round of suggestions, but that if someone didn't want to make one, they didn't have to.

Ms. McGinley: So what was happening a few minutes ago? I saw Jason and Eric doing all the talking. Does that mean everyone else opted out?

Gurjita: No. Bryony opted out, but then they assumed that we all had.

Gemma: Probably 'cause we're girls.

Aiden (chiming in from the bench): Hey, I'm not a girl, and they ignored me too.

Ms. McGinley: Is that how you saw it, Jason and Eric?

Jason: Well, there isn't much time left in the lesson, so we thought it would be quicker if *we* decided so that we could all just get on and play.

Ms. McGinley: So was that fair?

She turns to the students on the bench.

>**Ms. McGinley:** Why are you letting these two take away your power?
>
>**Gurjita:** They always get their way—especially in PE. There's no point speaking.
>
>**Ms. McGinley (resisting the urge to remind them that this is the point of this lesson):** OK. When we get into moments like this when we get stuck, we need to see them as a way to learn something.

Eric and Jason roll their eyes. The other four wait.

>**Ms. McGinley (to the four on the bench):** OK. Take back your rights to speak and cocreate this game. I'm going to suggest that you all take a minute to jot some ideas down individually on paper and then share them. I'll be back to see how you've done.

This chapter offers ways to introduce the concepts and tactical problems unique to the invasion games category. It also addresses the fundamental democratic principles and issues of social justice that invasion games raise.

The inventing games process has 10 stages (Butler, 2013, 2005), which can be organized into units that flexibly address varying contexts: the number of classes, desired outcomes, grade levels, experience, and student ability. The outline offered here is not specific to any grade level, but table 1.2 (in chapter 1) offers a guide to the stages for various grade levels. Within each of the stages, progressions are also offered, which are intended for use in the same lesson. As we have already established, stages are not necessarily equal to lessons, but depend on lesson length, the speed of student adaptation to the approach, and emergent learning. For example, an eighth-grade class took 6 lessons to complete stage 7, whereas a sixth-grade class took only 2 lessons to complete the stage. The eighth-grade class took time to make two variations on the suggested sequence of stages: (1) an examination of an issue that arose from stacking teams to win and (2) an expansion of the game showcases (each team taught its game to everyone else for an entire class).

Following this chapter, two chapters cover soccer (13) and touch football (14) as examples of the invasion category. The primary rule (intent) of invasion games is to invade the opponents' defending area to score a goal while simultaneously protecting one's own goal. Examples are basketball, hockey (field, floor, ice), football, lacrosse, netball, rugby, soccer, team handball, water polo, and ultimate. The strategic principles and tactics that form an external schema for invasion games and provide content for transfer across these games can be found in table 12.1. The inventing games stages used in this chapter are dependent on this table to help students understand game constructs within the invasion game category.

Table 12.1   Strategic Concepts, Skills, and Tactics for Invasion Games

Strategic concepts and skills	On-ball tactics	Off-ball tactics
Offense		
Keeping possession Skills: Sending, receiving, traveling Question: How do we keep possession?	Traveling with the ball Looking for a receiver Passing the ball Using deception	Moving into space to receive a pass Drawing defenders Reacting to a signal Reacting to deception
Distributing possession Skills: Sending skills to width and depth Question: How do we create scoring opportunities and keep possession?	Using width and depth in attack Supporting the attack	Providing cover in depth
Penetrating and invading the defense Skills: Scoring and hitting a target Question: How can we score?	Creating space to shoot and taking on defense Attacking the target	Drawing out defenders from the target area Supporting in width and depth
Defense		
Obtaining possession Skills: Anticipating, shuffling, changing speed, running in different directions Question: How can we regain possession?	Tackling or intercepting	Anticipating the pass
Closing down space or a specific player Denying shooting space and defending the target Skills: Footwork, anticipating, reading the game Question: How can we stop the attack and prevent scoring?	Preventing passing by close marking Preventing forward movement by tackling Staying on the target side and blocking the striker and the shot	Supporting other defenders Staying close and on the target side Maintaining depth and covering angles Defending a player or a space
Transition		
Obtaining possession (moving from defense to offense) Skills: Peripheral vision, footwork, running, quick direction changes	Tackling or intercepting Moving forward solo and looking for the pass	Moving quickly into offense mode (available for a pass or to support depth)
Losing possession (offense to defense)	Applying immediate pressure back on the ball handler to prevent a pass or close space	Dropping back to support other defenders

STAGE 1A:
Setting the Learning Environment

Focus: Setting up the learning environment for democracy in action while defining one of the game categories; establishing a group system, roles, and a policy for making decisions. Stage 1 is divided into two parts:

- 1A: Democracy in action
- 1B: Invasion games constructs

Learner focus:

- Discussing or brainstorming principles of democracy in action (cognitive)
- Creating a policy for making decisions (cognitive)
- Establishing and electing roles of recorder and equipment manager (cognitive)

Equipment: Pens, paper, charts, cards for the recorder and equipment manager

Setup: Students are at tables in groups of four to six, in a classroom if possible.

Learner Experiences

If any groups have an odd number of players (or injured players), someone can work as a referee. The intent of the group is to work cohesively to create a game by making ethical and fair decisions. The decision-making processes they construct can then transfer into sound decision making in game play. The decision-making process depends on the democracy-in-action principles discussed in chapter 1, as follows:

- Group process
- Personal and social responsibility
- Free inquiry
- Decision making
- Social justice

Any of these democratic principles can be the focus in the following stages.

Resist the temptation to help students come up with easy answers. In this stage, the process is just as important as the outcomes. Following are tips for successful group discussions:

- Contribute to your group discussion. You have the right and responsibility to do so.
- Listen respectfully to your peers until they have finished speaking.
- Be respectful of your peers' ideas, even if you don't agree.

- Whenever possible, contribute to the decision-making process in the group.
- Consider alternative ideas as the game unfolds.
- Use your vote wisely.

Establish two roles as follows (can be summarized on cards):

- Recorder of the group workbook: Records decisions about game setup (playing area, equipment size, ball type, goal dimensions, and rules).
- Equipment manager (EM): Collects and distributes game equipment and provides an equipment request list to the teacher.

Modifications

Students naturally make modifications as they create games that intrinsically suit their abilities. You can draw attention to how the game might be modified with different equipment (see table 4.4 for a table of modifications).

Democracy in Action

Decision making: Group policy

Central to the decision-making process is the creation of conditions that are respectful and safe. These conditions can be achieved by first working through inventing games processes in other categories. Alternatively, experiences such as experiential learning in outdoor settings, project adventure games involving problem solving, and cooperative learning activities can lay the foundations for success in this unit.

Students need to have answers to questions such as the following:

- How will individuals know when to speak? By shouting out at will? By taking turns? By raising a hand? By using a talking stick?
- How will decisions be made? By vote? Does there have to be a majority? By what percentage? Or does the decision have to be unanimous? What happens if it's not?

Check for Learning

- How did you contribute to the group process?
- What suggestions did you make?
- How did you help others to contribute?
- How would you rate your listening skills?
- What did you learn about group decision-making processes?
- Why is it important to contribute?

STAGE 1B:
Defining Invasion Game Constructs

Focus: Exploring game constructs

Learner Focus: Define the category of invasion games (cognitive)

Learner Experiences

In this stage, students explore the commonalties among invasion games. They are usually quick to arrive at the conclusion that there is a goal at each end and that the main purpose is to invade the opponents' defending area to score, while protecting their own. To help students understand the concept of inventing invasion games, you could draw on the example of James Naismith, who invented basketball. As a teacher at Springfield College, he was given the task by his boss (superintendent Gulick) of inventing a game suitable for physical education students between the football and baseball seasons. The constraints were that it had to be played safely indoors and without implements. You might also discuss the invention of pickleball (see the introduction in chapter 11).

Students need to understand the constructs of invasion games, as follows:

- Goal at each end
- Clear boundaries
- Scoring areas
- Attacking opponents' goal while defending one's own
- Offense: Maintaining possession and scoring goals
- Defense: Regaining possession and preventing scoring
- Transitions: Moving quickly to and from offense and defense

Older students can learn that the equipment and playing areas make up the regulations of the game and can be distinguished from its rules (which make it fair and accessible).

Democracy in Action (Continued From Stage 1A)

Decision making: Group policy

Groups continue to refine their decision-making policies and need time to test them on several occasions. A trial exercise to put their policies to the test might be helpful.

Check for Learning

- What is the main primary rule (intent) of invasion games?
- How does knowing this help you understand invasion games?
- What are some of the constructs of invasion games?
- What makes invasion games similar to and different from each other? Give some examples.

STAGE 2:
Establishing the Game Through the Democratic Process

Focus: Decision making and creating rules for inventing games

Learner focus:

- Defining the game by creating basic regulations and minimal rules (cognitive)
- Sharing ideas, negotiating, and making good decisions (cognitive)

Equipment: A way to record game inventions (worksheets or game-design software on iPads)

Setup: Continue in the classroom or set up benches in the gym so the transition to game play can be quicker.

Learner Experiences

Create a rough game outline that includes boundaries, goals, a ball, a scoring system, a name, and (most important) approximately five rules, including a safety rule. The recorder fills in the details. These can be refined as the game develops. Rules serve the following functions:

- Allow the game to flow.
- Provide a structure.
- Provide a safe environment.
- Establish fairness.
- Involve everyone.
- Challenge everyone.
- Make the game fun.

Democracy in Action

Personal and social responsibility: Individual rights during group discussions

Students often need to be taught how to engage in group processes and make group decisions. Offer frequent reminders, such as the following:

- You have the right to speak and the right not to speak.
- There are consequences to not speaking or not voting—you might have to live with choices that you disagree with.
- Once decisions are made, everyone must support and own them without resentment. This is the essence of consensus.

Check for Learning

- How would you rate your group process when designing your game?
- Were the rules easy to establish?
- What criteria did you use to agree on the rules?

STAGE 3:
Playing the Game

Focus: Testing the negotiation system and the game

Learner focus:

- Playing the game and identifying what makes it fun (cognitive)
- Directing the game setup (recorder and equipment manager); discerning what makes the game fun (cognitive)

Equipment: Worksheet, designated group equipment collected by EM

Setup: Divide the gym into quarters across the length of the gym. Position goals against the walls to minimize stray balls.

Learner Experiences

- The EM shows you the completed workbook, collects the equipment, and directs group members to their assigned playing areas.
- Students play their games.
- Groups discuss what makes their games fun.

Democracy in Action

Personal and social responsibility: Group responsibilities to the individual

As the games begin, determine whether they flow, and whether they are fair and accessible. Quick interventions may be appropriate. If, for instance, a player is stuck in a restrictive role (such as goalie), you might question the group's reasoning. Will positions rotate, for instance? Questions may help, such as How can the group introduce a rule that results in more movement for everyone? and Why do we want everyone involved? Moments of tension, conflict, or stuckness (aporia) are more likely when students add or amend rules without the consent of others.

Check for Learning

- How is the game working?
- Is it fun? If so, what makes it fun? If not, why isn't it fun?
- Can you give an example of how adding a rule made the game more enjoyable?
- Why do we need rules?

STAGE 4:
Refining the Game

Focus: Understanding the relationship between the game and its rules

Learner focus:

- Appreciating the relationship of rules to game constructs (cognitive)
- Using trial and error to make rule adjustments (cognitive)
- Negotiating rules that need changing, deleting, or adding (affective)
- Changing regulations for such things as boundaries, equipment, and goals (cognitive)
- Differentiating between regulations and rules (cognitive)
- Appreciating the need for rule and regulation changes and understanding why rule changes happen in traditional games (affective)

Equipment: Worksheet, designated group equipment collected by the EM

Setup: A designated area of the gym defined by line markers.

Learner Experiences

Offer game time-outs as needed to invite groups to refine their games. If something is clearly awry, you may need to make a strong intervention. It's important that clear, fair group processes are in place. Following are suggested time-out topics:

- Does the game flow?
- Is it structured?
- Is it safe for everyone?
- Is it fair?
- Is everyone involved?
- Is everyone challenged?
- Is it fun?

These questions can be introduced as a package with older students or one at a time with younger ones. As students work through these questions, they consider improvements. Changes in regulations (court dimensions, ball size or type, goal size, and the scoring system) usually make the game easier or more challenging. Changes in rules usually influence flow, fairness, and accessibility. For example, a fourth-grade group invented a rule that demarked the center-line as a boundary for offense players, thus affording defensive players more time to strategize. Reversing this rule (by preventing defensive players from crossing the centerline) gives offensive players more time to take shots on goal. Rules can be defined as prescriptive (what players must do) and proscriptive (what players must not do). Older students can understand the importance of striking a balance between the two as they consider what restricts and what increases game flow.

To promote further discussion points and deflect potential arguments, a committee box can be introduced to the process. This allows any student to take one of the following cards to make proposals during time-outs:

- Change an existing rule card
- Add a rule card
- Drop an existing rule card
- Restate a rule card

For example, if a student wants to propose that a rule be changed in some way, she retrieves such a card during a time-out and quickly writes her argument. She then asks for the next time-out to be devoted to listening to her proposal.

The group discusses the cards, putting each idea to a vote or consensus decision. This promotes understanding of committee work and offers a glimpse into how national bodies modify rules (you can offer examples).

Modifications

You may need to facilitate game modifications to help make the game easier or more challenging (e.g., reduce playing space or rotate positions for all players).

Democracy in Action

Social justice: How can everyone be involved? What if they don't speak up?

Summarize individual and group responsibility. Discuss the importance of empathy (shown by listening respectfully and acknowledging contributions). Discuss rules, equipment, space, and the complicated roles of players.

Check for Learning

- What have you learned about the purpose of rules?
- How do they help you?
- How do they change the game?
- Did you have to add, delete, or edit rules?
- Did the process work? Why?

STAGE 5:
Identifying the Coach

Focus: Examining and identifying the role of the coach

Learner focus:

- Defining the role of a leader or coach (to guide equitable decision making; cognitive)
- Electing a coach using a democratic process (cognitive)

- Developing the leadership qualities coaches need (cognitive)
- Appreciating the role of a coach (affect)
- Improving communication skills (cognitive)

Equipment: Coach worksheet, designated group equipment collected by the EM

Learner Experiences

Once the games are refined and underway, the next step is to share them. First, however, each group elects a coach (nominating self or others) after they have discussed this role with your help, using the following questions:

- What is the role of a leader or coach?
- How can leaders help groups make decisions?
- What is clear communication?
- What is respectful communication?
- Why is it important to listen?

Establish a list of criteria and responsibilities for coaches, including the following:

- An understanding of the leadership or coaching role
- Tact and firmness in guiding peers through decision making
- Clarity of explanations
- Clear communication of rules

Modification

This stage may be a great opportunity to involve older students from other grades to participate as coaches, particularly those who are interested in leadership roles.

Democracy in Action

Free inquiry: Leadership styles

Discuss with students the types of leadership and coaching. A coach-centered style allows less player contribution to game decisions, but on the other hand, it is often useful to get feedback from an objective observer. What is the role of the coach? What style will they adopt or want in their coach?

Check for Learning

- What skills does a good coach need?
- Did your coach improve the game? How?
- How did your coach and your players interact? Did the player accept all of the coach's suggestions?

STAGE 6:
Identifying the Referee

Focus: Understanding the fundamental role and demands of a referee
Learner focus:

- Understanding the need for rules and appreciating the consequences of violating them (cognitive)
- Respecting referees' decisions (affective)

Equipment: A whistle for each referee

Learner Experiences

Serving as referees helps students understand the rules and develop empathy and respect for this often-difficult role. Identify students who will reinforce the rules and administer the consequences for violating them. Rotate this position often.

This is a good time to have students compile lists of penalties and signals for rule violations in their workbooks.

In the next phase of game playing, groups have student coaches and players take turns serving as referees.

Democracy in Action

Group process: Consequences, patience, and respect

As discussions of violations, infractions, and consequences begin, students need to understand that the referee's role is educational and informative rather than punitive. In a culture in which disrespectful behavior toward referees and referees is often condoned, students may need reminders that patience and tolerance are necessary.

Check for Learning

- What have you learned about the referee's role?
- What was your experience in this role?
- How would you rate yourself as a referee?
- What skills do you need to learn for this role?
- How might you prepare yourself for this role next time?
- How has the experience of playing changed with the inclusion of a coach and a referee?

The assessment for referees (table 12.2) can be used for observers or as part of the referee's own reflective process.

Table 12.2 Assessment for Referees

Referee's skills	Yes	How?	No	Why not?
Has developed the following officiating skills:				
Knows the rules.				
Sees infractions and uses the whistle quickly.				
Knows the appropriate consequences for the infraction.				
Moves to see the action clearly.				
Remains calm and explains the decision clearly when asked.				

From J.I. Butler, 2016, Playing fair (Champaign, IL: Human Kinetics).

STAGE 7:
Showcasing Games

Focus: Showcasing games and making observations

Learner focus:

- Making informed choices (cognitive)
- Learning the responsibility that goes with making choices (cognitive)
- Showcasing game for classmates respectfully (psychomotor and affective)

Equipment: The EM establishes the group's need

Learner Experiences

1. Initial setup
   - The coach from each group explains the game to the rest of the class.
   - The group shows the class the game.
   - The class is invited to comment or make suggestions.
2. Pair up groups until each group has tried and played every game (see table 12.3).
   - The group's coach explains and guides the process.
   - Students choose which game to play.
   - If all students prefer one game, both groups play it (however, students often choose their own games).

Table 12.3 Showcasing in Group Pairs

Showcase: Lesson 1 (date)		
	Scoop ball game (team 1)	**Hoop game (team 2)**
Time for each game:	1 teaches 3	2 teaches 4
Time for each game:	1 teaches 4	2 teaches 3
Showcase: Lesson 2 (date)		
	Circle game (team 3)	**Hopsters game (team 4)**
Time for each game:	3 teaches 1	4 teaches 2
Time for each game:	3 teaches 2	4 teaches 1
Showcase: Lesson 3 (date)		
	Scoop ball game (team 1)	**Hopsters game (team 4)**
Time for each game:	1 teaches 2	4 teaches 3
	Circle game (team 3)	**Hoop game (team 2)**
Time for each game:	3 teaches 4	2 teaches 1

Table 12.4 Sample Inventing Games Tournament Setup

	Lesson 1 (date)		Lesson 2 (date)	
	Scoop ball game (team 1)	**Hoop game (team 2)**	**Circle game (team 3)**	**Hopsters game (team 4)**
Time: 2:00-2:07	1v2	1v3	1v2	1v3
Time: 2:09-2:16	3v4	2v4	3v4	2v4
Time: 2:18-2:25	2v3	1v2	2v3	1v2
Time: 2:27-2:34	1v4	3v4	1v4	3v4
Time: 2:36-2:43	1v3	2v3	1v3	2v3
Time: 2:45-2:52	2v4	1v4	2v4	1v4

3. A tournament could be played that would be limited to one or two of the games chosen by the class. Table 12.4 shows a possible setup for four concurrent games played by all teams over two lessons.

4. Showcasing could be combined with peer assessment. Use one of the games created and have two teams play it as the other two teams observe. Observers observe the game for five minutes and then a designated player for five minutes. Teams play two of the four games over two lessons and observe using inventing games performance assessment instrument (IGPAI) forms for one game (see table 12.5 for a sample showcasing format).

Democracy in Action

Free inquiry: Constructive feedback

The IGPAI (see table 12.6) focuses students' attention, sharpens their critical awareness, and improves their performances. However, it explores

Table 12.5 Sample Showcasing Format

Showcase Lesson 1 (date)	
Scoop ball game (team 1)	
_____ Time for each game	1 plays 3
Observers	Teams 2 and 4
Hoop game (team 2)	
_____ Time for each game	2 plays 4
Observer	Teams 1 and 3
Showcase Lesson 2 (date)	
Circle game (team 3)	
_____ Time for each game	3 plays 1
Observers	Teams 2 and 4
Hopsters game (team 4)	
_____ Time for each game	4 plays 2
Observer	Teams 1 and 3

Table 12.6 Inventing Games Performance Assessment Instrument (IGPAI)

Game features	Yes	No	How do you know?
Does the game flow?			
Is it structured?			
Is it safe for everyone?			
Is it fair?			
Is everyone involved?			
Is everyone challenged?			
Is it fun?			
Individual observations	Yes	No	How do you know?
Is the player helping the game flow?			
Is the player playing safely and respecting others?			
Is the player playing fairly and listening to the referee?			
Is the player involved in the game?			
Is the player challenged by the game?			
Does the player seem to be having fun?			
Other comments?			

From J.I. Butler, 2016, *Playing fair* (Champaign, IL: Human Kinetics).

a sensitive area. The process is often hampered by students who do not want to offend their friends with negative feedback, and it can also be a site for covert bullying. Although offering constructive feedback can be challenging, even for adults, it is a vital part of the democratic process.

Guidelines for assessing peers and giving feedback are helpful. Here are some suggestions when teaching students about assessment and feedback:

- Identify the purpose of the peer assessment as part of the learning process, both as observed and observer.
- Explain that constructive feedback is supportive and helps people improve.
- Discuss how destructive feedback can be hurtful and damaging.

Consider your students' readiness for peer assessment. Decide whether to pair up students or let them make their own choices.

Check for Learning

- What did you learn from watching other groups' games?
- What suggestions did you hear about your own game?
- What suggestions did you accept?
- What do you think of your game now?
- What did you learn from using the assessment form?
- What did you learn from the feedback from others about your game and your playing ability?
- Was this helpful? Why?

End the inventing games process here for younger or less experienced learners.

STAGE 8:
Defense

Stage 8A: Strategies

Focus: Identifying defensive strategies and tactics

Learner focus:

- Problem solving in groups (cognitive)
- Discerning what works best, through trial and error (cognitive)
- Learning the roles of defensive players (cognitive)
- Distinguishing between on-ball and off-ball play (cognitive)
- Making decisions as a group—both while inventing games and during game play (cognitive and psychomotor)

Equipment: The EM collects the group's equipment

Learner Experiences

With the game established and somewhat developed, students move into developing game play through organized tactics. I start with defensive tactics. Although it is true that students are often more excited about scoring than about defending, a good offense takes the opponents' defense into consideration. How better to understand what opponents are trying to do than by considering their defensive systems?

The basic questions of defense are as follows:

- How can your team stop the other team from scoring?
- What are your opponents' defensive tactics?
- Why do you need to know?

Possible answers include the following:

- Covering, or marking, a player (full court, half court, sagging)
- Covering, or marking, an area
- Double-teaming

In their teams (not groups), students brainstorm answers to these questions. The coach lists ideas and decides which one to try first. During time-outs, players evaluate their success and consider improvements. Consider the following teacher prompts during time-outs:

- What ideas did you try?
- Did you need to modify any of them? How?
- How did your defensive strategy work?
- How did the offense manage to score?

During this problem-solving stage, encourage students to work through trial and error, noting why something worked and why it didn't. This helps them construct a schema for situational strategy planning.

Democracy in Action

Free inquiry: Active listening

- Groups discuss strategies. Remind them about the need for attentive listening and asking clarifying questions.
- Revisit the role of the coach by delegating the role to the whole team. Have them observe how their opponents are managing to score and whether their defense tactics are working, and why or why not.

Check for Learning

- What strategy were you working on?
- What was your tactic for this strategy?

- Did it work?
- What adjustments did you need to make?
- What is the difference between strategies and tactics?

Stage 8B: Skills

Focus: Refining defensive skills
Learner focus:

- Practicing skills in context (cognitive and psychomotor)
- Elevating the effectiveness of game play (cognitive and psychomotor)
- Identifying and practicing skills necessary for executing defensive strategies (cognitive and psychomotor)
- Improving observational skills (cognitive)
- Analyzing movement (cognitive)

Equipment: The EM collects the group's equipment

Learner Experiences

This sophisticated stage is best reserved for more experienced students (you can suggest it for some groups and not others). It helps players identify and develop defensive skills such as observing, analyzing movement, appreciating progressive skills practice, and making connections between practice and game play. Following is a sequence for developing defensive skills:

1. Students list the possible defensive skills.
2. Students design a practice that isolates these skills. They should start with a slow version and build up to full game-like speed.
3. The coach watches the drill and offers ideas for improving the practice.
4. Students develop the skill until it is almost gamelike.
5. Students go back to the game and try the refined skill within the game context. Does it help? Following are some defensive tactics possibilities they can use:

   - Staying with the opponent player
   - Staying goal side of the player
   - Tackling
   - Anticipating, intercepting, reading actions
   - Covering, or marking, a player (full court, half court, sagging)
   - Covering, or marking, an area
   - Double-teaming

Table 12.7 lists the steps in this stage along with teacher and learner roles.

Table 12.7 Possible Learning Experiences for Stage 8B

Experience	Teacher role	Learner role
Students design a practice that isolates the skills, starting slow and building to game speed.	Offer suggestions where needed.	Discuss, identify a plan, and implement it.
The coach watches the drill and offers ideas for improvement.	Talk individually to coaches.	Listen to and consider the coach's ideas. Try them out.
Students develop the skill until it is gamelike.	Offer suggestions and encouragement.	Build the intensity of the activity.
Students go back to the game and try the refined skills in context. They then answer the question Does it help?	Observe the game and offer feedback.	Focus on the practice skills and apply them to the game; be observant.

Modifications

In order to accommodate ranges of ability, students are encouraged to consider the use of more accessible equipment (e.g. different size balls for easier handling) or changes to the court or field dimensions or rules.

Democracy in Action

Group process: Consensus building

Once decisions are made, all parties need to get behind the decision.

Check for Learning

- Did the skill practice help? How? If not, why not?
- What did you decide to focus on in your practice?
- Did you build progressions in your practice?
- How did that help?

Stage 8C: Transitions

Focus: Creating defensive transitional strategies (defense to offense)

Learner focus: Building defensive strategies into offensive strategies (cognitive)

Learner Experiences

This stage is best reserved for more experienced players. Often, players win the ball on defense but move into offense slowly, thus losing possession. Changing from defense to offense requires team organization. Following are some questions for students to consider:

- How does your team gain possession of the ball (or object) from the other team? Possibilities:
  - ► Using intuition.
  - ► Reading the game.
  - ► Considering offense options.
  - ► Closing down passing lanes.
  - ► Forcing an error with defensive pressure.

- What have you noticed about your opponents' defense that would allow your team to penetrate it?
- Once in possession, what system or organization helps you to move quickly into offense?

Democracy in Action

Personal and social responsibility: Trust

In team play, it is important to observe both the opponents and one's own team members. It is also vital to build strong relationships, which depend on trust, communication, and understanding. Explain that a teammate is like a good friend—you can predict how she will react, or know that she will support you, even when you make a move that is outside the box. If you call or ask for help, you know that your teammate will listen and respond.

Check for Learning

- What is one clear concept or idea you learned today about transitioning from defense to offense?
- How did your team get organized?
- What qualities make a good team player in defense?

STAGE 9:
Offense

Stage 9A: Strategies

Focus: Identifying offensive strategies and tactics

Learner focus:

- Developing tactics from the basic strategies of offense (cognitive)
- Distinguishing between on-ball and off-ball play (cognitive)
- Assisting the player with the ball (psychomotor)
- Enhancing decision making from decisions made in groups to decision made in game play (cognitive)

Learner Experiences

Like the defensive stage, this stage begins by asking key questions:

1. How do you keep possession of the ball (or object) to set up scoring opportunities?
2. How can your team score more points or goals than your opponents? Possibilities:

   - Keep the ball moving with short, safe, controlled passes.
   - Player on the ball.
     - What do you do with the ball?
   - Players off the ball.
     - Where do you go to be available for pass?
     - How do you create space for the player with the ball?
   - Divide roles to cover the goal.
   - Use transitional awareness.
     - Be aware of the risk of losing possession.
     - Create space for opportunities.
     - Think two or three moves ahead.

3. The same method of trial and error is used with offensive and defensive strategies. Digitally recorded game play can help students analyze what is going according to plan, what isn't, and why.
4. Time-outs can be used at the teams' discretion as strategies become refined and adapted.
5. A coaching session may be appropriate for distinguishing between on-ball and off-ball play.
6. Follow-ups might include discussions of player support and assistance for the player with the ball.

Table 12.8 provides a quick summary of the possible learning experiences in this stage along with teacher and learner roles.

Table 12.8 Possible Learning Experiences for Stage 9A

Experience	Teacher role	Learner role
Discuss ideas for an offensive strategy; then choose one and plan to implement it.	Define offensive strategy and remind coaches of their roles.	Contribute ideas; be involved in team decision making.
Play the game focusing on one plan. Use time-outs for refining and reorganizing.	Observe and inquire what the plan is for each team; write them down.	Identify the individual role within the team structure for offense.
Observe opponents' game play, and define tactics within the chosen strategy.	Focus groups' observations using questioning.	Observe and share.

Democracy in Action

Personal and social responsibility: Individual self-reflection to assess team play

Individual players begin self-analyses by keeping logs of their contributions to offensive play (assists, passes, opening up space, encouragement, support of moves, being in position for a pass). They can seek help from coaches or watch digital recordings.

Check for Learning

- What strategy were you working on?
- What was your tactic for this strategy?
- Did it work?
- What adjustments did you need to make?
- What is the difference between strategies and tactics?

Table 12.9 is a useful assessment tool for the teacher to collect at the end of the lesson. It might also be used as a log for students to keep track of their progress as they develop offensive strategies.

Stage 9B: Skills

Focus: Refining offensive skills

Learner focus:

- Practicing skills in context to elevate game play (psychomotor)
- Identifying and practicing the skills necessary for execution (cognitive and psychomotor)

Table 12.9 Log or Assessment for Identifying Offensive Strategies and Tactics

Identifying offensive strategies	Yes	How?	No	Why not?
How can your team score more points or goals than your opponents? How do you keep possession of the ball (or object) to set up scoring opportunities?				
Develop a plan for scoring and keeping possession.				
Try out ideas and discuss their effectiveness.				
Modify the plan.				
Identify specific player roles.				
Identify specific on-ball and off-ball actions.				
Build support systems for the player with the ball.				

From J.I. Butler, 2016, *Playing fair* (Champaign, IL: Human Kinetics).

- Designing offensive strategies (cognitive and psychomotor)
- Improving observational skills (cognitive)
- Analyzing movement (cognitive)

Learner Experiences

1. Students identify and list skills that are required to use offensive strategies effectively. Possibilities:
   - Move to receive a pass.
   - Pass to open players.
   - Support other players.
   - Create open spaces.
   - Develop skills in carrying, passing, receiving, and shooting.
   - Combine locomotor and manipulative skills.
2. Students design a practice that isolates these skills, starting slow and building to full speed.
3. The coach watches the drill and offers ideas for improvement.
4. Students develop the skill until it is almost gamelike.
5. Students go back to the game and try the refined skills within the game context. They answer the question Do they help?

Democracy in Action

Group process: Consensus building

Once decisions are made, all parties need to get behind them.

Check for Learning

- Did the skill practice help? How? If not, why not?
- What did you decide to focus on in your practice?
- Did you build progressions in your practice?
- How did that help?

Stage 9C: Transitions

Focus: Using offensive transitional strategies (offense to defense)

Learner focus:

Students build offensive strategies into defensive strategies (cognitive).

Learner Experiences

Students should focus on the following question: If your team loses possession, how will you switch quickly to defensive mode? Possible answers:

- Intercepting
- Using intuition
- Reading the game
- Closing down passing lanes
- Forcing an error by using defensive pressure

Table 12.10 lists the possible learning experiences in this stage along with teacher and learner roles

Table 12.10 Possible Learning Experiences for Stage 9C

Experience	Teacher role	Learner role
The defensive team discusses a system for moving into defense (i.e., organizing players).	Facilitate idea sharing.	Identify concepts, offer solutions, listen to others' ideas.
Implement a plan for offense once possession is won.	Observe, provide feedback, and encourage.	Anticipate, react, and implement the plan.
Debrief and discuss.	Offer suggestions where needed.	Analyze and discuss solutions.
Practice and refine the transitional tactic.	Coach.	Play, discuss, play.

Check for Learning

- What is one clear concept or idea you learned today about transitioning from offense to defense?
- How did your team get organized?

STAGE 10:
Transferring Concepts From Inventing Games to Institutionalized Sports

Focus: Identifying concepts for transfer

Learner focus:

- Appreciating the value of inventing and refining their own games (affective)
- Identifying similarities between their owns game to national games in terms of strategies, rules, player roles, concepts, regulations, and concepts (cognitive)
- Noticing transfer effects (affective and cognitive)

Learner Experiences

- Teach invasion games before teaching national invasion games.
- Students can then make sense of national games by using their games as yardsticks.
- Identify key concepts that are easily transferable (e.g., rules, modified behaviors, referees, keeping possession, passing the ball ahead of teammates, player-to-player defense).
- Teachers guide discussion to establish skills that enable these concepts to be implemented.
- Students identify progressive drills and practices for this purpose.

Democracy in Action

Social justice: Making modifications and adaptations for equal access

Students can compare their invented games to institutionalized invasion sports. How inclusive are they? When and why is it fair to make allowances and modifications to games (e.g., using a smaller ball for women in basketball, using a lower net for wheelchair basketball)? What kind of allowances and modifications do we make elsewhere in society (wheelchair ramps, special seats on buses, support for students with different learning needs)?

Check for Learning

Rubrics based on the outcomes can be created for each stage. GPAI instruments work really well with this approach, particularly at the end of the game-making stage and then after each of the three stages in either defense or offense.

SUMMARY

For learning to be sustainable and transferable, experiences need to be meaningful and thus memorable. Chalking up their own blueprint game for each of the categories helps students fully understand and appreciate the constructs of the subsequent games they learn. The next two chapters will continue to explore the opportunities offered by invasion games and help make connections between the invasion game constructs through their own invented game and those established for soccer and touch football.

Invasion Game: Soccer

Steve Mitchell

Mr. Beckham's fifth-grade class is in a soccer unit. The environment is learning oriented, but players can get competitive when games are close. During one 3v3 game, Mr. Beckham sees that Ray just tried to dribble the length of the field to score, but lost the ball as he got closer to the goal. Mr. Beckham then hears the following exchange between Ray and Jack, a teammate:

Ray: C'mon, help me out here, will ya?

Jack: How can I help when you never try to pass the ball?

Ray: How can I pass when you just stand around?

Jack: Well, you're such a ball hog that there's no point in moving because you won't pass it anyway.

Clearly we have a moment of aporia here, so Mr. Beckham intervenes. He brings the team in for a short discussion.

Mr. Beckham: So, what's the problem?

Jack: Ray never passes!

Ray: Jack never moves so I can pass to him!

Mr. Beckham: So we have a problem, because you can only really be successful in soccer if you play as a team, yes? You have to rely on each other! Why don't you spend a few minutes talking this through. I'll come back in a little while and ask you to give me three things that will help you work more as a team and less as individuals.

Mr. Beckham moves away to observe other games while subtly keeping an eye on the ensuing discussion. He returns a few minutes later.

Mr. Beckham: So what did you decide?

Jack: Well, Ray says he'll pass if we all move, so we decided that if a teammate has the ball, the rest of us have to be moving.

Ray: And I need to play more with my head up so I can see my team-mates, and I need to trust them more.

Jack: And we need to call for the ball as well.

Mr. Beckham: Great. Let's see it happen then.

Soccer provides a great opportunity for young learners to engage in creative, social, and democratic processes. Each lesson in this chapter is planned for groups of six students, which allows game or practice designs with several numerical permutations (e.g., 3v3 or multiple pair or triad activities). These present realistic situations that are representative of those found on a soccer field and ensure that players have a full range of decision-making opportunities in multiple ongoing games played simultaneously on adjacent fields or playing spaces. This setup might also allow for 6v6 game play. Importantly, of course, this small-sided setup also facilitates the social and democratic processes so fundamental to inventing games. Players inevitably discuss and negotiate as they develop their ideas for game play and practice situations. This works particularly well in a sport education framework (Siedentop, Hastie, and van der Mars, 2011), in which all team members accept roles and responsibilities, and each contributes to the effective functioning of the team.

As in all invasion games, the aim of soccer is to invade the opponents' defending area to score a goal while simultaneously protecting one's own goal. However, the principal primary rule (which distinguishes soccer from invasion games such as team handball, hockey, and lacrosse) is, of course, that the ball must be propelled by any part of the body other than the hands. Most commonly, outfield players kick the ball. Secondary rules are perhaps more important for teachers to understand, because these can be changed depending on the type of soccer game, players' abilities, or desired responses. These secondary rules are many and varied and often amount to the conditions that teachers place on a game to elicit particular responses related to either game performance or behavior. These conditions include the number of touches players have before passing or shooting, the height at which the ball can be played, the way a game is restarted after the ball goes out of bounds, and the method of scoring.

The block plan in table 13.1 is for an eight-lesson unit focused primarily on offensive concepts, but also on defensive and transitional concepts. Following this plan results in a well-shaped, but modified, game of soccer. Note that game play is 3v3 for most of the unit, meaning that several games are going on simultaneously. Keeping students on the same three-person team builds trust and familiarity and allows for combining teams for 6v6 play later in the unit.

Table 13.1 Block Plan for a Soccer Unit

Lesson number and topic	Learner experiences	Democracy-in-action focus
Lesson 1	Play the game: Learning rules Skill: Throw-ins	**Group process and decision making:** Group decision making and consensus building
Introduction	Establish a team decision-making process. Play 3v3 (no goalkeepers) with primary rules	
Development	Learn rules for restarts after goals and balls sent out of play	
Culmination	Make decisions regarding rules	
Lesson 2	Offensive concept 1: Keeping possession Skill: Dribbling, passing, receiving	**Personal and social responsibility:** Individual responsibilities to the group
Introduction	Individual possession (1v1) focusing on dribbling under control	
Development	Team possession: Passing, receiving, and moving to receive	
Culmination	3v3 possession games without goals	
Lesson 3	Offensive concept 2: Distribution of possession (width and depth) Skill: Crossing and shooting	**Free inquiry:** Communication
Introduction	3v3 games (short and wide field) using width to attack	
Development	Team practice: Feeding the wings and finishing	
Culmination	6v6 games with goalkeepers with a focus on width and depth and timing attacking runs to goal	
Lesson 4	Offensive concept 3: Penetration and scoring Skill: Shooting	**Decision making:** Group policy applied to team tactics
Introduction	3v3 games in a narrow field with goals but no goalkeepers	
Development	Play penetrating passes Shoot a rolling ball from a pass	
Culmination	6v6 games with goalkeepers	
Lesson 5	Defensive concept 1: Stopping the opposing team from scoring Skill: Shot stopping	**Personal and social responsibility:** Individual responsibilities to the group
Introduction	1v1v1 goalkeeping game	
Development	Goalkeeping practice: Stopping and gathering the ball	
Culmination	3v3 game with rotating goalkeepers	

(continued)

Table 13.1 *(continued)*

Lesson number and topic	Learner experiences	Democracy-in-action focus
Lesson 6	Defensive concept 2: Denying space Skill: Pressuring the ball carrier	**Personal and social responsibility:** Interpersonal communication
Introduction	3v3 game with rotating goalkeepers and an emphasis on marking opposing players	
Development	1v1 practice on pressuring the ball carrier (closing down)	
Culmination	6v6 with rotating goalkeepers	
Lesson 7	Transitional concept 1: Obtaining possession (high pressure and winning the ball back early)	**Personal and social responsibility:** Communication and individual responsibility
Introduction	3v3 dribble-in game: Players must dribble into an end zone to score	
Development	Block tackling practice	
Culmination	3v3 dribble-in game: Players must dribble into an end zone to score	
Lesson 8	Transitional concept 2: Regaining possession Skill: Dictating play defensively	**Personal and social responsibility:** Team communication and cooperation
Introduction	3v3 dribble-in game: Players must dribble into an end zone to score	
Development	Practice delaying attacks and dictating the direction of play (extend to recovery runs)	
Culmination	6v6 game including goalkeepers with an emphasis on team defending	

LESSON 1:
Play the Game—Learning Rules

Focus: Playing the game using appropriate restart rules

Skill focus: Performing throw-ins

Learner focus:

- Accepting others' input in discussions and decision-making processes regarding restart rules (affective)
- Understanding a 3v3 game setup, particularly restarting play with a pass in from out of bounds (cognitive)

Equipment: Soccer balls, cones, and goals

Setup: Playing areas of about 30 by 20 yards (for each game).

Learner Experiences

1. In preselected, mixed-ability teams, students play 3v3 games. Each team defends a small goal (2 yards wide) but may not use a goalkeeper. Fields can be adjacent to each other and can share a common sideline if necessary (in this case, rules should prevent players from running into an adjacent game to retrieve a ball).
2. Methods of restarting play are decided on by the players in each game. This needs to occur soon after the game begins since the ball will go out of play quite soon. Traditionally, soccer is restarted with a throw-in when the ball goes out of bounds. However, students might be prompted to reconsider this rule because balls bouncing from a throw-in can be hard to control, especially on a small field. Roll-ins are easier to control because the ball is already on the ground.
3. Teams discuss the best restart rules for balls out of bounds.
4. Require that opponents rotate (play different teams) to create further discussions regarding restarts.
5. Facilitate a class discussion on restarts and the relative merits of throw-ins, pass-ins, and roll-ins. Use convergent discovery (i.e., asking questions that lead to students arriving at a specific conclusion) to guide students to the conclusions that pass-ins and roll-ins are easier to control in this modified game.
6. Students play until lesson closure, rotating opponents.

Modifications

Because students play modified 3v3 games in the first six lessons of the unit, it is important that they learn to play independently as they organize themselves and make their own officiating calls. The 3v3 game creates many more decision-making situations than larger-sided games do, because players have more on-ball opportunities. Goalkeepers are not used at this stage to provide maximal moderate-to-vigorous physical activity (MVPA), but goals should be small so that scoring is not too easy.

Democracy in Action

Group process and decision making: Group decision making and consensus building

Presenting students with three options for restarts provides early opportunities for small group discussions and decision making. As indicated in chapter 12, stage 1 of this decision-making process might be to develop a system for making group decisions. Initially, students must reach consensus within their 3v3 games, and then do so again after rotating opponents. In a later class discussion, you can guide the class in choosing the best restart method. More experienced soccer players usually have the loudest voices and often prefer officially sanctioned methods, such as for throw-ins. However, you can help them recognize that a bouncing ball resulting from a throw-in is harder to control, and that a roll-in or a pass-in is a much better option. The rule change challenges students to think outside the box in adapting secondary rules to facilitate better game play.

Check for Learning

■ What are the key rules you need to follow in this game?
■ What are some rules you could change to make the game better?

Instrument for Formal Assessment

Although restarting play effectively is important for success in the modified 3v3 game, the most important focus of this initial lesson is the process by which teams negotiate this decision and the team dynamics that result. Successful team discussion requires that students respect each other's opinions. You can use the rubric in table 13.2 to check the extent to which your students have been able to do this in the discussion segments of the lesson.

Table 13.2 Rubric for Evaluating Team Process

Below expectations	Meets expectations	Exceeds expectations
• Does not recognize and/or evaluate the effects of personal behavior to ensure positive effects on others. • Sometimes uses put-downs or comments that are hurtful. • Has difficulty in respecting the rights and feelings of those who may be of different background or different skill level.	• Evaluates personal behavior to ensure positive effects on others and refines behavior with prompts from others. • Provides some positive comments to classmates and does not use put-downs or comments that are hurtful. • Respects the rights and feelings of those who may be of different background or different skill level.	• Evaluates personal behaviors and refines behavior to ensure positive effects on others without prompts. • Provides frequent positive comments to classmates without prompts. Never uses put-downs or comments that are hurtful. • Respects the rights and feelings of those who may be of different background or different skill level by encouraging others or other behaviors to include all students.

Reprinted from *The Ohio Physical Education Evaluation.*

LESSON 2:
Offensive Concept 1—Keeping Possession

Focus: Keeping possession of the ball on an individual and team basis
Learner focus:

■ Dribbling the ball under control to keep possession (psychomotor)
■ Passing accurately to teammates' feet and out ahead of a moving receiver (psychomotor)

■ Receiving the ball under control and setting up for the next move (psychomotor)

Equipment: Soccer balls and cones to mark off playing areas

Setup: Multiple 20- by 10-yard playing areas marked off next to each other for 1v1 games and 30- by 20-yard areas for 3v3.

Learner Experiences

1. Students play 1v1 games with the goal of keeping the ball for as long as possible.
2. Students discuss the best ways to keep the ball away from an opponent.
3. Students practice individual dribbling and turning on command, using as many foot surfaces as possible.
4. Students play 3v3 games (in 30- by 20-yard areas) and discuss the requirements for team possession.
5. Pairs practice passing and receiving, and then passing and moving to space.
6. Students play 3v3 games.

Modifications

Modifications focus on making the small-sided 3v3 game as challenging as possible for all students.

■ For higher-skilled students, limit the number of touches by having them play three touch (i.e., two touches to control the ball and one more to pass it) each time they are in contact with the ball.

■ For very highly skilled students, decrease the size of the playing area.

■ For those who are less skilled, increase the size of the playing area (if more space is available) to give them more time and space in which to receive and control the ball.

Democracy in Action

Personal and social responsibility: Individual responsibilities to the group

In discussions, students can choose the techniques they need to play their modified games. They also come to recognize that they are individually responsible to the team for keeping possession of the ball when they have it, and that they can help the team keep possession by making accurate and well-weighted passes. Use student responses to develop appropriate skill practice segments for the individual dribbling and pairs practices.

Check for Learning

- What ways did you find to keep the ball away from your opponents?
- What are the important things to remember about receiving the ball?

Instrument for Formal Assessment

A skill assessment (that is as gamelike as possible) is very helpful in this lesson. To save time, incorporate as many of the relevant skills as is feasible into one assessment. The following assessment task, assessed using the rubric in table 13.3, might fit the bill:

- Assessment goal: To demonstrate the critical elements of the fundamental soccer skills of receiving, dribbling, and passing.
- Skill and task: Receive, dribble, and pass with the feet. Observe multiple repetitions of your students in a soccer practice setting. This can be done in pairs with one student acting as the feeder who rolls the ball to the performer. The performer receives the ball with the foot, dribbles 20 or 30 feet (6 or 9 m) to a designated line, and then passes the ball to a target (about 10 ft, or 3 m, wide) from a distance of 15 to 20 feet (4.6 to 6 m). If performed indoors, the target can be against a wall; if performed outside, this is best done in groups of three with the third player acting as the target.

Table 13.3 Rubric for Assessing Receiving, Dribbling, and Passing

Level	Criteria
Exceeds expectations	Demonstrates correct receiving technique.
	Dribbles with speed and passes with power to the target.
Meets expectations	Demonstrates correct receiving, dribbling. and passing technique (moves into line with the ball, uses the receiving foot to steer the ball in the required direction, keeps the ball close, passes with the inside or laces of the foot to the target).
Below expectations	Demonstrates incorrect receiving, dribbling, and passing technique.

LESSON 3:
Offensive Concept 2—Distribution of Possession

Focus: Distribution of possession (width in attack)

Learner focus:

- Using wide areas of the field to attack and get behind the opponents' defense (psychomotor and cognitive)
- Attacking the center of the goal area so that shooters are moving onto a crossed pass (psychomotor and cognitive)
- Cooperating with teammates to design an appropriate skill practice (cognitive)

Equipment: Soccer balls and cones

Setup: Multiple soccer fields of about 30 by 40 yards, if possible.

Learner Experiences

1. Students play 3v3 games on short and wide fields using width to attack.
2. Groups discuss how to use the width of the field to attack the goal.
3. Teams practice feeding the wings and finishing. Teams of six can use this time to create their own practices that combine passing out to the wing and then finishing with an attack on goal in the middle of the goal area. After a practice is started, ask the students how they can make it better or harder (figure 13.1 shows one possibility).
4. Students play 6v6 games with goalkeepers (with a width and depth focus), timing attacking runs to goal. Because the size of the teams has increased, the size of the field must also.

Modifications

Thoughtful groups develop a practice that involves passing to a wide player, who then crosses the ball for an oncoming shooter. Here are other modification ideas:

- To increase the level of challenge in the practice setting, require crossing from the other side of the field.
- Require really advanced students to cross the ball in the air.
- Place cones on the halfway line, about 10 yards from the sideline, and require that players move the ball around the outside of the cone before the team can attack the goal. This modification exaggerates the need for players to use the width of the field.

S = Shooters (pass to the crosser and move forward to receive and shoot)
C = Crossers (receive, dribble, and cross to the shooter)
R = Ball retriever
---➤ = Movement of players
⟶ = Path of ball

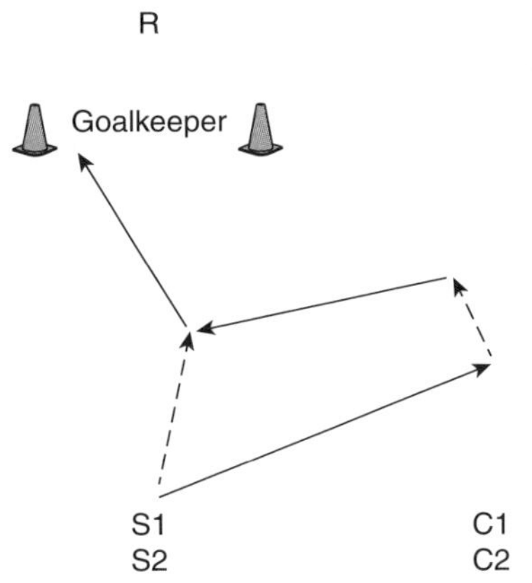

Figure 13.1 Finishing practice from a crossed pass.

Democracy in Action

Free inquiry: Communication

In the two previous lessons, students were involved in small and larger group discussions. In this lesson, they engage in the democratic process at a higher level by working within their teams to design their own practice tasks. This provides a strong test of the skills of communication, group dynamics, leadership, and cooperation.

Check for Learning

- What is the value of using the width of the field?
- What modifications did your team use to make the practice better?

Instruments for Formal Assessment

Learning outcomes for this lesson are varied, calling for varied means of assessment. The rubric in table 13.4 can be used to assess the performance outcomes related to using wide areas of the field.

The rubric in table 13.5 can be used to assess players' ability to cooperate appropriately as they develop skill practices within their teams.

Table 13.4 Rubric for Using Wide Areas of the Field

Level	Criteria
Exceeds expectations	In 3v3 (or 6v6) game play, students use wide areas of the field appropriately by passing the ball to a player in space, and then moving to shoot the crossed ball as it comes into the middle.
Meets expectations	In 3v3 (or 6v6) game play, students use wide areas of the field appropriately by passing the ball to a player in space and then moving to meet the crossed ball.
Below expectations	In 3v3 (or 6v6) game play, students play only through central areas of the field and ignore opportunities to use the space in wide areas of the field for attacking purposes.

Table 13.5 Rubric for Assessing Cooperation

Level	Criteria
Exceeds expectations	Leads, follows, and supports group members to improve play in cooperative and competitive settings.
Meets expectations	Consistently engages in appropriate cooperative behaviors in partnerships and groups. Behaviors include leading, following, and supporting group members to improve play in cooperative and competitive settings.
Below expectations	Engages in behaviors that are helpful to others after prompts or direction from the teacher, or does not engage in behaviors that are helpful to others.

LESSON 4:
Offensive Concept 3—Penetration and Scoring

Focus: The concept of penetration relates to players' ability to get the ball through the defense. This builds on lesson 3, which focused on getting the ball around the defense by using the more easily accessible wide areas of the field.

Learner focus:

- Attacking with penetrating passes between defenders (psychomotor and cognitive)
- Passing forward and moving into potential shooting positions (psychomotor and cognitive)

Equipment: Soccer balls and cones

Setup: 3v3 games in 30- by 20-yard areas with goals but no goalkeepers.

Learner Experiences

1. The narrow field requires that players make penetrating passes to move the ball forward into shooting positions. The field can be split into thirds with each team of three required to leave a player, designated as a target forward, in the attacking third. This player can receive the ball but cannot turn with it and cannot score.
2. Team discussions focus on ways to use the target forward to create scoring opportunities when that forward is not allowed to score. Supporting runs are needed by other players, and the forward needs to redistribute the ball to players making those runs. Practices can be done in teams of six in preparation for the next game.
3. In a team practice (figure 13.2), the shooter (S) passes to a target forward (T), makes a run for a return pass to position S2, and shoots on goal.
4. Students play 6v6 games with goalkeepers, in 50- by 30-yard areas. The aim in this game is to transfer the skill practice work into a larger game on a larger field.

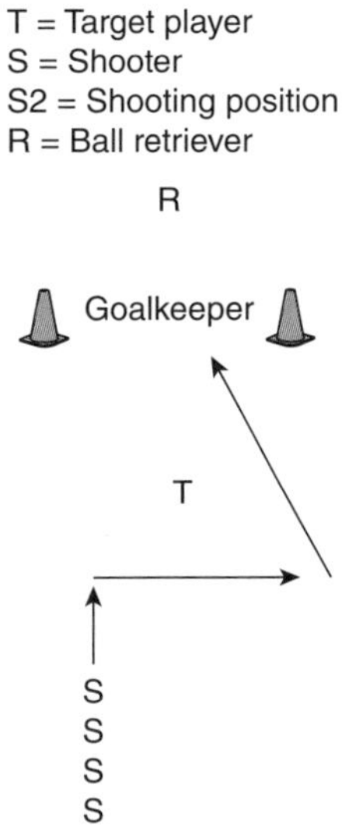

T = Target player
S = Shooter
S2 = Shooting position
R = Ball retriever

Figure 13.2 Shooting practice using a target forward.

Modifications

The condition, or enabling constraint, in the initial game (in which the target forward cannot score) is important because it forces players to think about ways to use that player to set up scoring opportunities for others. This can lead to good discussions as teams seek solutions. The condition can also be applied to the closing 6v6 game, but should be relaxed for a while before the conclusion of the lesson to see whether players can retain their tactical thinking in the absence of game conditions.

Democracy in Action

Decision making: Applying group policies to team tactics

As they address the problem of how to attack by using a target forward who is not allowed to score, teams of six can have some interesting and challenging discussions. The 6v6 game provides an opportunity to implement what they have discussed and practiced.

Check for Learning

- How did you solve the problem of using the target player to set up scoring chances?
- What is important about the passes you played to reach the target player, especially given that the field was narrow and a bit crowded?

Instrument for Formal Assessment

Although execution of the required skills during game play would be ideal, perhaps the most important and realistic outcome of this lesson is the cognitive learning related to positioning and decision making. Penetrating a defense is difficult, particularly on a narrow field; doing so first requires sound tactical decision making related to movement and skill selection. The rubric in table 13.6 can be used to evaluate decision making and movement in game situations.

Table 13.6   Rubric for Assessing Decision Making and Movement

Level	Decision making	Movement
Exceeds expectations	Consistently looks to make penetrating passes to the target forward.	Consistently supports the target forward by moving to receive a pass in a shooting position.
Meets expectations	Usually looks to make penetrating passes to the target forward.	Usually supports the target forward by moving to receive a pass in a shooting position.
Below expectations	Rarely looks to make penetrating passes to the target forward.	Rarely supports the target forward by moving to receive a pass in a shooting position.

LESSON 5:
Defensive Concept 1—Stopping the Opposing Team From Scoring

Focus: In this lesson we move from addressing offensive concepts to addressing defensive concepts, perhaps the most important of which is to prevent opponents from scoring. Clearly, this involves a goalkeeper, arguably the most important position on the field.

Learner focus:

- As goalkeepers, moving to narrow the angle for the shooter (cutting down the angle so the shooter has less of the goal to aim for; psychomotor and cognitive)
- Gathering the ball successfully at feet, waist, and head height (psychomotor)

Equipment: Soccer balls and cones

Setup: For the goalie challenge game (figure 13.3), set up three goals facing each other in a triangle. The goals are about 5 to 6 yards wide and about 10 to 15 yards apart.

Learner Experiences

1. Goalie challenge: Three goalies defend their own goals (goals are set up in a triangle). When in possession, each goalie rolls the ball to try to score through either of the other goals (figure 13.3).
2. Students discuss how to give the other goalies less of their own goals to shoot at.
3. Students continue to play goalie challenge.
4. Students discuss how best to gather the ball.

   - Feet: Get in line with the ball, place feet together, and gather the ball into the arms.
   - Waist: Get in line with the ball, keep the elbows in, catch the ball in the arms, and cradle it.

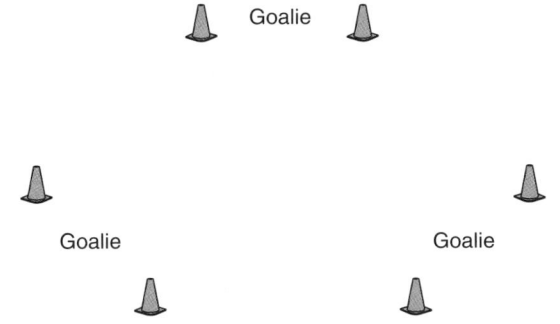

Figure 13.3 Positioning for goalie challenge.

- Head: Get in line with the ball, make a W with the hands, catch with the hands, and cradle it.

5. Students practice in pairs or triads gathering hand-fed balls at feet, waist, and head height.
6. Students play 3v3 with rotating goalkeepers.

Modifications

- In goalie challenge, the goals can be narrowed, widened, brought closer together, or spread farther apart as needed to challenge players or simplify the game.
- In goalie practice, vary the strength and distance of feeds.

Democracy in Action

Personal and social responsibility: Individual responsibilities to the group

Two discussion segments in this lesson provide opportunities for students to give input, share ideas, and listen to others' opinions. Students become aware of the importance of the goalkeeper as the last line of defense, and the responsibility this player has to the team.

Check for Learning

- In goalie challenge, what strategies did you use to make it harder for your opponents to score?
- What would goalies have to do if they cannot make a save and stay on their feet?

Instrument of Formal Assessment

Assessment of goalkeeping proficiency is best done using simple statistics related to goals conceded and rebounds given up from shots.

LESSON 6:
Defensive Concept 2—Denying Space

Focus: Defending 1v1 and denying space
Learner focus:

- Marking opponents as they move into attacking positions (psychomotor and cognitive)
- Pressuring the ball carrier and dictating the direction of play (psychomotor and cognitive)

Equipment: One soccer ball and four cones per group of six

Setup: 3v3 fields of about 30 by 20 yards, and 1v1 fields of about 20 by 10 yards.

Learner Experiences

1. Students play 3v3 games with rotating goalkeepers, with an emphasis on marking opposing players when the other team has the ball.
2. Students discuss marking positions, emphasizing getting closer to opponents when they get closer to the goal or to the ball.
3. Students continue 3v3 game play.
4. Students discuss how to make it more difficult for ball carriers to attack goal by channeling them into specific areas of the field (e.g., toward the sideline).
5. Students play 1v1 in 20- by 10-yard areas, practicing pressuring the ball carrier (closing down) and dictating the direction of play. Each player defends a 10-yard line; the two lines are 20 yards apart.
6. Students play 6v6 with rotating goalkeepers, emphasizing marking and pressuring the ball carrier.

Modifications

The following modifications might necessitate grouping teams according to playing ability.

- For higher-ability players, enlarge the playing area to make marking more difficult.
- For lower-ability players, decrease the size of the playing area to make marking easier.

Democracy in Action

Personal and social responsibility: Interpersonal communication

Discussions provide opportunities for players to give their input. The defensive focus also requires that players communicate with each other to ensure that all opposing players are marked.

Check for Learning

- How did you work as a team to defend the spaces close to your goal?
- What sorts of things did you need to communicate to each other?
- How did you defend individually in a 1v1 situation?

Instrument for Formal Assessment

Checking for learning in this lesson requires observing student performance in a game setting. The rubric in table 13.7 would be appropriate.

Table 13.7   Rubric for Assessing Defending Space

Level	Defending space
Exceeds expectations	Consistently moves to mark or guard opponents, to deny space, and to prevent opponents from attacking and scoring.
Meets expectations	Usually moves to mark or guard opponents, to deny space, and to prevent opponents from attacking and scoring.
Below expectations	Rarely moves to mark or guard opponents, to deny space, and to prevent opponents from attacking and scoring.

LESSON 7:
Transitional Concept 1—Obtaining Possession

Focus: Obtaining possession (high pressure and winning the ball back early)

Learner focus:

- After losing the ball, putting immediate pressure on opponents to regain possession
- Regaining possession of the ball with strong tackles in 50/50 situations.

Equipment: Soccer balls and cones

Setup: Fields of about 30 by 30 yards with end zones marked with cones.

Learner Experiences

1. In a 3v3 dribble-in game, players must dribble into an end zone to score. This provides many opportunities for defenses to win the ball back because the team in possession must keep the ball and move forward to score.
2. Students discuss the best place and time for a team to try to regain possession of the ball after losing it. Clearly, the sooner teams win the ball back, the less danger their own goal is in and the sooner they can attack again.
3. The 3v3 game continues with a focus on winning the ball back quickly.
4. Students discuss appropriate tackling technique (staying on the feet, getting close to the ball, having relaxed knees and firm ankles, blocking tackles with the inside of the foot).
5. Block tackling practice progresses to 1v1 in 10- by 10-yard spaces. The player who starts with the ball must try to get from one side of the square to the other without losing the ball. The defender's goal is to win the ball.
6. Students play a 3v3 dribble-in game.

Modifications

- Make game play and practice situations more difficult from a defensive point of view by enlarging the playing area.
- Make defending easier by shrinking the playing area.

Democracy in Action

Personal and social responsibility: Communication and individual responsibility

Student interactions take place mostly during game situations when players must communicate as they apply defensive pressure as a unit. Ultimately, players must accept responsibility individually for winning the ball back with solid block tackling when the opportunity presents itself.

Check for Learning

- How did you have to work as a team to defend your end zone?
- What did teammates need to do when the defender nearest the ball moved to close down an opponent?

Formal Assessment

In this lesson, as in lesson 5, the primary outcomes can be determined using simple statistics of the number of successful tackles recorded for both individuals and teams.

LESSON 8:
Transitional Concept 2—Regaining Possession

Focus: Defending as individuals and as a team
Learner focus:

- Delaying an attack or allowing time for teammates to recover (psychomotor and cognitive)
- Returning to a goal-side position to provide defensive cover for a teammate (psychomotor and cognitive)

Equipment: One soccer ball and four cones per group of six
Setup: Fields of about 30 by 30 yards with end zones marked with cones.

Learner Experiences

1. Students play a 3v3 dribble-in game in which they dribble into an end zone to score.

2. Students discuss what to do when defending against more than one attacker. The emphasis is on the first defender delaying an attack to give teammates time to recover.

3. Students play 2v1 in 20- by 10-yard areas. The goal is for the two attackers to get the ball from one end to the other as quickly as possible. The defender delays them as long as possible. See figure 13.4.

4. Extend the 2v1 games to include a recovering defender who starts level with the two attackers and has to get back behind a teammate as soon as possible, making it 2v2. Now, the two defenders try to win the ball back.

5. Students play 6v6, including goalkeepers, with an emphasis on team defending.

Modifications

Again, space can be modified to challenge or simplify the game. From a defensive point of view, larger spaces are more difficult to defend and smaller spaces are easier.

Democracy in Action

Personal and social responsibility: Team communication and cooperation

The focus on team defending necessitates small-group communication as players try to solve issues in the 2v1 situation. Cooperation among defending players is also important to ensure successful team defense.

Check for Learning

Successful tackles and accurate score keeping can be the most effective way to check for learning in this lesson. You might ask yourself, How did you and your teammate work together to make it harder for the attacking pair?

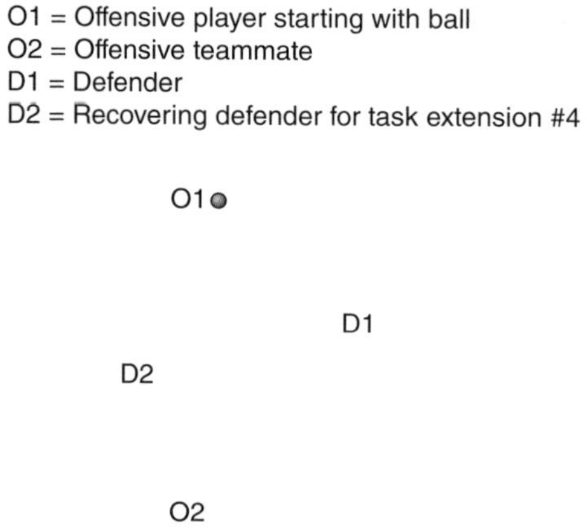

O1 = Offensive player starting with ball
O2 = Offensive teammate
D1 = Defender
D2 = Recovering defender for task extension #4

O1●

D1

D2

O2

Figure 13.4 Team defending practice.

SUMMARY

Much of the student learning in these lessons takes place during game play. Many teachers, particularly those early in their careers or without extensive games expertise, feel unsure of themselves during game play. However, focused game play provides the ideal context in which to experience the communication and collaborative processes of invasion games and to develop effective decision-making capabilities. So what does the process of teaching within the game involve?

First, it is important to observe students closely. As you do, ask yourself the following questions:

What is happening in the game(s)?

Is this what I want?

What changes do I need to make to help students play more effectively? Do I need to change the conditions? If so, do I need to change the conditions for the whole class or just for individuals?

Second, use two important strategies: freezing the game and reconstruction and rehearsal (which usually follow freezing the game). Either or both strategies are valuable tools, regardless of the type of game, but particularly in dynamic, free-flowing invasion games.

Freezing the game. Use freezing the game (stopping game play) to point out (in a constructive manner) appropriate and inappropriate performance. Players must freeze immediately in place so that the context of the situation is not lost. This requires using a prearranged signal for freezing promptly when a teachable moment occurs.

Reconstruction and rehearsal. Once the game is frozen, use the process of reconstruction to identify what happened, demonstrate appropriate performance, or critique inappropriate performance. If reconstruction is used for critique, then rehearsal can follow to facilitate learning the appropriate performance, taking a "this is what could happen" approach. Reconstruction and rehearsal are potentially useful for teaching decision making, a critical component of game performance. To many, this is synonymous with coaching. Indeed, I have heard teachers comment, "I do [reconstruction and rehearsal] all the time when I coach, but it never crossed my mind to do it during PE classes as well."

Invasion Game: Touch Football

Bobby Gibson

Mr. Gibson knows something is up with the class. The students are usually bright and bubbly at the start of a new games unit, looking forward to fun games and their teacher's on-the-fly ideas and changes. Today, everyone looks uninspired.

Mr. Gibson: Hi, Wayne. Ready to play? What's up?

Wayne (picking up a football from the equipment pile): Are we playing this?

Mr. Gibson: That's the plan. Why? Don't you like it?

Wayne: Not so much.

So that's it. Mr. Gibson looks around at his students.

Mr. Gibson: OK. Let's talk about football.

Yasmina: It's a boys' game. Girls can't play.

Don: 'Cause girls are too small.

Wayne: Some boys are too small, too. I've played with my brother's friends and I just got knocked over all the time.

Jo: Why can't they use a proper ball instead of these things?

Will: Those are regulation footballs. Come on, guys! Football is great. Everyone knows that. Look at the Super Bowl—it's the biggest thing on TV!

Jo: They're stupid. They bounce all weird and funny so you can't catch them. They're impossible to throw, except for people with giant hands. And the Super Bowl . . . . Throw the stupid ball. Stop. Talk. Throw the stupid ball again. Stop. Run on and off the field. I don't think anyone understands football. Even those who pretend they do. Do we *have* to play it?

The two things I hear from students in my physical education classes when I say we're going to be looking at football are usually *I don't like football* and *I'm not good at football*. Although it can be a lot of fun, football can also be confusing, and many students are quick to discount their ability. When we dig down into their experiences, their negative associations usually come from past experiences in which they felt too small to play or couldn't throw the ball. As a result, they don't want to play it again. The challenge is making the football experience novel and changing negative mind-sets and associations.

Football has important outcomes for students: working together as a team, mutual support, leadership, and determination. Modifying the game to highlight these benefits can result in students understanding the essence of the game, wanting to get better at it, and ideally continuing playing when they leave school. Enjoyment and engagement have an enormous impact on learning and long-term involvement in activity. When students like what they do in class, they may pursue it on their own time. Teaching as much as possible through active game play and inserting short drills in context can help students understand the purpose of drills and be more willing to give them a try.

Football can be complex and confusing or really simple. The common principle in all forms of football is that players have a specified number of attempts to cover at least 10 yards in trying to achieve the offensive focus: getting the ball across the goal line. Football is in the Teaching Games for Understanding (TGfU) invasion games category because it is based on territorial dominance as players attempt to score and restrict their opponents' opportunities to score. Football is, however, much more static than other invasion games such as basketball, soccer, and rugby; these games are in constant motion with few stoppages. Football's stop-and-start style of play is what most people unfamiliar with the sport find confusing and boring. Many people do not understand the need for so many stoppages, and neither do students, until they can create meaning for themselves. Sometimes students even ask for rules that require the game to stop more often to ensure that it is fair for both offense and defense and to allow for better competition.

PEDAGOGY

Much of my teaching is based on emergent and collective learning. Lessons are structured so that students learn from each other and create meaning together. Students actively work together to find solutions based on multiple possibilities. Emphasizing that there may be more than one correct answer (or no one correct answer) forces students to examine what they are doing in class and why. This helps immensely with developing class cohesion, mutual respect, and responsibility. Everyone has the potential to clarify, to make sense of what is going on in class, to contribute ideas, and to be accountable.

Students need encouragement to be creative when making decisions and making sense of what they are learning. Open-ended games and activities provide opportunities to create their own boundaries and rules. I encourage my students to look for loopholes in each activity; some of these may need to be closed to create smoother game play, whereas others enhance game play in ways I had not foreseen. As a result of exaggerating game concepts, students often request new rules to ensure fairness and promote challenging competition.

DEMOCRACY IN ACTION

The activities in this chapter place students in situations in which they create strategies and goals collectively. Free inquiry is a major part of the process: all students need to feel safe and comfortable voicing their opinions, to be heard, and to have the group work with their suggestions. The group process should not be restricted in how it looks and operates; all problems and obstacles should occur organically as the class takes shape. The result is that students genuinely work together and solve problems as a group, using skills they will need throughout their lives. Football provides excellent opportunities to discuss some of the complexities of leadership. Once a play is called, it can work only if members of the team implement it effectively, adapt and adjust creatively to changes that happen moment by moment, and support and encourage each other.

UNIT PLAN STRUCTURE

The lessons in this chapter are broken down into concepts, games, and activities (see table 14.1). Time lines and sequencing are absent, because each class

Table 14.1   Strategic Concepts and Skills for Touch Football

Lesson number and topic	Learner experiences	Democracy-in-action focus
1: Ultimate Football	Attacking the goal line by throwing, catching, and finding open space	**Personal and social responsibility:** Individual responsibilities to the group; group responsibilities to individuals; role of the leader and supporting players
	Establishing a team decision-making process and flickerball	
	Skill enhancement: Throwing, catching	
	Flickerball with extensions: Decision making regarding rules	
2: Flickerball	Creating and taking away space, dodging and evading, and tagging	**Decision making:** Group policy
	Flickerball extensions	
	Skill enhancement: Square tag	
	Flickerball extensions	
3: Flickerball Extended	Using the line of scrimmage (LOS), getting open, and defending a pass	**Personal and social responsibility and free inquiry:** Creating and taking opportunities; giving and receiving feedback
	Flickerball extensions: LOS	
	Skill enhancement: Defending a pass	
	Flickerball extensions	
	Minigames	

(continued)

Table 14.1 *(continued)*

Lesson number and topic	Learner experiences	Democracy-in-action focus
4: Team Concepts	Offensive and defensive team concepts	**Group process, decision making, and free inquiry:** Individual rights and responsibilities to the group; depending on good leadership; deciding when and when not to speak one's mind
	Minigames from lesson 3	
	Skill enhancement: Running pass patterns	
	Minigames	
5: Gamelike Situations	Concepts of downs and play design	**Group process:** Role of the official
	Three to score	
	Skill enhancement: Play design	
	Three to score	
6: Kicking	Territorial advantage and the role of kicking	**Personal and social responsibility:** Supporting team members who are in the spotlight
	Gainer's yards	
	Skill enhancement: Kicking the football	
	Three-down football	
7: Team Formation and Playbook Design	Team formation and playbook design	**Group process, decision making, and social justice:** Responsibilities of individuals to contribute; fairness in choosing plays; representing everyone in the playbook design
	Organizing teams	
	Playbook design	
	Scrimmage and playbook editing	
8: Game Play and Game Management	Game play and game management	**Free inquiry:** Peer assessment and group reflection
	Tournament play	
	Skill enhancement: Modifying playbooks	
	Tournament play and unit summary	

is unique. I've had some classes play an introductory game for an entire period, building off the initial concept, introducing new rule changes, and constantly adapting the game to keep it fresh for a full period. With the same lesson, another class may lose interest or motivation within the first 10 minutes. The students drive the timing and tempo; I provide an initial direction and a goal. I have discovered that when my students help me decide how to reach our goals, their experiences are more meaningful. I like to ask them for modifications or extensions before I introduce the ones I have; they are playing the game, so they will probably know what changes need to be made. In this unit, I want the students to invent the game of football. I do this by starting with a simpler game and adding or changing rules as necessary until we have reached our goal.

LESSON 1:
Ultimate Football

Focus: Attacking the goal line by throwing, catching, and finding open space

Learner focus:

- Understanding how to march or drive the ball (psychomotor)
- Throwing the ball downfield and catching it in the end zone (psychomotor)

Equipment: Cones, bibs, one football per pair

Setup: 3v3 in 20- by 20-yard fields, or 5v5 in 30- by 40-yard fields.

Sequence:

1. Flickerball
2. Skill enhancement: Throwing and catching
3. Flickerball with extensions

Learner Experiences

1. Students play flickerball the same way and with the same rules as ultimate (Frisbee), except with a football. Teams do not change sides after a score. The quarterback gets a 5-yard radius in which to throw the ball.
2. Skill enhancement work for throwing and catching a football can be accomplished with stationary partner passing.

Modifications

- Allow for one dropped ball to be reset where it would have been caught.
- Provide more time and space in which to throw the ball.
- After each completed pass, require that all players reset on their side of the ball. This introduces the line of scrimmage (LOS) and offside penalty.
- Require a certain number of tries to score (3-7, depending on class and skill level; number can be determined by the class) before it is their opponent's turn
- Assign one player as quarterback. Receivers place the ball on the ground where it was caught, and the quarterback runs up to restart play.
- Allow the receiver a certain number of steps or a certain distance or time period after catching the ball; the receiver turns into a ball carrier when in possession of the ball. The defense can stop the ball carrier with a tag.

Democracy in Action

Personal and social responsibility: Individual responsibilities to the group; group responsibilities to individuals; role of the leader and supporting players

In this game, the quarterback decides the play, although only by paying attention to the receiver who is open. Good leaders do not dominate the field; they are sensitive to changing conditions and opportunities. The quarterback role should be rotated, so that everyone can experience it. Students can consider the following questions:

- What are the qualities of a good quarterback? (Possible answers: Calmness under pressure, ability to see the big picture quickly, courageous risk taking, forward thinking)
- How does the team help the quarterback? (Answer: By being an available receiver)
- How does the quarterback improve his or performance? What kind of feedback might be helpful? How can other players make suggestions?

Check for Learning

Q: Which passes are the easiest to make?

A: Short passes.

Q: How can you separate from your defender?

A: Get the offensive player moving away from the ball, change direction, and come back to the ball.

LESSON 2:
Flickerball

Focus: Creating and taking away space, dodging and evading, and tagging

Learner focus: Understanding being open from both offensive and defensive perspectives (cognitive)

Setup: 3v3 in 20- by 20-yard fields, or 5v5 in 30- by 40-yard fields.

Sequence:

1. Flickerball
2. Skill enhancement: Square tag
3. Flickerball with extensions

Learner Experiences

1. Students play an extension of flickerball from the previous class that includes running with the ball. Following are rule additions:
   - Incomplete passes are turnovers.
   - When tagged (one hand), the ball carrier must stop and has 10 seconds to throw the ball.

2. Students play square tag focusing on both offensive skills (evading, advancing to the goal line) and defensive skills (taking away space, tagging).

- The alternative game of 10-yard square is played 1v1 (ball carrier vs. defender). The ball carrier starts with the ball, opposite the defender (each on an end line). Play starts when the ball carrier moves.
- Make the square bigger to increase the chance of offensive success.
- Introduce a pass to start the game.
- Make the playing field bigger (10 yards wide, 20 yards long) and award offensive points (1 point for every 5 yards of progress) and defensive points (1 point for every 5 yards away from the end zone).

3. Students resume playing flickerball.

Modifications

- Introduce the concept of downs (every incomplete pass or tag counts as a down). Players have a predetermined number of downs to get across the halfway line and then to score. Students should determine the number; if it is too low or too high, they can adapt it.
- Introduce the line of scrimmage (LOS).
- Require that only forward passes can be made after a tag, and everyone has to reset on the LOS.

Democracy in Action

Decision-making: Group policy

This unit should begin with students establishing a clear process for making decisions (see chapter 12). Students should answer the following questions:

- How will individuals know when to speak?
- How will decisions be made?
- How did you contribute to the group process?
- How did you help others to contribute?
- How would you rate your listening skills?
- What did you learn about group decision-making processes?
- Why is contributing important?

Check for Learning

Q: Why run with the ball instead of throwing it?
A: Less chance of a turnover—you are in control of the ball.
Q: Should you throw the ball before or after you are tagged?

A: After—you have time and space to make a good throw.

A: Before—if you have lots of time and space and you see someone who is open and has a better opportunity to advance the ball or score.

LESSON 3:
Flickerball Extended

Focus: Using the line of scrimmage (LOS), getting open, and defending a pass

Learner focus: Understanding why the line of scrimmage exists (cognitive)

Setup: 1v1 in a 10-yard square, or 2v2 in a field 20 yards wide and 15 yards long.

Sequence:

1. Warm-up: Flickerball extensions, introducing LOS
2. Skill enhancement: Square tag with a focus on defending pass
3. Skill insertion
4. Minigames
5. Flickerball with extensions

Learner Experiences

1. Students play square tag with a defensive focus in groups of three: one receiver, one defender, and one quarterback (change roles every one to three plays). Following is a point system:

   • Receiver: 1 point for a catch, 1 point for forward progress, 1 point for a score
   • Defender: 1 point for knocking down the ball, tagging, or preventing a score, 2 points for an interception
   • Quarterback: 1 point if the receiver touches the ball, 1 point for a catch

Students change groups regularly to have opportunities to work with different players.

The skill insertion for this lesson focuses on defending a receiver, as follows:

■ Backward running (students need to feel comfortable moving backward and changing direction)
■ Shadow games: Students are in pairs (one receiver, one defender). The receiver jogs from one end line to the other in a zigzag manner. The defender moves backward, keeping the receiver in front of him while trying to mirror his movements. This drill is for the benefit of defenders; receivers should try make them work hard, not just run past them.

Modifications

- Permit hand-offs to remove the need to catch.
- Require that the defender wait on the goal line until the ball is caught; this aids hesitant or unskilled receivers.
- Make the square bigger to provide more options for the receiver and make the task more difficult for the defender.
- Introduce the concept of downs, and limit the number of downs to score.
- Allow defenders to start wherever they want.

Democracy in Action

Personal and social responsibility and free inquiry: Creating and taking opportunities; giving and receiving feedback

Feedback is a kind of mirroring or active noticing of someone's behavior and actions. Feedforward builds on such noticing with constructive suggestions. After each game of square tag, each player can offer one piece of feedback and one piece of feedforward to each of the other two players. Feedback could include something done well (I found it hard to defend you because you changed direction quickly). Feedforward could include a suggestion for the next round (What would happen if you ran slower at first; then sped up?).

Check for Learning

Q: What is the line of scrimmage?

A: It is an imaginary line on the ground on which the ball is placed at the beginning of the play.

Q: When defending a receiver, should you be looking at the receiver or the quarterback?

A: You should be watching the receiver.

Q: What kind of things do you do as a receiver to fake out the defender?

A: Head fakes, flashing hands, changing speed, changing direction.

Q: What was the best kind of feedback or feedforward you got?

Q: Did giving feedback make you see anything differently?

LESSON 4:
Offensive and Defensive Team Concepts

Focus: Offensive and defensive systems, running pass patterns, 1v1 defensive cover

Learner focus:

- Understanding pass patterns and offensive strategy (psychomotor and cognitive)
- Continuing to develop defensive cover (psychomotor and cognitive)

Sequence:

1. Warm-up: Flickerball, using the rules from the last class
2. Square minigames from lesson 3
3. Skill enhancement: Running pass patterns
4. Minigames

Learner Experiences

1. Students do skill work focused on running pass patterns (see figure 14.1), as follows:

   - They are in groups of five or six.
   - One player is a quarterback; the others are receivers.
   - Receivers run the pass pattern, taking turns, and the quarterback throws the pass.
   - Once all students have run the pattern, a new quarterback is chosen.
   - The easiest patterns are: fly, in, out, and hook. In these patterns the receiver moves in all four directions: left, right, downfield, and back to the quarterback.

Passing Tree
0. **Hitch:** 1 step, turn to QB; if not there, run 9
1. **5 yard out**
2. **Quick slant:** Break at 2 yards
3. **Deep out:** Break at 10 yards
4. **Hook:** Break at 10 yards, work back to QB
5. **Corner:** Break at 10 yards
6. **Deep in:** Break at 10 yards
7. **Post corner:** First break at 10 yards, second after two or three steps (turn DBs hips)
8. **Post:** Break at 10 yards
9. **Fly:** Get down field, look at 10 yards

For all pass patterns
- Mark sharp, deliberate cuts
- When you cut, lower hips, turn head first, and show the QB your hands

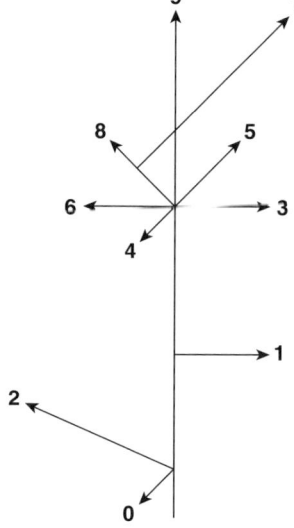

Figure 14.1 Running pass patterns.

2. The focus of the minigames is the communication between the quarterback and the receiver. Use two groups of three at the same square: one receiver, one defender, and one quarterback (change roles regularly). The receiver must get pass patterns from the quarterback. Quarterbacks call the plays because they are in charge in the huddle, so it is good practice to start now. Use the following point system:

   • Receiver: 1 point each for catching, making forward progress, and scoring (maximum of 3 points per play)
   • Defender: 1 point for knocking down the ball, tagging, or preventing a score, 2 points for intercepting
   • Quarterback: 1 point if the receiver touches the ball, 1 point for catching (maximum of 2 points per play)

Modifications

- Have no defender, to assist the quarterback with throwing.
- Require that the defender wait on the goal line until the ball is caught.
- Use two receivers and one defender. The defender chooses one receiver to cover and leaves the other open. This helps the quarterback with decision making.
- Have students play downs to score. Let them determine how many tries they get to score.
- Allow defenders to start wherever they want.
- Increase the field size or the number of receivers or defenders.

Democracy in Action

Group process, decision making, and free inquiry: Individual rights and responsibilities to the group; depending on good leadership; deciding when and when not to speak one's mind

Sometimes there just isn't time to process things to death! The huddle in football provides a good example. Members of a strong team have practiced cooperation, understand the capabilities and strengths of individual players, and have had input into the team's strategies and directions. In the huddle, the quarterback draws on this history to make the best decision for the next play. The quarterback's job is to make the best possible decision given the circumstances. The team's job is to carry it out. This is an excellent opportunity for learners to consider when it is OK to argue and debate, and when it's necessary to trust someone else.

Check for Learning

Q: Why is it important for both the quarterback and the receiver to know what pattern the receiver is running?

A: This gives the offense an advantage over the defense; the quarterback shouldn't have to guess.

Q: As a receiver, how do you get open when running your pattern?

A: Head fakes, change of speed or direction, running the pass pattern at full speed.

Q: When playing quarterback, how do you know when to throw the ball?

A: When the receiver has made a break and shows me his hands.

Q: Why does the quarterback call the plays in a huddle?

A: There isn't time for debate.

Q: What qualities does the quarterback need?

A: Knowledge of teammates' individual strengths, decisiveness, clear communication.

LESSON 5:
Gamelike Situations

Focus: Game rules, understanding the concept of downs, play design

Learner focus: Creating gamelike situations (psychomotor and cognitive)

Setup: Three players per team play in a field 20 yards wide and 15 yards long; a cone designates the line of scrimmage.

Sequence:

1. Warm-up: Flickerball using the rules from the last class
2. Three to score game
3. Skill enhancement: Play design
4. Three to score game

Learner Experiences

1. The goals of the game three to score are as follows:

   - The offense tries to get the ball across the goal line in three or fewer plays.
   - The defense tries to prevent the ball from crossing the goal line for three plays.

   Use the following guidelines to play:

   - Team A is on offense to start and has three downs to get the ball across the goal line.
   - Team B is on defense to start and tries to prevent team A from scoring.
   - Offense: All three players are involved in the play (one quarterback and two receivers); the quarterback must pass within five seconds.

- Defense: Only two players are involved in the play; the other player is the referee, whose job is to count the five seconds, spot the tag, and call interference.
- On a completed pass and tag, the ball advances to the spot of the tag, and a new down begins.
- If the defending team intercepts a pass, it is a turnover, and it is that team's turn to try to score.
- Points for offense only: One score = 1 point

2. Skill work focuses on designing a play. Players can think of the field as divided into four quadrants (for quarterbacks who cannot throw the ball very far) or as a tic-tac-toe board (for quarterbacks who have stronger arms). The idea is to have one receiver in each zone before having more than one receiver in any one zone. This is a tactical insertion that requires a short discussion and time for students to develop some plays.

Modifications

Introduce one extension at a time to give students ample time to explore the changes and develop their strategies.

- Allow one hand-off per three downs.
- Give the quarterback unlimited time to throw the ball.
- Create a no-defense zone; defenders may not cross the line until the ball has been caught.
- Increase the size of the field or the number of players per team, or both.
- Give the offense more plays.
- Add a defender as a rusher (starting 5 to 10 yards from the LOS), and allow the quarterback to run if the rusher crosses the LOS.

Democracy in Action

Group process: Role of the official

This is the first time, in this unit, that learners have officially served as referees, so this is a good time to consider this role. Before playing, students (with teacher guidance) decide on the nature of the infractions and appropriate signals for them. It is also necessary to consider the referee's role in general (see chapter 12).

Check for Learning

Q: Do you have to try to score on every play?

A: No. If you make three shorter plays and score, it is worth the same number of points.

Q: How does the team decide who will run what pattern?

A: The quarterback makes the decision in the huddle.

Q: Why do you huddle before every play?

A: So that all players know their roles.

Q: What have you learned about the official's role?

Q: What skills do you need to learn for this role?

Q: How has the experience of playing changed with the inclusion of the official?

LESSON 6:
Kicking

Focus: Understanding the role of kicking in football

Learner focus: Using kicks in football to maintain a territorial advantage (psychomotor and cognitive)

Sequence:

1. Gainer's yards game
2. Skill insertion: Kicking practice
3. Three-down football game

Learner Experiences

1. Students play gainer's yards on 30- by 50-yard fields. The goal is to kick the ball across the opponent's goal line without them catching it. Following are the rules:

   - Three players per team are in an alternating order for kicking the ball (regardless of who catches it or touches it first).
   - One team starts with the ball on its goal line and tries to kick it across the opponents' goal line. If successful, the team gets 1 point.
   - If the ball hits the ground, the opposing team picks it up and kicks it back from where the player picked the ball up (or where it went out of bounds).
   - If a player on the receiving team catches the ball, she can advance the ball five big steps before trying a kick. If a player catches the ball after it crosses the goal line, she gets five big steps forward; if she manages to get back past her goal line, the other team does not get a point.

2. Skill work focuses on punting, as follows:

   - Partners practice punt passing.
   - Students engage in punt-pass relays.
   - Students play 500 in groups of three to five (one kicker; the others are receivers). The kicker calls out point values for kicks (e.g., 100, 50); if the kick is caught, the receiver gets those points. Whoever gets to 500 first is the new kicker.

3. Students play three-down football on 30- by 50-yard fields. The goal is to run or catch the ball across the opponents' goal line. Following are the rules:

- Five people are on each team (offense: one quarterback, four receivers; defense: four defenders, one referee).
- The game starts with one team kicking the ball to the other team. If the ball is caught, the receiving team gets to take five steps forward and marks a new LOS.
- The offense has three downs to make 10 yards or to score. If the offense is on their side of half, they must kick the ball on the third down. If they are the other side of half, they can choose to kick or gamble (try to make the 10 yards or score), but they must tell their opponents what they are going to do.
- If the defending team intercepts the ball, it starts from the spot of the tag after the catch.
- The quarterback must pass within five seconds and may not run with the ball.
- Hand-offs are not allowed.

Modifications

Gainer's Yards

Introduce one extension at a time, giving the students ample time to explore the changes and develop their strategies.

- Allow the kicker to take steps forward before kicking the ball.
- Have a minimum distance the ball needs to travel. No matter how far the ball is kicked, the other team must treat it as though it has been kicked at least 20 yards.
- Allow for a throw instead of a kick.
- Do not award steps for catching the ball.
- Require three steps forward for a ball that is kicked out of bounds.
- Require steps backward for kicks that are not caught.

Three-Down Football

Introduce one extension at a time.

- Increase the number of downs to make 10 yards or to score.
- Allow for a throw instead of a kick.
- Introduce a rusher, who must start 5 yards back from the LOS on his abdomen.

Democracy in Action

Personal and social responsibility: Supporting team members who are in the spotlight

Any player who has to perform an action under the spotlight will experience peer pressure. For many students (especially those who are physically self-conscious or unathletic), performing under peer scrutiny feels like the ultimate humiliation. This is a good time to talk about how the team supports individual players. How do we encourage someone who is up to take a kick (or free hit, or penalty, or penalty corner, or is simply up at bat)? How do we respond if the performance is less than perfect?

Check for Learning

Q: Where do you try to kick the ball?

A: Where the opponent cannot easily get to it.

Q: Is it better to kick the ball really high in the air or to have it bounce?

A: Whichever way gets you the most distance.

Q: Why should the receiving team catch the ball?

A: It gives them an immediate chance to advance the ball.

Q: How can you encourage someone who is going up to take a kick?

A: By showing strong support.

Q: How should you react if someone makes a poor kick?

A: Turn poor play or mistakes into an opportunity to galvanize the team, creating an "It's us against the world!" mentality.

LESSON 7:
Team Formation and Playbook Design

Focus: Team formation

Learner focus: Football game play (psychomotor and cognitive)

Sequence:

1. Volunteer quarterbacks
2. Team selection
3. Playbook design
4. Scrimmage
5. Playbook editing

Learner Experiences

Ask for students willing to play the quarterback position (some may feel more comfortable if they know someone else on their team is also willing to play quarterback). Anyone can play quarterback. They just need to ensure that all teams have a quarterback.

The goal is to design a playbook for the tournament to take place in the following class. Give students a sample playbook, and provide feedback on their work as needed. Make sure they understand why it's important to have a playbook (so everyone knows what the team's plan is and there is time to practice). The game is played as follows:

- The field is 30 yards wide by 50 yards long.
- Teams have three downs to make 10 yards. Failure to make 10 yards results in a turnover at the spot of the ball.
- The defense must count five seconds for the quarterback to throw the ball, at which point, the quarterback must throw.
- Hand-offs are not permitted.
- On the third down, the offense must declare either a kick or a gamble. If kicking, the defense goes back to catch it and starts on offense from where the ball is caught or from where it went out of bounds.

Democracy in Action

Group process, decision making, and social justice: Responsibilities of individuals to contribute; fairness in choosing plays; representing everyone in the playbook design

As team members make decisions about strategies, to design a playbook, this is a good time to revisit the group decision-making processes begun in lesson 2. As described in chapter 12, the next step is to consider individual accountability within the group process. Following are guidelines:

- You have the right to speak or not to speak in group discussions.
- There are consequences to not speaking or not voting; you have to accept choices that you were not involved in making.
- Once decisions are made, it is important that everyone supports and owns them. This is the essence of consensus, and it helps to avoid resentment.

Check For Learning

Q: How can you be involved on every play?
A: By running my route as best I can.
Q: How would you rate your team's process in designing the playbook?
Q: Did your playbook draw on the strengths of all team members?

LESSON 8:
Game Play and Game Management

Focus: Game play, self-management, self-officiating
Learner focus: Applying the skills and tactics learned in the unit in a game setting (psychomotor and cognitive)

Setup: Teams of five students. Each game to played on a field area 30 yards wide by 50 yards long.

Sequence:

1. Tournament play
2. Time to modify plays and make changes to the game
3. Resume tournament play

Learner Experiences

The goal is to execute the playbook and win the tournament. Game time depends on all teams getting to play against each other during the class in a round-robin tournament. The team with the best record wins. Offense starts by receiving a kick from the opposing team. They scrimmage from where they catch the ball or from where it goes out of bounds. Teams can make rule changes to create better competition and greater involvement. See lesson 7 for rules and adaptations.

Modifications

- Introduce one extension at a time.
- Allow for one hand-off every set of three downs.
- Remove kicking from the game and go back to a predetermined number of downs to score from a certain point (e.g., from the half way line or 25 yards from the end zone). If a team doesn't score, the other team takes the ball back to the starting line and has a turn.
- Increase the number of downs to make 10 yards (to either four or five).
- Add a rusher and remove the five-second rule.
- Do not require teams to declare whether they are going to kick or gamble. The defense has to be ready for either scenario.
- Make hand-offs legal at any time.

Democracy in Action

Free inquiry: Peer assessment and group reflection

The end-of-unit tournament tests the capacity of each team to play intelligently, coherently, and determinedly. It offers players the chance to put what they have learned into practice and to contribute to the team. Possibilities for assessment include peer assessment and teammate review (see tables 14.2 and 14.3); a final team debrief after peer assessments have been shared (What did we do well? What could we have improved?); MVP awards (recognizing affective and cognitive as well as psychomotor skills); and individual reflections or journaling. Assessment is also done through teacher observation, formative questioning, and analyzing the final playbook.

Table 14.2 Touch Football Rubric

	5	4	3	2	1
Team offense	Runs all pass patterns with full effort. Runs pass patterns in the correct zone or area. Is more concerned about team success than individual glory. Fully understands team strategy.	Runs all pass patterns with full effort. Runs pass patterns in the correct zone or area. Is more concerned about team success than individual glory. Is not concerned with team strategy, only with his or her role.	Runs all pass patterns with full effort. Grumbles a little about not getting the ball. Is not concerned with team strategy, only with his or her role.	Runs hard only when in a position to get the ball. Complains about not getting the ball enough.	Concerned only with being the person in the spotlight. Does not know the playbook. Does not understand what the team strategy is.
Team defense	Understands role within the team concept. Fulfills his or her job to the team first and then helps others. Can play both zone defense and cover 1.	Fulfills his or her job to the team, but may not comprehend the overall strategy. Can play both zone defense and cover 1.	Does not comprehend the team strategy and needs to be told what to do. Can play both zone defense and cover 1.	Does not comprehend the team strategy and has trouble following team directions. Can play either zone defense or cover 1, but not both.	Does not understand what they are supposed to be doing on defense.
Football concepts	Completely understands the rules of football: • Offside • Three or four downs • Huddle • Forward pass • Territorial advantage	Understands most of the concepts covered in class.	Understands a couple of the concepts covered in class.	Is still confused about some of the concepts covered in class.	Does not really seem to understand what is going on.
Team concepts	Helps teammates. Is more concerned about fair play than winning. Helps to manage the game. Is willing to accept whatever role asked to play within the team. Tries to identify teammates' strengths. Takes on a leadership role.	Helps teammates. Is more concerned about fair play than winning. Takes on a leadership role.	Tries to help teammates. Will take on a leadership role only if asked. Cannot help with game management.	Does not work well with teammates. Will not accept a leadership role.	Needs to be given directions every play. Does not care about what the team is doing. Does not understand the game well enough to help manage it.

Table 14.3 Touch Football Peer Evaluation

Instance or situation	Offense													Defense						
	Maintains possession of the ball						Off-ball		On-ball				Off-the-ball	
	Receives and controls the ball.		Passes the ball.		Advances the ball into opponents' territory.		Advances to open space in opponents' territory.		Forces opponent to make fast decisions.		Forces opponent into space away from own goal.		Forces opponent away from own goal.	
	Yes	No	Yes	No	Yes	No	Yes	No	Yes	No	Yes	No	Yes	No
1														
2														
3														
4														
5														
Total														

From J.I. Butler, 2016, *Playing fair* (Champaign, IL: Human Kinetics).

SUMMARY

My experiences with TGfU have helped me to look at football from a new angle—to find the many small games within the larger game and to break down the skills and concepts football shares with other games in the TGfU invasion games classification. Combining TGfU with democracy in action is a great way to tangibly and explicitly teach many of the life skills attributed to being inherent in sports: leadership, decision making, teamwork, taking initiative, and democratic processes. What you see in this chapter is by no means intended as the final product of my exploration of teaching football. It is merely a snapshot of the current framework for my classes, and it changes with every new group of students I see.

15

Final Thoughts

The Teaching Games for Understanding (TGfU) approach, which focuses on connection and transfer, takes several steps away from the more traditional focus of physical educators on proficiency in techniques and skills in isolation. The inventing games process embedded in the TGfU approach takes even larger steps toward a bigger educational purpose. This move helps learners to develop across physical, ethical, cognitive, and social dimensions and to practice critical analyses, interpretations, dispositions, and attributes that they will find useful as engaged global citizens. As TGfU focuses more on the why before the how, so inventing games encourages students to think and feel before they do. The classroom becomes more participatory and democratic as learners embrace both autonomy and responsibility. The decision-making processes that emerge from the authentic, adaptive learning culture central to the inventing games process transfer to conduct and decision making in the playing arena and, by extension, to other life skills.

In physical education, we owe a debt to Thorpe, Bunker, and Almond, who founded TGfU in the 1980s. Since then, there have been many interpretations and iterations of the original model across the globe that we can refer to as games-centered approaches (GCAs). TGfU's biannual international conferences (TGfU seminar and AIESEP world congresses), website, and many publications attest to the fact the movement is alive and well (www.tgfuinfo.weebly.com). Although time spent in physical education has been, sadly, reduced, because administrators believe that they must obey the imperatives of quantifiable outcomes and standardized testing in other subject areas, good practice is, thankfully, alive and well. It is for this reason that I leave the final words where they belong, in the hearts and minds of teachers, coaches, and students committed to experiential learning across the educational domains.

> In our study [on inventing games], both elementary and secondary teachers initially believed that a controlled class was conducive to learning. "Control" in this sense was defined as the teacher giving instruction or demonstrating and the students doing what they are told. In preparation for teaching their inventing games and TGfU units, the teachers worked hard to redefine "control" as "controlled chaos."
>
> *Sarah Taylor, graduate research assistant,*
> *now physical educator, Whitehorse, BC*

■ ■ ■ ■ ■

Writing a unit and teaching has become a very complex and dynamic process for me. I am slowly learning to balance student learning and understanding with motivation and engagement level, assessment and the context of PE, my school, and the district, not to mention the needs of every individual student. I think I am well on my way if my classroom remains a place of teacher inquiry, communication, observation, and exploration involving teacher AND students, while I try to stay current with methodology and content.

Anja Berning, head of a physical education department

■ ■ ■ ■ ■

An issue that I have always struggled with is how Physical Education (PE) teachers group students for games. Our inventing games (IG) unit provided an excellent venue to see what would happen if I addressed this with students. What students learned from the first showcase was that a game where teams are unbalanced in terms of skill, development and/or experience will be ruined. I challenged each group to think about a better team-making policy.

Kevin Sandher, secondary school teacher

■ ■ ■ ■ ■

As a result of teaching and coaching through an altered lens—TGfU and Inventing Games—as well as co-coaching and mentoring, I have noticed a change in my pedagogical awareness. I'm able to make quicker and more conscious decisions about the way I teach PE and coach sport. In fact, I'm more aware of being a facilitator during Inventing Games units, being a coach during extracurricular activities, and being a teacher during new lessons. I'm working on wearing and switching those three hats within units or lessons in order to best meet the needs of my students and in a variety of specific situations.

Sarah Marshall, elementary school teacher

■ ■ ■ ■ ■

When teachers and coaches problem-solve too much for their students and their players, they create students and players who are more dependent on their teachers and coaches than on their own ability to search, problem-solve and create. Problem-solving and creativity are life skills, and it has become more and more critical for students to be exposed to them as they progress through school or a team season. The skills we are discussing transfer on and off the volleyball court, from the volleyball court to the classroom, and to daily life. As the global environment becomes more technologically advanced, the need for increased exposure to opportunities to solve problems and be creative is more profound.

Adriano DeSouza, Louisiana Tech University coach

■ ■ ■ ■ ■

References

Allison, P., & Barrett, K. (2000). Constructing children's physical education experiences. Boston: Allyn & Bacon.

Almond, L. (1983). Games making. *Bulletin of Physical Education*, 19 (1), 32-35.

Almond, L. (2010). Revisiting the TGfU brand. In J. Butler & L. Griffin L. (Eds.), *More Teaching Games for Understanding: Moving globally* (pp. VII-X). Champaign, IL: Human Kinetics.

Bailey, L. (1983). Striking/fielding games. In L. Spackman (Ed.), *Teaching Games for Understanding* (pp. 53-55). Cheltenham, UK: The College of St. Paul & St. Mary, Curriculum Development Centre.

Balyi, I., Way, R., & Higgs, C. (2013). Long-Term Athlete Development. Champaign, IL, USA: Human Kinetics. Retrieved from http://www.ebrary.com

Bandura, A. (1986). *Social foundations of thought and action: A social cognitive theory*. Englewood Cliffs, NJ: Prentice Hall.

Boyce, W.F., King, M.A., & Roche, J. (2008). *Healthy settings for young people in Canada*. Ottawa, ON: Public Health Agency of Canada. www.publichealth.gc.ca.

Bruner, J.S. (1977). *The process of education: A landmark in educational theory*. Cambridge, MA: Harvard University Press.

Bunker, D., & Thorpe, R. (1982). A model for the teaching of games in secondary schools. *Bulletin of Physical Education*, 10 (1), 9-16.

Bunker, D., & Thorpe, R. (1986a). The curriculum model. In R. Thorpe, D. Bunker, & L. Almond (Eds.), *Rethinking games teaching* (pp. 7-10). Loughborough, UK: Loughborough University of Technology.

Bunker, D., & Thorpe, R. (1986b). From theory to practice. In D. Bunker, & R. Thorpe (Eds.), *Rethinking games teaching* (pp. 11-14). Loughborough, UK: Loughborough University of Technology.

Butler, J. (1993) Teacher change in sport education. Dissertation Abstracts International, 54 02A, (UMI No. 9318198)

Butler, J. (2005). *Democracy in action using an inventing games unit.* Paper presented at International Conference (3rd) of Teaching Games for Understanding (TGfU) in Physical Education and Sport. Hong Kong, China.

Butler, J. (2006a). *Coaching softball using a constructivist approach*. Richmond, BC: International Softball Coaches Symposium.

Butler, J. (2006b). Curriculum constructions of ability: Enhancing learning through teaching games for understanding (TGfU) as a curriculum model. *Sport, Education and Society*, 11 (3), 243-258. doi:10.1080/13573320600813408

Butler, J. (2013). Stages for children inventing games. *Journal of Physical Education, Recreation and Dance*, 84 (4), 48-53.

Butler, J., Sullivan, S., McGinley, S., & Vjanjes, M. (2007). Teaching Danish longball to introduce striking games. *The Physical and Health Education Journal*, 73 (3), 29-33.

Calaprice, A. (2011). *The ultimate quotable Einstein*. Princeton, New Jersey: Princeton University Press.

Castle, K. (1990). Children's invented games. *Childhood Education,* 67 (2), 82-85. doi: 10.1080/00094056.1990.10521587

Centres, C. S. (2005). *Canadian sport for life: Long-term athlete development: Resource paper V2* Canadian Sport Centres.

Corbin, C.B. (2002). Physical activity for everyone: What every physical educator should know about promoting lifelong physical activity. *Journal of Teaching in Physical Education,* 21 (2), 128-144.

Cragg, S., Cameron, C., Craig, C., & Russell, S. (1999). Canada's children and youth: A physical activity profile. Ottawa, ON: Canadian Fitness and Lifestyle Research Institute.

Curtner-Smith, M.D. (1996). Teaching for understanding: Using games invention with elementary children. *Journal of Physical Education, Recreation & Dance,* 67 (3), 33-37. doi:10.1080/07303084.1996.10607218

Davis, B., Sumara, D., & Luce-Kapler, R. (2008). *Engaging minds: Changing teaching in a complex world* (2nd ed.). New York: Routledge.

De Castell, S., & Jenson, J. (2003). OP-ED serious play. *Journal of Curriculum Studies,* 35(6), 649-665. doi:10.1080/0022027032000145552

Den Duyn, N. (1997). *Game sense - Developing thinking players workbook*, Australian Sports Commission, Canberra.

Donnelly, F.C., Mueller, S., & Gallahue, D.L. (2016). *Developmental physical education for all children.* Champaign, IL: Human Kinetics.

Ellis, M. (1983). A games classification system, Paper presented at AIESEP International Conference on Team Games, Rome, Italy.

Ellis, M. (1986). Making and shaping games. In R. Thorpe, D. Bunker, & L. Almond (Eds.), *Rethinking games teaching* (pp. 61-65). Loughborough, UK: Department of Physical Education and Sports Science, Loughborough University of Technology.

Emdin, C. (2013). 5 reasons why current anti-bullying initiatives don't work. Retrieved from www.huffingtonpost.com/christopher-emdin/5-reasons-why-antibullyin_b_1017810.html

Fitts, P.M., & Posner, M.I. (1967). *Human performance.* Belmont, CA: Brooks/Cole.

Freire, P. (1989). *Pedagogy of the oppressed.* New York: Continuum.

García López, L. M., Contreras Jordán, O. R., Penney, D., & Chandler, T. (2009). The role of transfer in games teaching: Implications for the development of the sports curriculum. *European Physical Education Review,* 15(1), 47-63.

Gilligan, C. (1982). *In a different voice: Psychological theory and women's development.* Cambridge, MA: Harvard University Press.

Goodlad, J.I., Mantle-Bromley, C., & Goodlad, S.J. (2004). *Education for everyone: Agenda for education in a democracy.* San Francisco: Jossey-Bass.

Graf, C., Koch, B., Kretschmann-Kandel, E., Falkowski, G., Christ, H., Coburger, S., & Tokarski, W. (2004). Correlation between BMI, leisure habits and motor abilities in childhood (CHILT-project). *International Journal of Obesity,* 28 (1), 22-26.

Gregg, M., Seigworth, G.J. (2010). The affect theory reader. Durham & London: Duke University Press.

Hellison, D., & Martinek, T. (2006). Social and individual responsibility programs. In D. Kirk, D. Macdonald, & M. O'Sullivan (Eds.), *The handbook of physical education* (pp. 610-626). Thousand Oaks, CA: Sage.

Hofferth, S.L., & Sandberg, J.F. (2001). How American children spend their time. *Journal of Marriage and Family*, 63 (2), 295-308.

Hopper, T. (2003). Four Rs for tactical awareness: Applying game performance assessment in net/wall games. *Journal of Teaching Elementary Physical Education,* 4 (2), 16-21.

Hopper, T. (2007). Teaching tennis with assessment "for" and "as" learning: A TGfU net/wall example. *Journal of Physical and Health Education*, 73 (3), 22-28.

Hopper, T. (2011). Game-as-teacher: Modification by adaptation in learning through game-play. *Asia-Pacific Journal of Health, Sport and Physical Education,* 2 (2), 3-21. doi:10.1080/18377122.2011.9730348

Horowitz, F. D. (2000). Child development and the PITS: Simple questions, complex answers, and developmental theory. *Child Development*, 71(1), 1-10.

Howarth, K., Fisette, J., Sweeney, M., & Griffin, L. (2010). Unpacking tactical problems in invasion games: Integrating movement concepts into games education. In J. Butler & L. Griffin L. (Eds.), *More Teaching Games for Understanding: Moving globally* (pp. 245-256). Champaign, IL: Human Kinetics.

Ifedi, F., Canadian Government EBook Collection, & Statistics Canada. Culture, Tourism and the Centre for Education Statistics. (2008). *Sport participation in canada, 2005.* Ottawa, ON: Statistics Canada, Culture, Tourism and the Centre for Education Statistics.

International Olympic Committee (2015). Olympic Charter, Lausanne, Switzerland: DidWeDo S.a.r.l.

Jacobson, L. (2008). Children's lack of playtime seen as troubling health, school issue. Ed Week on line. Retrieved from http://www.edweek.org/ew/articles/2008/11/17/14play.h28.html?print=1

Jewett, B.L., & Ennis, C. (1995). *The curriculum process in physical education*. Madison, IA: Brown and Benchmark.

Kretchmar, S. (2005). Teaching games for understanding and the delights of human activity. In L. Griffin, & J.I. Butler (Eds.), *Teaching games for understanding: Theory, research and practice* (pp. 199-212). Champaign, IL: Human Kinetics.

Lockwood, A. (2000). Breadth and balance in the physical education curriculum. In S. Capel & S. Piotrowski (Eds.), *Issues in Physical Education* (pp. 117-130) London: Routledge.

Luce-Kapler, R., Sumara, D., & Davis, B. (2002). Rhythms of knowing: Toward an ecological theory of learning in action research. *Educational Action Research,* 10 (3), 353-372. doi:10.1080/09650790200200191

Mallon, R. (2015). Boccia International Sports Federation. *Competition rules.* http://www.bisfed.com/wp-content/uploads/2014/01/Competition-Rules_English1.pdf

Mandigo, J.L. (2003). Using problem based learning to enhance tactical awareness in target games. In J. Butler, L. Griffin, B. Lombardo, & R. Nastasi (Eds.), *Teaching Games for Understanding in physical education and sport: An international perspective* (pp. 15-28). Oxon Hill, MD: National Association for Sport and Physical Education.

Mandigo, J., Francis, N., & Lodewyk. (2009). *Position paper: Physical literacy for educators* Physical and Health Education Canada.

Mathews, D. (1996). Reviewing and previewing civics. In W.C. Parker (Ed.), *Educating the democratic mind* (pp. 265-286) Albany, NY: State University of New York Press.

Méndez, G.A., Fernández, R.J., & Casey, A. (2012). Using the TGfU tactical hierarchy to enhance students understanding of game play: Expanding the target games category. *Cultura Ciencia y Deporte, 8* (7), 135-141.

Metzler, M. W. (2005). *Instructional models for physical education.* Boston: Allyn and Bacon.

Mitchell, S. A., Oslin, J. L., & Griffin, L. L. (2006). *Teaching sport concepts and skills: A tactical games approach.* Champaign, IL: Human Kinetics.

Mitchell, S.A., Oslin, J.L., & Griffin, L.L. (2013). *Teaching sport concepts and skills: A tactical games approach for ages 7 to 18* (3rd ed). Champaign, IL: Human Kinetics.

Mitchell, S.A., Oslin, J.L., & Tannehill, D. (1999). *Assessment in games teaching.* Reston, VA: National Association for Sport and Physical Education.

Morris, H.H. (2002). Fundamentals of teaching open and closed skills. *Panel Metġnlerġ,* 115. 7.uluslararasi spor bilïmlerï kongresï 27-29 ekïm, mirage park resort hotel antalya

Nastasi, R.J. (1992). Distinguishing conflict and competition: A model for understanding some teaching interactions in athletics. *Educational Considerations*, 19 (2), 45-48.

Nichols, B. (1994). *Moving and learning* (3rd ed.). St. Louis: Mosby.

Nieto, S. (2000). Placing equity front and center: Some thoughts on transforming teacher education for a new century. *Journal of Teacher Education, 51* (3), 180-187. doi:10.1177/0022487100051003004

Ophea (2013). Teaching games for understanding activity support package. Toronto, ON: Author. Available online at http://growingyoungmovers.com/+pub/document/TGfU/PLAY_TGfUActivitySupportPkg_20NV13.pdf

Ophea (2014). PlaySport [website]. Retrieved from http://www.playsport.net/.

PlaySport, Ophea (2014): www.playsport.net/activity/croquet-ball

Payne, V.G., & Isaacs, L.D. (2008). *Human motor development: A lifespan approach.* Boston: McGraw-Hill.

Piaget, J. (1952). *The origins of intelligence in children.* NY: Basic Books.

Prinstein, M. (2013). Why current anti-bullying campaigns will be unsuccessful, but could be improved. Psychology Today. Retrieved from www.psychologytoday.com/blog/the-modern-teen/201103/why-current-anti-bullying-campaigns-will-be-unsuccessful-could-be-improved

Richard, J., Godbout, P., & Griffin, L. (2002). Assessing game performance. *Physical and Health Education Journal, 68* (1), 12-18.

Rink, J. (2014). Teaching physical education for learning (7th ed.). Boston: McGraw-Hill.

Schmidt, R.A. (1977). Schema theory: Implications for movement education. *Motor Skills: Theory into Practice, 2* (1), 36-48.

Schmidt, R.A. (2003). Motor schema theory after 27 years: Reflections and implications for a new theory. *Research quarterly for exercise and sport, 74*(4), 366-375.

Schunk, D.H. (1996). Goal and self-evaluative influences during children's cognitive skill learning. *American Educational Research Journal, 33* (2), 359-382. doi:10.3102/00028312033002359

Seaman, B. (2010). Re-defining competition in sport: The "freedom of excess." *Law Now, 34* (3), 1-5.

Seefeldt, V.D., Ewing, M.E (1997). Youth sports in America: An overview. *Physical Activity and Fitness Research Digest, 2,* 1-11.

Sheppard, J. (2007). Ready, aim, target games! *Physical & Health Education Journal, 73* (3), 34-39.

Shogan, D. (2007). *Sport ethics in context*. Toronto, ON: Canadian Scholars' Press.

Siedentop, D. (2002). Sport education: A retrospective. *Journal of Teaching in Physical Education*, 21 (4), 409-418.

Siedentop, D., Hastie, P.A., & van der Mars, H. (2011). *Complete guide to sport education*. Champaign, IL: Human Kinetics.

Singapore Ministry of Education. (2003). Teaching Games for Understanding. Educational technology division. Retrieved from https://www.moe.gov.sg/docs/default-source/document/education/syllabuses/aesthetics-health-and-moral-education/files/physical-education.pdf, p.24.

SportsKnowHow.com. (n.d.). Pickleball history. Retrieved from www.sportsknowhow.com/pickleball/history/pickleball-history.shtml

Starhawk. (2011). *The empowerment manual: A guide for collaborative groups*. Gabriola Island, BC: New Society Publishers.

Stoll, S., & Beller, J. (2000). Do sports build character? In J.R. Gerdy (Ed.), *Sports in school: The future of an institution* (pp. 18-31). New York: Teachers College Press.

Thorpe, R. (2001). Rod Thorpe on Teaching Games for Understanding. In L. Kidman, (Ed.), *Developing decision makers: An empowerment approach to coaching* (pp. 22-36). Worcester, UK: IPC Print Resources.

Thorpe, R., & Bunker, D. (1986). Is there a need to reflect on our games teaching? In R.D. Thorpe, D.J. Bunker & L. Almond (Eds.), *Rethinking games teaching* (pp. 25-34). Loughborough, UK: Department of Physical Education and Sports Science, Loughborough University of Technology.

Thorpe, R.D., & Bunker, D.J. (1989). A changing focus in games teaching. In L. Almond (Ed.), *The place of physical education in schools* (pp. 42-71). London: Kogan Page.

Thorpe, R., Bunker, D., & Almond, L. (1986). *Rethinking games teaching*. Loughborough, UK. Department of Physical Education and Sports Science, Loughborough University of Technology.

Tuckman, B. W. (2001). Developmental sequence in small groups. *Group Facilitation*, (3), 66.

Varela, F.J. (1999). *Ethical know-how: Action, wisdom, and cognition*. Stanford, CA: Stanford University Press.

Visek, A.J., Achrati, S.M., Manning, H., McDonnell, K, Harris, B.S. & DiPietro, L. (2015). The fun integration theory: Towards sustaining children and adolescents sport participation. *Journal of Physical Activity & Health*, 12 (3): 424-433.

Vossen, D.P. (2004). The nature and classification of games. *Avante-Ontario*, 10 (1), 53-68.

Vygotsky, L. (1981). The genesis of higher mental functions. IN J.V. Wertsch (ED.). The concept of activity in Soviet psychology (pp. 144-188). White Plains, NY: Sharpe.

Wall, M., & Cote, J. (2007). Developmental activities that lead to dropout and investment in sport. *Physical Education and Sport Pedagogy*, 12 (1), 77-87. doi:10.1080/17408980601060358

Wallion, N. (2005). Assessing learning as an understanding: Towards a semioconstructivist approach in ball games. Paper presented at the meeting of the International Teaching Games for Understanding Conference, Hong Kong.

Young, I.M. (1990). *Justice and the politics of difference*. Princeton, NJ: Princeton University Press.

About the Author

Joy Butler, EdD, is a professor in the department of curriculum and pedagogy at the University of British Columbia in Vancouver. She is coordinator of physical education teacher education (PETE), outdoor education, and health programs at the undergraduate and graduate levels. Born in the United Kingdom, Butler taught secondary school physical education there for 10 years and coached three basketball teams to national finals.

Butler is active in international scholarship, organization, and advocacy for TGfU (Teaching Games for Understanding). She founded and chaired the TGfU Task Force in 2002 and aided its evolution into the TGfU SIG in 2006. She directed the 1st and 4th International TGfU conferences in 2001 and 2008. Butler has been invited to give presentations and workshops on TGfU in Finland, Singapore, Australia, Spain, Taiwan, Hong Kong, the UK, Colombia, and Germany. In 2012 she created and has since chaired the TGfU International Advisory Board, composed of 19 individual country representatives.

Butler has edited or coedited seven TGfU books.

Photo courtesy of Patti Morrison, ImageStrategist.com

About the Contributors

Linda L. Griffin, PhD, is a professor in the College of Education at the University of Massachusetts at Amherst. Her research and scholarly interest for over 25 years has been on the teaching and learning of sport related games through a games-centered approach grounded in constructivist learning. She has coauthored several books and articles and has coedited two books with colleague Joy Butler from the University of British Columbia. Linda has spoken and presented all over the world. She has also received several honors and awards for her work in games centered approaches.

James Mandigo, PhD, is a professor and member of the faculty of applied health sciences at Brock University in Ontario. He has served as interim dean and associate dean for the faculty and as the codirector for the Centre for Healthy Development. His scholarly body of work encompasses the areas of physical literacy, Teaching Games for Understanding (TGfU), and the development of life skills through sport and physical education.

Kevin Sandher, **MA,** grew up in Burnaby, British Columbia and was influenced to play cricket by his father, who grew up in India. Kevin played in Vancouver since he was 9 years old and at the age of 18 was selected to the Canadian national team, where he played for 10 years. He currently teaches physical education at Lord Byng Secondary School in Vancouver.

Tim Hopper, PhD, is an associate professor in the School of Exercise Science, Physical and Health Education in the faculty of education at the University of Victoria, British Columbia. He received his master's degree and PhD from the University of Alberta. Dr. Hopper's scholarly work focuses on teacher education in physical education and the use of digital portfolios to support teacher development. His research explores the use of complexity thinking in teacher education and physical education.

Steve Mitchell, PhD, is a professor and PE professional programs coordinator and sits on the SHAPE America Board of Directors. He has been at Kent State University in Ohio since 1992. He has authored numerous articles and book chapters related to standards-based teaching in physical education. Dr. Mitchell has also coauthored two textbooks related to Teaching Games for Understanding in public school physical education, including one that is now in its third edition.

Robert Murray Gibson, BSc, BEd, MEd, grew up on hockey, football, and music in Saskatoon, Saskatchewan, and has a varied teaching background with experiences in Ireland, South Korea, Saskatoon, and China. He has taught in mainstream, alternative, and special education programs. Robert currently teaches physical education in Vancouver, where he lives with his wife, Emily, and their children, Ava and Nate.

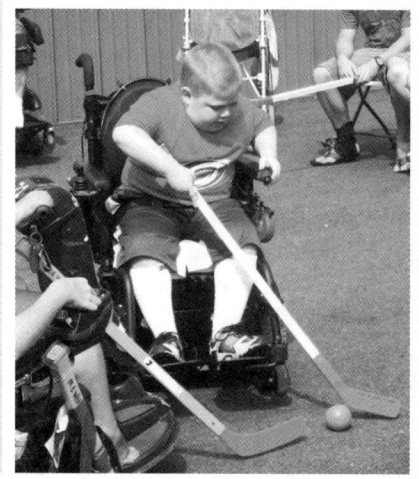

You'll find other outstanding
physical education resources at

www.HumanKinetics.com